P9-CDB-825

WHOLE LIVES
Shapers of Modern Biography

W·H·O·L·E
L·I·V·E·S

Shapers of Modern Biography

REED WHITTEMORE

The Johns Hopkins University Press
Baltimore and London

The Johns Hopkins University Press, 701 West 40th Street, Baltimore, Maryland 21211
The Johns Hopkins Press Ltd., London

The paper used in this publication meets the minimum requirements of
American National Standard for Information Sciences—Permanence of Paper for
Printed Library Materials, ANSI Z39.48–1984.

Library of Congress Cataloging-in-Publication Data
Whittemore, Reed, 1919–
Whole lives : shapers of modern biography / Reed Whittemore.
p.   cm.
Companion vol. to : Pure lives.
Bibliography : p.
Includes index.
ISBN 0-8018-3817-7 (alk. paper)
1. Biography (as a literary form) 2. Biographers—History. I. Title.
CT21.W52   1989
920'.02—dc19   89-31338
CIP

Again to
HELEN, CATE, NED, JACK, DAISY

I was looking at the flower bed by the front door;
"That is the whole," I said.
I was looking at a spread of leaves; that a ring enclosed
what was the flower; and that was the real flower;
part earth; part flower. I felt that I had made a discovery.
I felt that I had put away in my mind something
that I should go back to, to turn over and explore.
—Virginia Woolf

Contents

Acknowledgments

I am grateful to a number of kindly librarians at the Library of Congress, the public library in Hyattsville, Maryland, and the McKeldin Library of the University of Maryland for their good will as I rifled their resources. I am also indebted to Terrie Hruzd for her careful typing and retyping—or should I say disking?—of the manuscript. (Elsewhere I may later rave against the destructive effect—from which Terrie partly saved me—of "desk-top publishing" upon authors of the Old School, and perhaps all schools.) And I thank Professor Morris Freedman for reading an early draft and making many useful suggestions.

The poem "Who's Who," on pages 102–3 (copyright 1937 and renewed 1965 by W. H. Auden) is reprinted from *W. H. Auden: Collected Poems*, edited by Edward Mendelson, by permission of Random House, Inc.

WHOLE LIVES
Shapers of Modern Biography

Introduction

Biography and autobiography are so conspicuously present in the high finance world of modern American publishing that high-minded opponents of the industry's practices find it easy to think of the genres as split down the middle, between serious books and promotional stunts. To do so may be snobbish, but there is enough wrong with the promotional dominance in modern book publishing to make snobbery almost a virtue.

The chief drawback to being virtuous like this is that there seems no place to stop. What industry in America is not dominated by forces that even a teaspoonful of virtue might improve? The soundest approach would seem to be, then, at root historical rather than ethical. One should look at the past of these long-lived genres with the intent of ferreting out their most pervasive elements. At least that approach was what I took in this book's predecessor, *Pure Lives*.

In *Pure Lives* I began far back, as one does when being ambitious, but I soon found out that not many modern students of the genres, ambitious or not, have dug deeper than Samuel Johnson and James Boswell. Their common assumption has been that biography did not really get up steam until modern times, and that autobiography—though represented earlier by such oddities as Saint Augustine's *Confessions* and Benvenuto Cellini's famous personal outpourings—was not a genre with a clear shape and intent until modernity set in, with its sudden respect for the self and the probing of self.

The assumption was a lucky one for me. Not a classical or medieval scholar, and claiming only an ordinary English teacher's grasp of the "great tradition," I was able to go back to many familiar texts in that tradition, and to look at them in a relatively unfamiliar way. In *Pure Lives* I imposed the history of these genres upon some elements of that tradition in ancient cultures, and then carried the history hastily forward from Plutarch through the hagiographers and chroniclers— with way stops for Machiavelli, Cellini, Shakespeare, and Laurence Sterne—*to* Johnson and Boswell. With this volume I move relentlessly forward from there, but into a world where the scholars of genres are many and busy. I must watch my step, and not only historically. Value judgments of all kinds become important as soon as one nears one's own world. The result is that I have not been able to avoid being virtuous here, though being so about Freud and Norman Mailer is more dangerous than being so about Plutarch. At least I have tried to be virtuous quietly.

But to return again to Plutarch for a moment. His relative lack of interest in the self, characteristic of the classical period, was the product of an attentiveness to public lives—that is, lives dedicated to public, social service. Plutarch and his contemporaries rendered incidental—because they thought it *was* incidental—the kind of domestic detail that we now think central to biography and autobiography, especially detail about the self's childhood and maturing years. They did not explore the home sources of Alexander the Great's greatness, but the signs in the heavens at his birth.

What was true in Greece and Rome was also true of biblical lives, for though the biographers of the Bible were always ready to report conflict among the children of patriarchs, they paid little attention to the *causes* of conflict. And as for the public figures in Egyptian and oriental cultures, they could well have had no childhoods.

Neglect of the domestic being did not mean lack of knowledge about it, and about its maturing, though curious notions were common. It meant that the authors of early lives had a different sense of their mission than do modern authors. The cultures of Greece and Rome produced a few works in which private affairs were seriously studied—think of *Oedipus*—yet the Oedipus of Sophocles has little in common with Freud's modern version of him. The Oedipus of Sophocles is ruled by forces outside himself, while Freud's Oedipus rules, though subconsciously, his own fate.

The modern mind, though still surrounded by astrologists, is resistant to heavenly causation other than, loosely, fate. It does not readily accept the presence of outside givens other than those supplied by sociologists and biologists, and in biography and autobiography it looks steadily in rather than out. It is therefore baffled by the functions and roles of the old gods and goddesses, since those deities were symbols not just of givens, but also of mysterious overseers playing a positive role in the formation of human character and in its conduct at maturity.

Homer's description of the siege of Troy is an early instance of the classical point of view, with gods and goddesses overrunning the battlefields, and much extrinsic influence can still be seen at work in Plutarch's *Lives of the Noble Grecians and Romans* (about 50 A.D.). For his time Plutarch was a sophisticate, but he was no skeptic about heavenly influence. He could sometimes sound like a modern man, but not when he discussed, for hundreds of words, whether Brutus was physically confronted with his "evil genius" the night before his death, or whether Lycurgus in old age ascended directly to heaven after abandoning his governance of Sparta and walking out of town.

The Metamorphoses of Ovid (about 10 A.D.) is probably the fullest rendering we have of the mythical weaving of classical selves with outside forces. Ovid was satirical about the gods, but no disbeliever. He could not have ascribed so much human fate, even figuratively, to Jove's lecherousness, Juno's jealousy and so on, if he had not assumed that qualities of earthly character had sources other than earthly conditioning. He did not describe Io becoming a cow, Arachne a spider, and Hyacinthus a flower by their own choosing. He was always careful to place their destinies in higher hands and make them self-modest.

But there is one story not in Ovid that may, with a little squeezing and molding, be said to represent a significant shift in the classical view of self: the tale of Cupid and Psyche. The tale nearest to it in Ovid is that of Narcissus, but the fates of Narcissus and Cupid were very different. When Narcissus looked into a reflecting pool, "neither desire of food or sleep" could lure him away, and he was soon defunct; but when Cupid made love to Psyche, their affair became, after a rocky start, a fine romance, so satisfying to Jupiter that he made Psyche immortal.

And Psyche, unlike the empty pool loved by Narcissus, was a positive something. She was the soul, and the soul, I must insist, cannot be winnowed away from the self itself—though many have tried.

The Cupid-Psyche story as we have it comes from Apuleius, a

century after Ovid. Like Ovid he was a satirist, and Edith Hamilton says of his tale, "The writer is entertained by what he writes; he believes none of it." Yet this complicated, variously interpreted tale suggestively contains a view of the soul or self that was a novelty for its time. Usually it is described as a forerunner of romances like that of Cinderella and the Prince, and of Romeo and Juliet, tales of lovers evading wicked sisters and angry parents, in short the Establishment; but since Cupid's love is not for a clear "other" but for the self, the Cupid tale should perhaps be allied instead to the likes of the story of Hamlet or, among the story's less noble progeny, tales of the later bourgeois apostles of unlimited individualism. Jack Lindsay, an excellent modern translator of *The Golden Ass*, in which the Cupid-Psyche story appears, describes the story's theme as that of "the soul's progress," a phrase that would be a suitable title for this book if I did not fear being taken for a man of the cloth. In the story the fabled Psyche comes, as it were, of age.

Psyche was a beautiful mortal, to whom Cupid made love, though he had been told by his mother, Venus—who was jealous of Psyche's beauty—not to do that at all, but to mate her somehow with a low, beastly type (perhaps someone similar to Apuleius's image of himself). Cupid came to Psyche only in darkness, and she did not know his identity (though her wicked sisters told her they had heard—and from a high source, Apollo—that he was a serpent and would eat her up). Incurably curious, she at last held a lamp over him while he was sleeping, and was, briefly, delighted. Cupid was not. In the first place she had inadvertently wounded him by spilling hot lamp oil on his shoulder while he was sleeping, and in the second place he knew that in loving her he was breaking his mother's command, that his indulgence would now be evident, and that both he and Psyche would now be punished. They were. Psyche was obliged to do several odd jobs for Venus, like sorting innumerable seeds (of course Psyche arranged to have innumerable ants do this), and the wounded Cupid was placed as near to death's door, by the angry mother, as a god can be. Yet the conclusion was no more tragic than the essentially comic narrative itself. The Establishment at last relented and blessed their relationship. So a question arises. Why did the gods change their minds?

An answer of sorts was given in the simplistic finale that Apuleius gave the tale, details of which Edith Hamilton omits in her rendering. Apuleius declared Cupid and Psyche to be incorrigibly loving lovers who handled the world's assaults so well that eventually their body-and-soul relationship was found by Jupiter to be "perfectly in accord with usage and the civil code." Apuleius added that their union was productive of a child named Joy, thus affirming—as I read the tale—respect and love for the privacy, dignity, and beauty of the soul or self, and declaring that an ethical revolution in heaven and on earth had occurred.

Do I thus twist the tale? A little, but others have done so, including Robert Bridges. What I am doing with it is pointing it, as I think it asks to be pointed, in the direction of two overlapping archetypal moments in human history that are much discussed in our time. The first moment is, in theology and also psychology, that of spiritual conversion or second birth. (The psychologists differ from the theologians only, or chiefly, in their tying the moment to the physical maturation process of adolescence.) The second, hard-to-distinguish moment is the moment of truth, when an individual sees for the first time something basic about his life that he has not seen before. In the Apuleius story these two moments converge. Cupid and Psyche succeed in breaking away and also, simultaneously, in discovering a great truth about the self. For biography the convergence is vital because it widens the base for the genre, to *include* the self life. Before Cupid and Psyche had their affair the genre was, because of custom's heavy hand, censorious about all but the public life—that is, it did not normally allow private life to enter its domains. After the affair the biographer could conventionally ask, while presenting the public life of his hero, what was he *really* like? Or he could even forget about the public life entirely.

But why do I propose the Cupid-Psyche story as my example of these themes, when even early Greek tragedy contained moments of truth, and when all the early Christian martyrs, of the same period as Apuleius, are more obvious cases of conversion than his little sexual bedtime tale? Were not the martyrs' opposition, upon conversion, to the things that were Caesar's, and their resultant instant ascension to heaven, more important historical symptoms of cultural change than the tale?

Perhaps, but the martyrs' rebirths, as described by the early hagiographers, remained conspicuously impersonal. Each Christian convert's greatest mission was to relinquish individuality, abandon the selfness of soul, with the result that hagiographic "lives" had as little in them of the private life as the pagans'. The Protestants had yet to come, but they would not uniformly approve of the Cupid-Psyche kind of independence either. The rise of the middle class had to come along too, as well as the Renaissance, Copernicus, and dozens of other forces in sophomore surveys, before there was consensus in the West that a man's soul was, or could be sometimes, and with many reservations, his own.

Those forces spoke slowly, so slowly that they are still speaking, often without conviction. What cultural evidence is there, even now, that Psyche should not keep sorting seeds? Yet in biography—and particularly English and American biography—attention to the self has come to be at the center of things, with the biographer sometimes playing the role of Psyche herself, by holding the lamp over Cupid and, as his temporary soulmate, discovering (and telling the world of) his true identity.

Yet this attention to self, while widening the base of the genre, has not changed the primary motivating force behind it. Biography has always been, and remains, chiefly dedicated to celebrating individual human success. It would not be read, would not exist, if it had not brought news down the centuries of the fulfillment of human hopes by great achievement. It has been read because the creators of biographies have had such hopes with the rest of us and have written of individuals who have, with hundreds of greatly flawed exceptions, fulfilled those hopes. The shift of attention to private lives has altered our hope quotient little; it has simply altered the biographers' focus as they proceed with their celebrations. Now a common biographical formula is, for instance, to look for a moment of truth in infancy and to find that it was a hidden moment, an unexpected private moment, not at all a moment out of which success would seemingly proceed. And another, related formula is to delve into a biographee's writings and actions, to find in them repetitive motifs and concerns lying beneath their surface. In thus shifting attention from the evident to the submerged the biographer partly alters his own function; he becomes not merely a recorder, a commemorator, an evaluator of performance, but also an analyst of the sources of performance.

But when those sources are, as they so frequently are, dismal, traumatic experience, and when the biographee's subsequent successes therefore become clouded over with all sorts of psychic misery, then questions begin to arise about the nature of success itself. They may be happy questions for a reader who is not himself a success but shares the successful one's miseries, but they are definitely subversive questions for a genre traditionally committed to the study of performance *per se*. (See W. H. Auden's sonnet "Who's Who" in my Freud essay below for a poetic announcement of the kind of subversion I am talking about.)

So we have come far enough now, with this shift to self study, to produce the common assumption I have mentioned, that biography did not even exist until it began to be attentive to the self. In *Pure Lives*, I therefore took a partly opposed position, thinking it wrong to put good classical minds like Plutarch's back with the Neanderthals. But I agreed that in focusing upon public selves Plutarch omitted biographical matters of moment, matters that Apuleius did not omit. For, unlike Plutarch, Apuleius was an earthy writer in the comic tradition, a predecessor of Rabelais and Boccaccio, and he was more concerned with the humanity of Psyche and Cupid—even though Cupid was a god and Psyche a perambulating ideal—than anything else. In his recounting of their affair, Psyche was very human, and Cupid went to bed with her as a human. His tale was fanciful, but physical too, and he presented Venus's jealousy of Psyche's beauty as human and physical. Thus when Venus heard of her son Cupid's treachery in romancing her competitor in beauty, she raged at him (in the Lindsay translation) as follows: "You, a mere boy, entangle yourself in a lewd schoolboy affair—just to annoy me with a woman I hate for a daughter-in-law. But no doubt you presume, you jokester, you profligate, you disgusting fellow, that you are my only high-born son, and that I'm past the age of bearing another."

Oddly enough, not until the nineteenth century did this kind of comedy in literature and drama reach far into biography, since biography until then had taken its cues from the gospels of epic poetry and tragedy, and from historians of great-man performances. Not until then did the shift in focus take place in earnest.*

In this book I begin with Thomas Carlyle's inwardly driven (but

---

*And in poetry the shift did not occur even then, if Robert Bridges's version of the Apuleius tale—"a poem in twelve measures"—is representative of the late century. It appeared in 1885 without a smile in it. Presumably Bridges was offended by Apuleius's frivolity. He translated the passage quoted above as follows:

Thou too to burn with love, and love of her
Whom I did gate; and to thy bed to take
My rival, that my trusted officer
Might of mine enemy my daughter make!
Dost thou think my love for thee so fond,
And miserably doting, that the bond
By such dishonour strained will not break?
Or that I cannot bear another son
As good as thou? (Bridges, *Eros and Psyche*, 86.)

hardly sexually driven) heroes, and move from them—after discussing dictionary biographies of public personages as seen in Leslie Stephen's *Dictionary of National Biography*—to Freud's inward selves. And with Freud and his successors I come to our world of capitalism, individualism, and the subconscious, where all biographers must now be diligent students of self even if not lovers of it.

In the eighteenth century and early nineteenth, these students were not psychologists because psychology had not been invented. One earthly school was Lockeian and thought of mental conditioning as a sure way to mankind's progress upward, dismissing intractable subjects like the will and the spirit. Another school was heavenly and took its lead from German philosophers who demonstrated, with invulnerable logic, the superior reality of the will and spirit. In time, the earthly school begat utilitarians, positivists, and most of the varieties of socialist. In time, the heavenly school produced the transcendentalists and even, circuitously, Hitler. We should not blame these originals, though of course we do, for what was later derived from them. We should instead be properly cautious in assigning blame, and simply note that by the early nineteenth century both schools were present throughout Western culture and were trying to understand and guide the massive social and technological revolutions taking place around them. We should also note that the culture of the time was more deeply influenced by these essentially social-political schools than by anything remotely resembling modern psychology.

In England Thomas Carlyle and John Stuart Mill represented the opposed schools handsomely, and made the conflict between them dramatic by being, for a time, good friends. What needs to be kept in mind about both of them is that despite their differences they talked about the self as if it were a philosophical concept. Freud, perhaps oddly, later read and admired both of them,* but if he had settled down to analyze either, he would probably have described their conceptual lives as mere sublimations of their "real" lives. In any event, he went out and started his own school of the self,† and with him more

---

*Freud seems to have named his son Oliver after Cromwell, of whose work (in readmitting the Jews to England) he may have been made aware by Carlyle. See my Freud essay, below, for his feelings about Mill.

†Or soul. Bruno Bettelheim is particularly insistent that when Freud talked of psychoanalysis, he was not thinking, as his English translators have insisted, of something medical, but of the root meaning for *psyche*. (Bettelheim, *Freud and Man's Soul*, 53.)

than with any other individual, psychology became an intellectual force in the private life of Psyche and Eros. And an intellectual force in biography too.

Then too, with Freud, perhaps unfortunately, psychology became a *profession* in earnest, though it was hardly the only intellectual field to do so as the nineteenth century came to a close. The great age of professionalism was upon us then, and with its arrival somebody was sure to make private lives professional matters even if Freud did not. But for biography, no matter who was to blame, professionalism has not always been—or so this volume tries to show—the wonderful solution to its "prolonged immaturity" that some modern biographers have claimed.* I should not be snide, but there is something about the arrogance and assertiveness of the modern, professional, analytical mind that has annoyed me throughout my readings for this book, with the annoyance being stirred about equally by the various professions I have confronted, including my English-department own. My doubtless prejudiced conclusion is (here is where my virtue becomes troublesome) that in our world the professionals have generally come to feel obliged to deal as *specialists* with private lives, and that while they vary widely in the range of their vision, few seem ready to admit that other professions have knowledge and talent equal to their own. Each seems fixed in his own wondrous way of "taking hold" of the genre of biography, a phrase that Freud once used and with which I begin my essay on him.

The taking-hold is sometimes impressive and persuasive, but it is sometimes also absurdly self-serving, dedicated to promoting the biographer's welfare within his profession. The results can be dismal. With the most professionally driven of the biographers one can imagine, for example, all sorts of tragicomic versions of the Cupid-Psyche story emerging, were they to put their minds to it. Some might discover that the delights to which the lovers addressed themselves were mere channels into which their subconscious resistance to their elders had blindly flowed, hence not really delights at all. Some might dwell learnedly on the *complex* character of the *multifaceted* forces, earthly and divine, opposing the lovers' union. Some might even probe Psyche's own psyche, discovering—how could they avoid it?—that she was not what she was. And of course some connoisseurs of best-sellerdom and the

*The phrase is Richard Altick's in his *Lives and Letters*, 186.

dollar might uncover nasty pornographic perversions beneath the lovers' ostensibly romantic affections.

My dander is therefore up, intermittently, against authorities and authoritarianism in biography, the how-to-do-it people who would take hold of the genre with firm hands as if it were somehow *their* genre. If ever there was a genre resistant to such narrowing of its domain, biography is it. It is a genre whose long, complicated history has indeed been that of the soul's progress, a progress toward wholeness in the sense of inclusiveness. It is therefore a genre in which, finally, humility must be the best policy, allowing the soul to progress without being told how to.

Yet even that cautionary pronouncement needs qualification. A biographer cannot, aspiring to humility, simply pile up detail like scholarly cordwood, believing that he has no discriminatory function. His artistic role in the proceedings must remain, or he is *only* a woodpiler. I hope that in my fulminations against specialist excesses I will not myself seem authoritarian about them. Professionalism breeds the vice, and I confess that with this, my fourth book of biography (one, a kind of private training ground, has not been published), I am beginning to feel like a biographer professional.

I

Carlyle and His Great Men

First paragraphs can be dead weight, and a fine editor I know habitually strikes them out with two quick slashes, but in a paragraph introducing Thomas Carlyle (1795–1881) it is at least important to unsay what Carlyle's first biographer, James Anthony Froude, first said: "The river Annan, rising above Moffat in Hartfell, descends from the mountains through a valley, gradually widening and spreading out, as the falls are left behind, into the rich and well-cultivated district known as Annandale. Picturesque and broken in the upper part of its course, the stream, ..." The trouble with Froude's beginning is that the tone, though pleasant, is wholly un-Carlylean. Carlyle *was* from Annandale, and knew the river Annan, but as a biographer he never moved in on a subject as if he were a pastoral poet, or a reporter for the *National Geographic*. He went right to work. He was insistently thematic. Like most driven souls he reached for essences first, details later.

He wrote in a sound-proofed room (when he finally had enough money to have one made). While writing he was arrogant, bad-tempered, unpredictable. While writing he turned his home, said his wife, into a madhouse—and he was always writing. But he was a great historian and a great biographer. He was also a great, though dogmatic, social theorist, who managed to organize and explain human history with a handful of heroes as intensely directed as he.

For fifty or so writing years he had constant reference to these heroes, but he brought most of them together in just one early book, *On Heroes, Hero Worship, and the Heroic in History*, starting with the

Scandinavian god Odin. In his hands each of the figures represented an age or, more properly, became himself the spirit of an age.

So, at least, Carlyle said at age forty. By age sixty he had modified his theory and become furiously scholarly. Everything he did he did furiously. The early book was a collection of carefully revised lectures and needed only 250 pages for eleven heroes. The last books needed 5,000 pages for just two. But early and late, with and without the heroes' presence, he wrote of the need for their presence. The boy born by the river Annan always had more ideological matters than the Annan on his mind.

Yet biographer Froude did actually know the man. In old age Carlyle entrusted his papers to him, and asked him to be his biographer. So Froude is to be believed when he says that Carlyle had, to the last, "the manners of an Annandale peasant." All the best evidence about him suggests that the driven peasant could put the river Annan out of mind, but the river stayed with him anyway, a good Scotch river with severe rural Calvinists lining its banks.

Carlyle grew up with the values of the river folk, and then grew mature watching their values disintegrate in the larger world around them. In one of his first published polemics he told that world that "public principle is gone, private honesty is going, . . . and society, in short, is fast falling in pieces." Samuel Johnson became one of his early heroes because Johnson had tried to keep the pieces of eighteenth-century traditionalism together. Frederick the Great became a hero for him later for the same reason At sixty Carlyle was not as sure about Frederick as hero as, at forty, he had been about Johnson, but his authoritarianism stayed with him, even grew with age. By 1850 he had become so intolerant of democracy that he was thought of as an old curmudgeon, but he was not *just* that. In part of his mind he was of the new world too, the post–French Revolution world, the industrial world; and his hero ideas straddled the old and the new. Especially they straddled the old and new in biography, and his father was a key figure here, as fathers tend to be. Upon the father's death he wrote a forty-page encomiastic biography of him, describing him as an inspiring example. His repetitive phrase for him was "natural man." In the father the pastoral river Annan ran, and like most intense sons Carlyle was both attracted and repelled by the father's constant psychic presence.

James Carlyle, reported the son admiringly, never spent "more than three minutes in any school." Less admired was his finding literature "not only idle, but false and criminal," and taking religion as his "pole-star." He was "rude and uncultivated," and the son in adolescence rebelled against his father's stern Calvinism, first by giving up school-teaching, then by giving up university training in divinity, and last by giving up the law too, though all had been urged on him by the father. To do what? To do what the father did *not* recommend: set up shop as a lonely, not-quite man of letters in a room in Edinburgh. In other families the breaking away, especially from the father's church, might have been absolute, but Carlyle declared that it was never that at all; it was not a break with the father's convictions, but only with church forms. Nor, he added, did it offend the father: "When I declined going forward into the Church, (though his heart was set upon it) he respected my scruples, my volition, and patiently let me have my way. In after years . . . he had the forbearance to say at worst nothing, never to whisper discontent with me."

This father possessed, then, an essence that went beyond forms. He was "religious with his whole faculties." He was straightforward, clear, "singularly free from affectation." Thus, forty pages of biographical tribute. The pages will not convince many that there were no whispers of discontent between two hot Carlylean tempers and no guilt in the son as he wrote his praise, yet the praise should not be discounted either. Carlyle's complicated feelings for his father underlay his whole mystique about leadership. Between the stonemason Calvinist patriarch and the religious heroes of whom the son wrote there was a strong connection, and the connection was indeed of "whole faculties," not forms.

The connection was evident even when Carlyle wrote of secular greatness—of kings, poets, men of letters. The father image followed him up and down history, since he kept finding the father's essence in history's great ones; and when he himself became one of his great ones, his thoughts were still never far from the father he had rebelled against.

It should be added that his thoughts were never far from his mother either, especially after his father's death, but his mother fully supported the father's essence. She brought her son up on Bible readings while the father walked about setting an example. All in all, the son could only make a slow, unconvincing departure from the parental world, and the departure was a tearing experience for him, one he never gave over finding equivalents for in the lives of others.

For some years he was in limbo. When he settled in as a writer, he did so without knowing what kind, or for what purpose. By his own account his mind was finally straightened out by German idealistic philosophers, who gave him the new essence he was looking for, a lofty intellectual tie between the self and divinity that he would live with until death. He would *preach* the tie too, with particular effect on Americans, it being the transcendental tie that excited Emerson, Thoreau, and Melville. What the tie did not do, being so lofty, was move one mere human being toward another. About human ties he remained in limbo, perhaps because the stern father had left his mark.

The son's lack of warmth came to affect, most of all, one Jane Welsh. He pursued Miss Welsh to marry him (against her mother's wishes) shortly after he wedded the philosophers, and they all lived together, but not happily, for forty years. According to Froude, who said he had it from Geraldine Jewsbury, who said she had it from Jane Welsh, Carlyle was "one of those persons who ought never to have married"—the Victorian way of saying he was impotent. A modern Carlyle biographer, Fred Kaplan, doubts that he was,* though he also doubts a different story, from the Carlyle side of the family, that a few years after their marriage Jane had a miscarriage. The marriage, whatever the reasons, was a steady storm—and is still a feminist source for polemic, since Carlyle's German philosophers did not question the prerogatives of male genius. Neither did his own family's tradition. The genius was expected to sit up in his room, transcendent, writing, and the wife was expected to sit down below, or do her assigned chores there. Wives were not supposed to deal with German philosophers, though Jane Welsh was quite capable of doing so.

Among those philosophers Goethe was central, and Kaplan says that Carlyle came to take Goethe as a substitute father. But there were others, especially the poet-playwright-philosopher Schiller. Before his marriage Carlyle translated Goethe's *Wilhelm Meister*, but he also wrote a biography of Schiller—his first—and asserted, right in the opening paragraph, the heroic in Schiller. Schiller was among "that select number whose works belong not wholly to any age or nation, but who . . . are claimed as instructors by the great family of mankind." It seems to have been with Schiller, even more than Goethe, that Carlyle began to see himself as among the select number.

◆ ◆

*Kaplan (*Carlyle*, 117-19) merely documents much sexual anxiety on both sides.

Schiller's adolescent work, *Robbers*, had in it the outlines of Schiller's own life. A central figure in his upbringing was a disciplinarian who was not his own military father but, if anything, worse: the unpleasant duke of Württemberg, under whom the father served. The duke took charge of the child's education and made him unhappy for years, so unhappy that he wrote *Robbers*. The duke was scandalized by *Robbers*, finding himself in it, and was thinking of appropriate disciplinary measures when Schiller, then twenty-one, walked away from both the duke's measures and Württemberg. At age thirty Carlyle, writing of Schiller, must have been thinking of himself as in a comparable social fix: "Hitherto Schiller had passed for an unprofitable, a discontented and disobedient boy; but the time had now come when the gyves of school discipline could no longer cripple and distort the giant mind of his nature; he stood forth as a Man and wrenched asunder his fetters with a force that was felt at the extremities of Europe."

Carlyle also found the breaking-of-fetters theme in later Schiller works, and since he was himself alone in a garret as he wrote, he reflected at length upon Schiller's "hovering between the Empyrean of his fancy and the squalid desert of reality . . . spending his weary days in conflicts with obscure misery: harassed, chagrinned, or maddened." He was thus ready to identify with young revolution, but not yet ready to write a prose of revolution. His Schiller biography, except for the enthusiasm in it, was in style and form conventional compared with what was to follow.

It was a critical biography, mixing commentary on Schiller's works with dutiful chronological reporting of the life. His sentences were not yet Carlylean, but Johnsonian. He said that Schiller was "distinguished alike for the splendor of his intellectual faculties and the elevation of his tastes and feelings." He thought it "worth inquiring whether he who could represent noble actions so well, did himself act nobly." He thought also that "it would at once instruct and gratify us if we could transport ourselves into his circumstances outward and inward, could see as he saw, feel as he felt." The shape of the phrasing was Johnsonian in its balanced deliberateness. He would soon learn a more urgent style that would fit his own urgencies, and *be* his own.

Kaplan thinks that even the Carlyle style began with the Germans, as he slowly mastered the language; Kaplan quotes him as having found German "frightful" for the pedantic, but "supremely good" for the gifted. Kaplan may be right, but the process of translation is a creative one anyway, and the style that Carlyle at last mastered must be among the most individualized verbal creations in any language, a great mixture of irony, hyperbole, bathos *and* Goethe, Johnson, the rest. It was composed of all the available literary stances except pastoral simplicity, and it took on all subjects, great and small, with no flinching. Thus, in his next important first paragraph after the Schiller biography Carlyle hurried to cover our whole "advanced state of culture" and found it lacking any "fundamental" literature about clothes. And in the first paragraph of his *Heroes* volume, soon to come, he admitted, still without flinching, that his heroes were a large topic, "indeed an illimitable one," since "Universal History, the history of what man has accomplished in this world, is at bottom the History of the Great Men who have worked here." By then his style had become grandly, offhandedly special, right down to the capitalizations. It was a style designed to fit the strange grandeur of a Scotch peasant who had been given, as he said only partly mockingly, "a God-given mandate" and felt that "the Clay must now be vanquished."

◆ ◆

Asserting a giant Self against the Clay, or an unfriendly System, is not easy. Carlyle had to suffer dyspepsia endlessly and take castor oil. He also had to suffer being snubbed by the scholars of St. Andrews University, who turned him down for a professorship he had much counted on, apparently because of his excessive "zeal" (the word was Francis Jeffrey's, his dubious friend, and editor of the *Edinburgh Review*). Then in 1832 both his father and Goethe died. His marriage was becoming difficult. He was writing for a living and the living was difficult. He decided that "the net result of [his] workings amounted as yet simply to—Nothing." He moved himself and his unrural life into the barest and most desolate of rural houses, to struggle with the Nothing in the total silence he had taken for his own. And by then Jane had dyspepsia too. She was expected to be obedient, said Geraldine Jewsbury, to the "eternal maxim . . . that man should bear rule in the house and not woman." Ms. Jewsbury was of course an apologist for Jane, and a very advanced woman for her time, but the evidence is not all from her that both Carlyle and the barren house in Craigenputtoch were impossible, and that both husband and spouse worked hard at being hypochondriacs there, while *Sartor Resartus* gelled. The book was a semi-autobiographical account of rebirth: just what they needed. Jane said she "could hear the sheep nibbling the grass."

Sartor Resartus (published first in magazine installments in 1833) was heady, and clarity was not its forte, but it was Carlylean. Its priorities were the inner life, and it was the beginning, for Carlyle, of thirty years of mixing the biographer's private life with his subjects' lives. The life studied in *Sartor Resartus* was partly fictional and partly Carlyle's own, but where it was his own it was not reliable. It dealt with the hero's father and mother, for example, by omission.

Its hero was not *born* into this world, but *delivered*. He was brought to the door of one Andreas and his wife by a capitalized Stranger, "close-muffled in a wide mantle," who advised them that they had received an "invaluable Loan" and then "gracefully withdrew." Andreas and his wife uncovered the richly wrapped "little red-colored infant," finding beside it a roll of gold coins and a birth certificate. Nothing on the birth certificate was decipherable except the name: Diogenes Teufelsdröckh.

"Teufelsdröckh" means "devil's shit," but "Diogenes" means "heaven-born." Characters in transcendental tales are like this, and some of the short biographies that Carlyle was soon to write in the *Heroes* volume are also like this. They are and are not of this world, just as Teufelsdröckh was and was not of Carlyle. Unlike Carlyle, Teufelsdröckh had no family to worry about, but like Carlyle he had a long-standing unhappy relationship with the world's falsehoods and snubbings, and felt surrounded, early in his adulthood, by an Everlasting No. Then Teufelsdröckh, like Carlyle, saw the light of positive ideas, which were as bright as the No had been dark, helping him to hurtle from No to Everlasting Yea.

Teufelsdröckh was also like Carlyle in the way signalled by his name. The devil's shit in him was Carlyle's dyspepsia, of which Carlyle wrote miserably in letters to his brother, and could not help thinking of as his permanent earthly ill. And the Diogenes in Teufelsdröckh was in Carlyle too, the German transcendentalism in Carlyle. The lives of both Teufelsdröckh and Carlyle make classic studies of youth's voyage, filled with doubt and angst, through adolescence to the relative safety of maturity, though Carlyle was nearly forty when he finished the voyage, and the book.

As a Puritan and prospective Victorian he could not be directly autobiographical. He could not write in terms that would make him recognizable as the son of James Carlyle of the little town of Ecclefechan. He had to fudge. Mostly he fudged by adopting a radically inflated manner. Call it Carlylean hype, being made up of extravagance that could be deadly serious. In his early suitor letters he had already practiced the manner on Jane. For example, he had written her that while he was struggling with his "weary" life of Schiller, he received a letter from her and it was "as if" she had "lit up a blazing fire in the dark damp haunted chamber of some old ruined Gothic pile, scattering the ghosts and specters into the shades of Erebus and tinging the walls once more with the colors of jovial life and warm substantial cheer." He then *told* her that he was indulging in extravagance, calling it Slawkenbergian (straight out of book 4 of *Tristram Shandy*, one of Carlyle's favorite books in youth). Yet he liked the extravagance, and did, in a way, mean what he said, just as she liked what she read. So he went on and on, and they both soon learned how to live with extravagance, as with his other eccentricities.

At root the manner was a mode of concealment, a way of self-reticence, and for a modern reader it is an anomaly in a writer dedicated to essences, but the truth seems to be that he wished to conceal his interest in *some* essences. He wanted to exalt the self, not compromise it. The search involved deception but not as much as one might think. Certainly the earnestness of his private feelings was meant to be revealed, murkily, underneath.

The feelings were sufficiently genuine to be appreciated, some years later, by a young medical man in Vienna who had not yet even decided that he would become a student of the underneath. Sigmund Freud read *Sartor Resartus* at age eighteen, and commented favorably on it to a friend. He liked the mannered humor, liked the ridiculing of "us brooding Germans," and liked best the "great wisdom" under all the "funny names." His fragmentary summary seems a bit off track, yet points up an easily overlooked connection between Carlyle's and Freud's approaches to "lives": "What is said about the philosophy of clothes is partly in the form of parody, partly as a witty opinion which starts from the assumption that clothes are a representation of the apparent and physical, behind which the spiritual shamefully hides."

◆ ◆

The connection between them? First, consider where Freud was off track. In *Sartor Resartus* Teufelsdröckh did *not* say, as Freud said, that the spiritual hid away from the world in shame, but that it found itself overshadowed by, and subordinated to, pride and all the other human vices, as well as plain stupidity. Freud had fig leaves in mind, but Carlyle dealt with elaborate, civilized clothing, excesses of clothing that blanked out *soul* truth. He soon found the clothing figure insufficient to carry his theme, and for chapters on end he abandoned it, switching to dozens of other figures—life as an "immeasurable steam engine, rolling on . . . in dead indifference," life as a "Den of Lies," life as a place for grammarians and utilitarians (see below) and for all the arts of "Quackery, Puffery, Priestcraft [and] Kingcraft." What he and Freud would have agreed about was not that what was behind or underneath was shameful, but that it was basic.

But merely to agree that it was basic was in itself basic, a source of communion. *There* was the connection between them, a simple shared allegiance to a reality underneath. If they had served on a biography committee together, they would have found themselves voting together in favor of the biographer's duty to search out, like Psyche with her lamp seeking the identity of Cupid, the hidden essence of his subject.

Of course, voting on a committee is not at all like saying what one believes. Anyone who has served on one knows the wonder of reading afterwards, perhaps in a newspaper, the results of the committee's deliberations. He has seen on a strange page the conditions agreed upon, and the decisions made, and he has wondered where they could have possibly come from. He has asked himself, Could I have been part of *that*? Both Carlyle and Freud might have asked that question when reading my announcement that they agreed on essences, but I have put them on my essences committee anyway, knowing that if they were obliged to serve, they would at least have been likely to agree that they should not be on the *other* committee I am about to form.

The other committee, across the hall, is not a committee of essences but a committee for the study of structural or collational biography, a quite different genre. I will have to keep the two committees separate, lest voices be raised, but I hope that within each committee there will be the small measure of understanding that one can expect from committees. Meanwhile I am adding to the essences committee, to keep Carlyle and Freud company, Mr. Shandy and Captain Ahab (I will soon add others). Can one put fictional personages on a committee? I have, and they are at work.

Mr. Shandy has just located the soul *not* in the pineal gland but the cerebellum, and is wondering what will happen to Tristram's soul when his cerebellum is squeezed at the moment of birth. Across the table Ahab has just found his white whale spouting, a few leagues ahead of the *Pequod*, and is worrying too, as well he might. Both of them have achieved clarity of a sort about their essences, and if the committee were not in session they might be busy preparing for action, with Ahab lowering the whale boats, and Mr. Shandy complaining to Dr. Slop. But Carlyle is now speaking.

He is speaking in the voice of Teufelsdröckh. At great length he tells the committee that he has passed through the valley of the shadow of No, and also through the Center of Indifference, and has at last arrived. Where? At the essence. What essence? The essence of Yes. This essence, he says, is a great idea. It sits in a self, though not necessarily in the self's cerebellum, and *is*. It simply is. It is God-given and is spread through the whole culture by the agency of a hero possessed of both it and the capacity to promulgate it.

He stops, and Freud speaks, also at length. I will save what Freud says for my essay on him, except to say that he also is specific in locating the essence in a person's self, rather than in a person's actions or speeches.

Yes, so all the committee members have now located the essence. They now draw up a resolution to that effect and adjourn. They are a happy committee. They have found that they have something in common, being all busy striking behind the mask for the purpose of spotting "it." They do not worry that they have different notions of the nature of "it" and of how to approach it, if at all. (Was Melville recommending or damning Ahab's approach to the Whale?)

John Stuart Mill (1806–1873) now briefly enters here, though he is properly across the hall with the structural or collational committee. He enters because for some years he was a true friend of Carlyle's, and because Freud liked him too, except for his preaching about the equality of women, and translated some of his work into German. Mill was neither a transcendentalist nor a psychoanalyst, and he did not believe in such essence-hunting. His *Autobiography* is as far away from *Sartor Resartus* as two Scotch projects of the same era could be, and his friendship with Carlyle seems to have been based, originally, on a misunderstanding. The misunderstanding was Carlyle's, who took Mill to be a mystic when Mill was not. Mill, on the other hand, knew that Carlyle was a mystic, but didn't complain. The essence committee has adjourned, but greets the newcomer.

Carlyle and Mill remained friends through the big moment when Mill's servant—if it was the servant—inadvertently burned Carlyle's manuscript of *The French Revolution*. They moved apart when Carlyle's ways of saving the world turned sharply to the right, and he became an apologist for slavery in the United States. At about that time Mill sat down to write his autobiography (the first draft was complete in 1853), and in it spoke kindly of Carlyle. Carlyle, in letters and reminiscences, was less kind, since Mill was a (partly) Utilitarian son of a (wholly) Utilitarian father, and Utilitarians were the enemy. More to the point, neither Carlyle nor Jane felt kindly toward the woman Mill had by then married. Still, Mill and Carlyle were intellectual allies long enough to point up many interesting features of their own thinking selves, as well as of their confused intellectual era. A good place to begin with likeness and difference is, as always, with fathers.

As a Utilitarian, James Mill was, for Carlyle, one of the greatly misled rationalists of Britain, busy destroying such humanity as was left in human institutions. Carlyle raged at these rationalists as the dead hand on man's spirit of the new mechanical-industrial era, yet James Mill was a lively dead hand. He was out of a different world from Carlyle's father but equally committed to a stern work ethic. He wrote a complete history of English India in ten years, while supporting a large family by writing for periodicals and training son John Stuart on the side. He had John Stuart reading a number of Greek tomes before the age of eight and then settling in on the classics in earnest, as well as much heavy English literature. He did not forbid children's books—the son read and liked *Robinson Crusoe*, *Don Quixote*, and the *Arabian Nights*—but his emphasis was on Homer, Virgil, Horace, Livy, Ovid, Lucretius, Cicero, Polybius, and Aristotle. He also had the son translating Horace early, writing poems in English on his own, and reading English history, the history to be reported on each day when father and son walked out into the fields. Evenings he had the son doing mathematics, but not until the son was age twelve did he put him to "another and more advanced stage of instruction, in which the main object was no longer the aids and application of thought, but the thoughts themselves." Logic. Philosophy.

(In these years Carlyle's father had mostly taught his son how to divide, saying, "This is the divider, this, etc.," giving him "quite a clear notion how to do it.")

The capstone of Mill's home training was the reading, also at age twelve, of the father's history of India, learning from that his father's whole adult view of things. The view took in such matters as the English Constitution, democratic radicalism, the social roles of various parties and classes, and education itself.

(At that age, Carlyle reported, his father could do little for him intellectually other than to walk him down to Annan Academy, and once or twice sit with him in class when the master was absent.)

Carlyle came to despise formal education in most of its forms, but especially at the university level, and he ranted against it in *Sartor Resartus* as if it had been entirely in the hands of Utilitarians. In his tribute to his own father he said, expressing his vision of "natural" manhood, "Alas! such is the mis-education of these days, it is only among what are called the uneducated classes (those educated by experience) that you can look for a man." Yet Mill, living at the heart of such miseducation, was grateful for it, approving—with important reservations—his father's educational principles. In fact, he wrote his whole autobiography with education at its center:

> I have thought [he began, trying to justify the writing of an autobiography at all] that in an age in which education, and its improvement, are the subject of more, if not profounder study than at any former period in English history, it may be useful that there should be some record of an education which was unusual and remarkable, and which, whatever else I may have done, has proved how much more can be taught, and well taught, in those early years, which, in the common mode of what is called instruction, are little better than wasted.

Mill's father's precepts seem to have been these: start the student early, lay it on, but don't let the student think that "cram" is sufficient. Then he had another precept implicit in these: keep to a minimum "not only the ordinary corrupting influence which boys exercise over boys, but the contagion of vulgar modes of thought and feeling."

So the son grew up a loner with a "bookish turn" who was "inexpert in anything requiring manual dexterity," and inclined to "a general slackness of mind in matters of daily life." In the final version of the autobiography Mill seemed content with this destiny, but in an early, excised passage he was not so. He said that he and his siblings had a fear of the father's "severity [that] sooner or later swallowed up all the other feelings toward him." They "neither loved him, nor, with any warmth of affection, anyone else."

And Carlyle, despite the great parental difference, grew up with a similar handicap, learning to put daily affairs off on Jane, and to be finicky and demanding. Worse, he learned, like Mill, to hold himself in on important self-issues. All in all the two of them emerged as loners, together, in Scotland and then London, equally stunted but also driven, even inspired by parental principles.

Their two fathers were even equal in the severity of their religious faiths, though James Mill professed to have none. James Carlyle's Calvinism was present in the parlor at all times, and James Mill's agnosticism was present at all times too. James Mill made his son "one of the very few examples, in this country, of one who has, not thrown off religious belief, but never had it." He labored mightily to teach John Stuart to judge actions not by their moral worth, but by their capacity to produce pleasure or pain, yet he had "scarcely any belief in pleasure." He stuck to his Utilitarian guns to the last, lest he be taken for a Calvinist, but Calvinist in spirit he was.

And son John Stuart, who did not want to be a Calvinist, grew up one too. Similarly Carlyle, who did not want to be one, was one. This underground connection may have been mainly Scotch rather than theological, but it was certainly there. Carlyle could be a mystic, and Mill a rationalist, but they were both slaves to the gospel of work, work taken on with "regard for the public good" and productive of "a life of exertion, in contradiction to one of self-indulgent sloth."

Yet their writings were as different as their upbringings and characters. Carlyle was tendentious, metaphorical, intense. Mill was lucid, straightforward, dispassionate. Right away Mill thought of Carlyle as a special being, and envied him his "animation": "I felt that he was a poet, and that I was not; that he was a man of intuition, which I was not; and that as such, he not only saw many things long before me, which I could only, when they were pointed out to me, hobble after and prove, but that it was highly probable he could see many things which were not visible to me even after they were pointed out." In that paragraph Mill was being kind, overkind, trying to avoid suggesting that he could judge such a man. Carlyle was less modest, and came to speak of Mill in patronizing terms as extremely learned but also extremely naive, especially about women—which, though Carlyle was not the person to say so, must have been the case. They were not made for each other's company, and to think of them both working toward the same end in the study of human selves—that is, improvement of the whole human lot—is hard. That is why I have put them on different committees.

The great difference between them was the degree of their purposed abstraction from the humanity of their subjects. Mill could write of himself introspectively, though seldom descending to physical matters, but he did not move far into the selves of others. Even his autobiography is for the most part impersonal, and he seems to have had little interest in biography. So, with the aim of improving us he turned quickly to analyses of liberty, democracy, oligarchy, and so on. Carlyle meanwhile—who could be far less perceptive about himself than Mill—sought out instead giant selves, and with the two selves he chiefly chose, Cromwell and Frederick, he went into the details of their lives with the obsessed dedication of someone searching for the essence of all truth in a niche or corner.

Mill did not look for such essences, or for heroes possessing it, though he was an optimist and posited intelligent humans. In his opinion reason was that which produced truth, and reason was not an essence but a process, a structure within which selves found their being and moved through life. Reason, then, was greater than self, and individual selves were only incidentally resident in it. It might even have been described as transcendental, if the transcendentalists had not ignorantly walked off with that word and given it to the essences committee. Being a structure, reason was not to be quested after in particular souls or whales. It was to be surveyed from an appropriate distance. It was to be measured statistically, even polled. It was to be looked at dispassionately by sociologists, political scientists, and journalists rather than by biographers—or if by biographers, then by biographers who were sociologists, political scientists, journalists (and contributors to dictionaries of biography).

Of course Mill, writing in the mid-nineteenth century, did not know of the coming wonders of consensus thought, and Carlyle did not either; but Carlyle sensed them, disliked them, and tried to move the genre of biography away from them.

◆ ◆

Sartor Resartus was the beginning of the effort. It was followed by a diversion into history, The French Revolution (1837), that turned out not to be a diversion at all, but a piling up of further evidence of the need for finding heroic essence. In The French Revolution Carlyle fought his way through all the falsehoods that Teufelsdröckh had fought, and in doing so came upon a whole historic period in which, as he saw it, the essence was missing. He discovered that the ferocity of the Revolution had been brought about by the *absence* of a great man at the right time. (Rousseau, for instance, was a fine fomenter, but not a leader. Mirabeau was close to greatness, but could not maintain power.) Carlyle would not choose such a dismal period to write about again, except his own, but in a way the Revolutionary period *was* his own—or so he felt. He knew its chaos by osmosis as well as scholarship, and in writing about it he showed, perhaps inadvertently, that he was a genius in bringing to life something that was quite other than essence, that is, the wild configuration of leaderless human history. In Paris, in 1789 and after, what he described was the wildness of *sansculottism*, and he took it on rhetorically, page by page, by moving out from a focal point, such as a single personage, to its crowded background, and holding the crowd together by a series of parallel clauses. The "fairest unhappy Queen of Hearts" came to a great dinner with the "young Dauphin in her arms," and then the description panned out, camera-fashion, to grammatically orderly shots of surrounding insolence. Or he reversed the process, beginning with the wild surround and moving to a single figure, as when, during the "insurrection of Women," he described the "menads" bursting into an innermost court, overflowing staircases, massacring guards with "a hundred pikes" and, picking up a single corpse, depositing it on marble steps where its "livid face and smashed head, dumb forever, would *speak*." The writing was an exercise for him in documenting the fragility of selves and essences. He did it well, but after it he had to go back to the biographical drawing boards. There was no such person as a suitable biographee in such democracy.

In the book that followed, *On Heroes, Hero-Worship, and the Heroic in History*, he gorged himself, therefore, on eleven divinely sent personages who had in their times *made* history. The original occasion for the book was a lecture series, one of four that he had promoted for himself in London after the success of *The French Revolution*. The series before it, which also was published, had been primarily literary, with a historical base. He had moved grandly through the ages, from the earliest Greeks to Schiller, with way stops on various topics like Fame, Skepticism, and (his favorite) Quackery. For the next series he selected his eleven heroes for the more clearly directed thematic purpose of showing how a great presence may mold an age even as he is molded by it, saying, "Universal history, the history of what man has accomplished in this world, is at bottom the History of Great Men who have worked here." His heroes were Odin, Mahomet, Dante, Shakespeare, Luther, Knox, Johnson, Rousseau, Burns, Cromwell, and Napoleon. His historic ages did not quite come to eleven, but were all—except his own—accommodating to heroes, beginning with the hairy days of Scandinavian paganism, working through periods in which prophets, poets, priests, and men of letters were successively dominant, and arriving unchronologically at kings.

Obviously his biographees were not all equally accessible to him—
where did one pick up data about the life of Odin?—but he was good
at improvisation and had archetypes in mind as much as individuals.
He even had a format, casual but recurrent, in which the individual
hero was carefully subordinated to his ambiance. He began each
lecture with comments on the historical phase, moved to the ethnic
base for the phase, and then came to the hero or heroes he had
chosen for it. With figures that his audience knew well he was referential about the lives themselves, and with all the lives he purified
their essences by searching out material relevant to his now firm image
of a hero, one with divine urging up against great earthly impediments. Most importantly, he used each hero to show what it was that
his historic age gave him and drew from him. In each case the hero
arrived to "read the world and its laws" *for* the world, yet the world
was also there "to be read."

Predictably, he found striking similarities between his heroes in all
the phases. Without exception they were "natural," "sincere," and possessed of an inner guiding light that he insisted was divine, though
refusing to be sectarian about divinity. They were natural in the way
that Carlyle must have thought of himself (as well as his father) as
natural, springing up out of the common people, knowing the truths
that they knew without regard for the frills of schools and churches.
They were sincere because they could not help being sincere (their
sincerity did not depend upon themselves; they were "messengers sent
from the Infinite Unknown with tidings"); and, possessed of sincerity,
they were always safe from quackery. As for their divine urgings they
were, as Fichte had said, an idea-reality lying "at the bottom of all
appearance."

It was a very slippery idea-reality, immanent yet changing its spots
in accordance with historical phases, and not evident until the Great
Man came along to reveal it. Here again Carlyle borrowed from
Fichte, who had told him that the "mass of men" did not recognize it
when it was present, but lived merely "among the superficialities,
practicalities and shows of the world." And here it was that Carlyle's
image of himself, and of his role in life, proceeded on the same track
as his heroes. Or rather, his heroes, especially the religious ones,
proceeded with him. They too were simple, natural men who had
come upon the light while just sitting around being simple. Mahomet
was an uneducated Son of the Wilderness who lived in an "entirely
unexceptionable, entirely quiet and commonplace way" until he was

forty. Luther was of humble birth too, and quiescent until thirty-five. As for Knox, who was culturally closest to Carlyle, he lived in an "entirely obscure way" until forty. Then there were Cromwell, who also stepped forth at forty, and Robert Burns—"uninstructed, poor, born only to hard manual toil"—who, oddly, made it at twenty-seven. The nature of the illumination varied a good deal, the moment of illumination not much. In all cases the sleeping giant was awakened from his sleep well after adolescence, rose to the demands of unpleasant events by bringing forth his great Idea, was opposed by quackery and institutional fixity, but mastered opposition by his transparent power and sincerity.

Not all achieved total mastery. Burns for instance, though a great natural voice for his people, became tainted, Hollywood-fashion, by the plaudits of the people, who were his "ruin and death." Nor was Rousseau a clean-cut hero; his vice was egoism, and his "books, like himself, [were] unhealthy." As for the mighty Napoleon, he had a faith that was genuine so far as it went, as well as "an instinctive, ineradicable feeling for reality," yet was possessed of a "fatal charlatan-element." Quackery! Poor Napoleon ended up on St. Helena confused and astonished at what had happened to him, and in his final failure was not unlike some of Carlyle's more modest latter-day heroes. Carlyle was slowly discovering that modern civilization was an almost unmanageable chaos even for divine managers.

His Yea is to be seen in its simplest and happiest form in his description (in lecture 4) of sixteenth-century Scotland and what John Knox was able to do then for it and its future. It was "a poor barren country, full of continual broils, dissensions, massacrings." It was "a country as yet without a soul: nothing developed in it but what is rude, external, semi-animal." Then came the Reformation—and what was the Reformation? It was Knox, all Knox: "This that Knox did for his Nation, I say, we may really call a resurrection as from death. . . . the people began to live. . . . Scotch literature and thought, Scotch Industry; James Watt, David Hume, Walter Scott, Robert Burns: I find Knox and the Reformation acting in the heart's core of every one of these persons and phenomena." He then added that he found Knox at the heart's core of Puritanism in England and New England too.

All his heroes like Knox, and partial heroes like Burns, fitted his image of true spirituality by being theologically free of cant and superficial doctrine. They could be Christian or Mohammedan. They could be Lutheran or Catholic (though being Catholic was hard; one had to be medieval, and preferably named Dante). Nominally they could be what an age demanded, yet still draw their heroic powers from something beyond sect, denomination, institutional faith. The denominations came and went. What the heroes had that transcended the frills of faith were unnameable "vital relations to this mysterious Universe."

His final lecture, about kings, was meant to be the capstone lecture, since kings were, he said, "practically the summary for us of all the various figures of heroism." The trouble he had carrying through with the lecture was that after enunciating this ideal, of the king as an all-around "Able-man," he had to fade off into Napoleon, about whom he had much to complain and little to sing. How nice it would have been if he had been able to end with Cromwell. He could not. He kept finding that the modern age—and the heroic biographical genre for it that he was trying to establish—was not responding properly to his emerging theme. No one can know what he would have thought of Hitler and National Socialism in a later age, but the point is not to be argued here. What is to be noted is that his *Heroes* book, though perhaps his most influential creation, remained incomplete. It left him, at age forty-six, with an agenda for a younger writer, one still searching for his proper niche. The heroes he needed for his kind of biography were missing, so he was in effect still (not being the poet that Mill thought he was) without a suitable genre.

◆ ◆

As I imagine Carlyle he resembled, at age forty-six, Macbeth, though an innocent, literary Macbeth, possessed of no dagger. Macbeth, before murdering Duncan, took the signs around him as "happy prologues to the swelling act / Of the imperial theme." Carlyle's *Heroes* book was prologue too, and to an imperial theme too; and as with Macbeth's thinking it contained a flaw. By this time (1841) he was no longer a tormented, isolate scribbler on the moors with sheep, but had settled in London as a figure. Emerson's reaction to him, and beating of drums for him, signalled the range of his grandeur: America wanted him though he did not want America. The whole English-speaking world wanted him, and thought of him as a Man of Letters in the very heroic mold he was busy molding. It also thought of him as a highly provocative lecturer—in fact, preacher. For he was a good preacher, and the format of his *Heroes* volume was an excellent sermon format, with a thematic structure to which biographical and historical materials were illustrative, incidental. With such a reputation he could do pretty much what he wanted in the public eye, but what did he want? Was he to be a preacher?

Or biographer? Or historian?

Or what about fictional biography, as per Teufelsdröckh?

And what were the possible connections between all of these?

By its nature the *Heroes* book was not quite anything *except* prologue. It contained a program for Carlyle's writing future—find the Great Man and write about Him—but the program did not say how to do so. The Great Man had to be historical, for by this time Carlyle seems to have decided against fiction and poesy. But he also had to be a mythic figure, mythic in the sense of larger than life. Mill was right in saying of Carlyle that he was wholly on his own.

Mill knew of what he spoke, having admired Carlyle enough to try to imitate him, especially in an early essay, "On Genius." He felt later that the imitation was "boyish" and "written at the height of [his] Carlylism, a vice of style [he had] since striven to correct. . . . Carlyle's costume should be left to Carlyle." Fifty years later Leslie Stephen took the same position in the *DNB*, praising Carlyle's style while tagging it "the worst possible model." But more than style was at issue between Mill, or Stephen, and Carlyle. Carlyle moved in on his material in a way that put the writer himself in a role for which a Mill or a Stephen was by nature ill-equipped, that of earth-mover. Carlyle had a definite messianic itch and did not lightly choose for his lectures Mahomet, Luther, Cromwell. He kept identifying with them. He wanted his messages to sweep forth as he felt theirs had, and move whole peoples.

Luckily he also had a scholarly itch, and after the *Heroes* volume he was able to shift his attention from earth-moving to the plainer duties of a biographer.

◆ ◆

And eccentric though he was, he thus latched on to something that was very much a part of the nineteenth-century cultural climate in both Europe and America. So, in some measure, did Emerson, who travelled to Europe in the 1830s and again in the 1840s "to play bo-peep with literary scribes" but also with the world at large. Emerson found many of the scribes lacking in worldliness, but not Carlyle. Carlyle, even when isolated with Jane and the sheep, was conversant with the ills of the age and doing battle with them. Also he had the

advantage over Emerson of living close to them, so that when Emerson
visited him in Craigenputtock, they talked as much about slums and
"poor Irish folk wandering over these moors" as about the Soul.
Carlyle also had the advantage of living close to history, for on top of
his German idealism he was now in the history trade, having readied
himself to mix the duties of messiah with those of the not-so-mythical
scholar he had come to call Professor Dryasdust. What his idealism
and his historicity told him was that the century itself was in motion,
as were even the literary scribes.

The trouble with the scribes was that, unlike the historians, they
did not seem to *know* they were moving. They thought of themselves
as singular, isolated selves—in the woods perhaps—occasionally travel-
ling to town to be ideologically engaged. Carlyle was different from
them in feeling the outside motion steadily, the motion of the mass of
men that Thoreau, for one, worked hard to separate himself from.
Carlyle's feeling here distinguished him from most of his transcendental disciples as well as from his eighteenth-century predecessors. His
eighteenth-century inheritance, even from innovators like Sterne and
Boswell, was of thinking men in stasis. Sterne was a great early student
of the vagaries of self, but the selves he explored sat quietly in their
places, never growing up before their readers' eyes, nor basically responding to the cultural motion around them. Similarly, Boswell,
though thoroughly immersed in contemporaneity, presented a Johnson whose life role was that of a wise observer on the sidelines, a Man
of Letters who was not an earth-mover.

Carlyle, while admiring such men, acknowledged their incapacity
to "regulate . . . the manifold, inextricably complex, universal struggle
[that] constitutes, and must constitute, what is called the progress of
society." He thought of "royal Johnson languishing inactive in garrets,
. . . [of] Burns dying broken-hearted as a Gauger, . . . [and of] Rousseau driven in mad exasperation" into the manufacture of paradoxes.
But then he aggressively prophesied a busier future for Men of Letters,
a future as earth-movers. That future, he said "would have to be
possible." The trouble was that the earth-mover he had chiefly in mind
was himself. The time was 1841. He was forty-six.

◆ ◆

By this time he had managed to commit himself to social action, but
he had also become quite clear-headed about what a laborious action
it was to write either history *or* biography, his chief social weapons.

He had well-developed scholarly scruples, though he liked to rant against the world of dryasdust scholars, and he knew that his early lectures had been, to say the least, sweeping. Also, somewhere in the 1840s he made a decision against more lecturing. He had been tempted to go on circuit in America, but he decided not to, and in that hesitation lay the beginning of the end of his earth-moving. Aside from angry journalistic outbursts he would now take on just three more major works in the writing years remaining to him, all single biographies, none so blatantly controlled by the hero thesis as the lectures, and none so preacherly in tone. The first of the three revealed how conscious he was of how *unscholarly* he had been.

As with the *Heroes* book its title showed his generic precision. It was not described as biography, but as *Oliver Cromwell's Letters and Speeches, with Elucidations,* though the elucidations were so extensive as to be a partial biography of Cromwell. In fact they were the scraps of the full biography that he had first felt he *had* to do on Cromwell, and then had felt he could *not* do.* So with the imperative and impossible opus on his hands he made himself into a dryasdust scholar holed up with "Thirty to Fifty Thousand unread Pamphlets of the Civil War in the British Museum alone." He went through "huge piles of moldering wreck wherein, at the rate of perhaps one pennyweight per ton, lie things memorable." He found it "the most impossible" project of all his writing experience, four years of "abstruse toil, obscure speculation, futile wrestling and misery." And the toil was not made less miserable by the toilers before him. They perfectly represented Human Stupidity. "O Dryasdust, my voluminous friend," he raged, "surely at least you might have made an Index for these huge books!"

As he settled into the four volumes, he was at the top of his polemical bent, and he climaxed his attack on bad scholarship by calling a Cromwell biographer by the name of Noble "a man of extreme imbecility" whose judgment lay "dead asleep." The Reverend Noble plodded along in "an element of perennial dimness" and produced a book that was "in fact not properly a book, but rather an aggregate of bewildered jottings." Carlyle might well have been describ-

---

*"I have come," he had written to Emerson, "at last to the conclusion that I must write a book on Cromwell, that there is no rest for me till I do it. This point fixed, another is fixed thereto, that a Book on Cromwell is impossible." (Kaplan, *Carlyle,* 298.)

ing a good many modern academic biographies, but at any rate he
then set about bringing order to the Noble jottings about Cromwell
(to which, despite himself, he referred quite a bit). The result—about
half Carlyle and half Cromwell—was an excellent experiment in the
extensive use of source material, but it did not work. I doubt that he
would be amused today to know that the pages of the library volumes
of his *Cromwell* I have been reading (publication date, 1903) were still
uncut before I signed them out, but he might now agree that what he
rescued of Cromwell from the Reverend Noble and the British Museum was still not properly a book. He had only public speeches and
letters to work with, some perfunctory, some eloquent, but none
moving outside the narrow urgencies of national events that Cromwell, the Protector, lived with so long. The narrowness should in itself
have bothered him but did not. Bad stomach and all, he went ahead
with his slavery, annotating scores of references and providing pages
and pages of dryasdust topical background, doing so for no other
reason than that Cromwell was a hero, his particular hero, the "soul
of the Puritan revolt, without whom it had never been a revolt tran-
scendentally memorable, and Epoch in the world's history."

Perhaps Cromwell *was* the Puritan soul (though what of Knox?),
yet to compare the papers that Cromwell left behind with the "living
Iliad" of the Greeks was surely delusory. Carlyle did so. His Cromwell
volumes were not earth-movers but essentially the products of a sentimental commemorative chore, and the unreliability of his feelings
about them is pointed up by his own summary of the ideal he was
reaching for and failed to attain.

> Histories are as perfect as the Historian is wise, and is gifted with an
> eye and a soul! . . . The grand difference between a Dryasdust and a
> Sacred Poet, is very much even this: to distinguish well what does still
> reach to the surface, and is alive and frondent for us; and what reaches
> no longer to the surface, but molders safe underground, never to send
> forth leaves of fruit for mankind any more.

These are memorable words (I will return to the curious identification
of historian and sacred poet), but Cromwell's own words are mostly
not. Cromwell spewed forth pages and pages of military information
to the effect that such and such a gentleman "was taken with Sir
Marmaduke Langdale in their flight together," that there was "a design
to steal away the Duke of York from my Lord Northumberland," and
that "the money for disbanding Massey's men is gotten." He spewed

forth equally unreadable pages of praise to the Lord above for *His* assistance, and dispraise to the enemies of the Lord for their opposition, with the "Maligant Party . . . prevailing in the Parliament of Scotland" and the papist Spaniards taking the lead of the "Antichristian Interest" as prophesied by the Apostle Paul in his Epistle to the Thessalonians. With such texts Carlyle was able to bring forth no *Iliad* but, at great labor, mere chronological order and topical sense.

What he did do that was memorable was a by-product of what he had hoped to do. He created—as his 1903 editor Traill notes—a kind of *auto*biography, Cromwell's own, out of the thousands of moldering pamphlets. The collation had the obvious basic flaw of being autobiography of only the public Cromwell, revelatory of little about him except his public piety, efficiency, and force; yet it was a document with the hero himself speaking, and speaking in the heat of his acting and doing, not reflectively, not after the fact.

Here *was* a real novelty, and my guess is that the drama of such immediacies appealed to Carlyle's dramatic, anti-dryasdust sense of things, the sense that Mill admired but could not emulate. It was a good sense indeed—in a way it was his genius—but it should not have been expended on the public Cromwell.

Why did he do it? In the mid-nineteenth century Cromwell was, as a hero, a dead duck, and Carlyle, though a sentimentalist, knew that he was a dead duck, and wound up his four volumes about him bemoaning the death: "Oliver is gone; and with him England's Puritanism, laboriously built together by this man, and made a thing far-shining, miraculous to its own century." He even belabored the death in relation to the sad state of contemporary England, where the country's "Genius" was no longer inclined to soar, as in Cromwell's time, but instead to stand "like a greedy Ostrich intent on provender . . . with its Ostrich head stuck in the readiest bush." In his lectures some years earlier he had not pushed his heroes into the grave so, but had insistently affirmed the *life* of their spirit. They were the earthly shape taken by the Everlasting Yea.

It seems that in those Cromwell years Carlyle had himself aged, and his mythology, still operative, had shifted with his aging. The result was that he now looked upon his heroes in the past tense in just the way, presumably, that he now looked upon his own messianic life. The shift must have been what brought forth his bad-tempered late-life conservatism, in the form of polemical essays blasting away at all democrats and radicals in sight. Oddly, though, it also produced something quieter and less angry (if only intermittently) in the form of a biography of a nonhero, John Sterling.

❖ ❖

Sterling was a writer eleven years younger than Carlyle whose talent he could modestly praise and whose life he could equate at many points with those of his elder heroes, though only politely—for the book *was* a politeness largely, a tribute to a poet-friend who had died early. Sterling was a different dimension in biographees for Carlyle, someone physically real, someone he had known well. A less driven writer than Carlyle could have put world history and the future of man wholly to the side for Sterling, and while Carlyle could not keep his pressing themes out of the biography, he was at least relatively relaxed with them. He could spend most of his time doing, what biographers normally do, getting the life itself down and in focus.

But the life was a truly sad life. Sterling was consumptive, intermittently ill from birth, and constantly being shipped away from the English damps. One of Carlyle's strongest memories of him was of a long, wet walk in the country, after which, deathly ill, Sterling was removed to Madeira. His physical weakness kept sending Carlyle's connectivist mind off to spiritual equivalents, not only in Sterling but in Sterling's family and in the circumambient culture, all unhealthy, all invaded by the spiritual sickness Carlyle had been complaining about since his early essay "Sign of the Times." He could not let poor Sterling just be consumptive, but kept probing the greater ailment underneath.

A prime source of the ailment was Sterling's father, whom Carlyle had also come to know well and like. The father was clearly not possessed of Carlyle's father's spiritual vigor. Sterling's father was a rover through life, first as a military man and then as a successful journalist, who moved his family restlessly from place to place during the son's early years, and who was just not a soul factor, a Presence.

But Sterling's own soul weakness was the book's real subject. Carlyle traced his subject's development with care, found the pattern in it he was looking for—of adolescent indecision leading to a great moment of truth—and then found an evading of the truth. As preface to the evasion he sought out rebelliousness in Sterling's adolescence, found it in one incident comparable to childish incidents he had found in his heroes' lives, and reported on it in detail. At age thirteen Sterling ran away from home, as Schiller had run away, as Frederick the Great had run away (Carlyle would handle that in his next book), and probably as Carlyle himself had at some early time wanted to run away; but, unlike the heroes, Sterling ran away without fanfare and wrote his mother a letter from twenty or thirty miles away telling her he had done so. He was laconic in the letter, saying nothing about rebellion or deep causes. He told his mother that he had left home while the mother and father were at church, and had walked down Kent Road until he came to Gravesend; that he had found a friendly innkeeper who had bought him a seat in a coach to Dover; and that he had reached Dover about seven. He said that in Dover he had met a certain Captain Keys, who was going to put him up, preparatory to his sailing for France, until his mother answered the letter. He signed himself "J. Sterling." No world-saving was mentioned, and in reporting on the letter Carlyle was content to let it speak for itself, saying only that the steady historical style of the young runaway, who narrated "without in the least apologizing" was "noticeable." Obviously he admired the runaway's coolness, but he did not belabor Sterling's apparent lack of spiritual intensity, a lack that brought the runaway placidly home with no trip to France at all.

Then there was another, more momentous moment in Sterling's maturing, when he gave up his church assignment. He was twenty-nine—Carlyle had just met him—and had just finished reading *Sartor Resartus*. The theme of great life shifts was deep in the minds of both of them, with Sterling reminding Carlyle of when he too had given up the ministry. Sterling settled into a small house in London, as Carlyle had settled into rooms in Edinburgh, with "his outlooks sufficiently vague" until he found his life purpose "rising before him slowly in noble clearness." His purpose proved to have also been Carlyle's—to be a Man of Letters—so here were their two life patterns merging. "I loved him, as was natural," said Carlyle, "more and more."

And Jane liked him too, and played chess with him. The Sterling and Carlyle families became close.

There was, however, a literary difference that Carlyle tended to slur over but did not ignore. As a Man of Letters Carlyle was firmly a man of prose, and Sterling a poet. For obscure, surely complicated reasons poetry had come to be an evasion in Carlyle's mind, and though Mill had called Carlyle a poet, Carlyle was unhappy even reading verses. He kept telling Sterling that Sterling should be unhappy too, and turn to prose, since the proper function of a Man of Letters was to gain "superior excellence in delivery, by way of speech or prose, what thoughts were in him."

What *thoughts* were in him.

From Carlyle's now fixed point of view (he was fifty-five when he took on the biography), the trouble with Sterling had been that he had spent too much time on the singing of thoughts, not enough on the thoughts. Also he had "intrinsically no depth of tune." Also, his thoughts lacked depth, though their rebelliousness was appealing. At a halfway point in the biography Carlyle could say of him that "Artist not Saint was the real bent of his being," and say it as if the tag of artist was to be worn proudly. But elsewhere, the Sterling he delighted in kept disappointing him by emerging, in one way or another, as a dilettante. Carlyle decided that poetry was what encouraged the dilettante in him. His physical weakness had been aggravated by the spiritual contamination of a flaccid genre and led to a few dull evenings at the Carlyles when Sterling read his poems, with Carlyle noting that he did not read well and that his great facility "in any given form of meter" was not enough. It just did not lead where a Man of Letters ought to be led.

Too bad. To Carlyle, upon first meeting Sterling, there had seemed great missionary promise in the man, and he had watched him leaving the Anglicans for Letters for what seemed the right, earnest reasons, and had talked with him fervently about religion, finding him to be a man of essences. Then, somehow, he did not take hold. The underlying theme of Carlyle's biography of Sterling became, slowly, just that: the tragedy of not taking hold.

He reinforced the theme by excursions into contemporary English society, which he found equally soft. And he found the same softness in another Sterling biographer, an Anglican cleric whom Carlyle thought to be as bad as the Reverend Noble.

The cleric was the Archdeacon Hare. Hare had been Sterling's tutor at Trinity College, Cambridge, and had persuaded Sterling, helped by none other than Samuel Taylor Coleridge, to take Anglican orders in the first place. Carlyle disliked Hare and Coleridge about equally, finding both of them theologically frivolous in seeking a religious revival within a decadent church structure, one that Carlyle regarded as mere quackery. He felt that they had, like hypnotists, temporarily taken over Sterling's young mind, and from his walks with Sterling he was perfectly sure that Sterling had given up on the church long before his death. He therefore thought Hare was misrepresenting his biographee cruelly in announcing that a church position would have been a happy earthly destiny for him, had he lived.

But, having demolished Hare, Carlyle could not take the next step, and say that at death Sterling had taken hold elsewhere. He could only say that the Anglican interlude had been of the order of whim rather than commitment, like so much in Sterling's life.

It is strange to read this life after reading Carlyle's intensities elsewhere, and to see how comfortable Carlyle was with Sterling's *not* being a hero. For all his interest in seeking out the man's weakness—which I have overplayed here for the benefit of my own theme about him—he managed to make the book a calm book, from childhood up. In writing of the childhood period he was, it is true, aided in calmness by long pastoral reminiscences written by Sterling himself, but he was calm later too, even when Sterling showed a good deal of literary hutzpah in writing him a highly critical letter about *Sartor Resartus*. Carlyle included nearly the whole letter in his book and did not even take issue with Sterling when he said that *Sartor Resartus* was "Rhapsodio-Reflective," that its sentences displayed "lawless oddity," that some of the coined words were "positively barbarous," and that it was too abstract and speculative. Carlyle not only did not question the criticisms, but even praised the energy in Sterling's words, adding that in conversation he was even more vivacious.

Their friendship must have meant a good deal to Carlyle. Kaplan describes them as having been "like older and younger brother," which seems closer than father and son, since Carlyle leaned over backward not to be authoritative with him. If Carlyle played older brother, he probably played it as one being led astray, willingly, by precocious youth. The tone of the biography is so different from Carlyle's tone elsewhere that the prospect of a Carlyle who occasionally shared important human intimacies rises up pleasantly. His walks with Sterling may have been a way for him of being a runaway, for a bit, from his Great Man responsibilities.

◆ ◆

For a thinker like Carlyle—that is, roughly, anyone on the essences committee—forms are incidental, peripheral, diversionary. When Carlyle set out to be a Man of Letters he thought of history, he thought of biography, philosophy, and certainly theology, but he did not think seriously of them as intellectual categories. From the start, his mind was working beyond them; they were mere implements for him to pick up and discard at will.

And quite early he seems to have discovered that poetry, among the implements, could be discarded. He was willing to keep it in his toolshed while he was enjoying his friendship with Sterling, but he did not learn from Sterling anything about the genre that redeemed it for him. To the contrary, the genre demonstrated its faults forcibly to him *via* Sterling. It was a dilettante's genre; it got in the way.

If we consider the poetic intensities of early-nineteenth-century English poetry, such a view may at first seem odd. How could Wordsworthean seriousness and Shelleyan passion be shuffled off so casually? But we should remember that the nineteenth century was one of the most contrarious moments in history, a time when great new scientific and cultural postulates were shaping human thought, and at the same time disrupting it. When the Romantic poets set out to destroy heroic couplets and poetic "essays," they were hardly the only rebels at work. The Western mind in the large was in motion, with consequences for all the professions, disciplines, genres.

Biography was in flux too, but since it had never achieved the formal precisions of other genres, its formal properties were belabored little. At least the critics seem not to have worried about it often between the days of Boswell and those of the "national biographies" (of which the English *Dictionary of National Biography* is to be our specimen here). Its relative structural innocence may, thus, have been an important negative reason for Carlyle's attraction to it, Carlyle the scourge of forms. Yet the choice of a genre, a medium for one's own psyche to perform in, is a major event in an artist's life, even if the artist doesn't think so. Sometimes the event occurs, or is foreseen, early, as apparently it was in Milton's case, and sometimes the event is repeated many times, as the unsure, unsettled artist keeps experimenting, trying out his talent in unfamiliar territory. But in either case every choice he makes is produced by a complicated mixture of changing influences inside him and around him, and in turn the choice influences those influences.

Among the outside influences impinging on Carlyle were those he dealt with in his early lectures on heroes and hero-worship, when he hurried through history spotting what he thought to be the dominant expressive professions of each cultural age. If he had followed this procedure for our own time, he might well have become an exponent (he would have been a noisy one) of "the medium is the message," and have turned himself into a media personage prophesying the end not just of print but of writing too. Yet, as his own life went on, his *inner* forces did not always phase well with such outer ones as these. He was not a consensus thinker, not one to go along with external imperatives, at least consciously. He had, for his own reasons, rejected the ministry and the law, and then climbed to his Edinburgh garret to become a Man of Letters of his own determining. Though he knew that Goethe and his other eighteenth-century heroes had somehow made Men of Letters generically a cultural force, he also had his own singular imperatives telling him that he was his own kind of Man of Letters, not one for instance who was, by some categorical definition, a man of poetry and/or fiction. Even Mill thought of him as a poet because he was intuitive, not because Mill had seen Carlylean verses. (What would the verses have been like?) And Carlyle's only real brush with fiction was *Sartor Resartus*, a mode of expression that, despite the book's success, he then backed away from. One can insist on the Calvinist influence here, and how it helped determine what constituted serious statement for him, as distinguished from Quackery, Puffery, and the like; certainly his criticisms of Sterling, though benign, suggest that his dislike of the established forms of church and state extended to poetic forms. Yet he was not consistent here. If he had been, he surely would not have chosen to cap his life's Man-of-Letters efforts with a scholarly immensity about Frederick the Great.

After all, the endless labors of blindly dutiful scholarship had been for years a prime target for him among the forms, with his Professor Dryasdust's attention to tons of trivia being the bull's-eye he mostly chose. From the beginning, his *Frederick the Great* was an oddly conventional project for such an iconoclast as he. That he did undertake it tells us that he was aging, but also says something about the state of biography in the mid-nineteenth century. By that time the genre had achieved immensity and formlessness, with the result that even though it was the center of much academic frivolity, Carlyle must have felt that he could be true to himself in it, to himself and his essences.

Since he was not a poet or a novelist, his choice did not result in a song of himself, or an autobiographical fiction, but in six volumes of his own turbulent kind of academic historicity. He must have chosen the slavery partly so that he could tell himself that he was not being personal in it, and could not be accused of being so while hiding in the library stacks. He had begun his research about 1851, though he had thought about the man for twenty years before that. Doing the

eight volumes would take another thirteen, and require two trips to
Germany to look at prime sources and battlefields while developing a
sense of German character (he found he did not like it much). It
would also aggravate his neuroses. He sat in his sound-proofed study
in Cheyne Walk suffering, and came out of it complaining. He kept
saying he did not *want* to do Frederick, and kept doing him. Despite
the ostensibly selfless tedium, the Carlyle self was having its day.

All over Europe and America he had become, by the mid-1850s,
one of his own Great Men, and not because of biography either. He
was known as a noisy seer, an anti-church bell ringing out spiritual
alarms, and his reputation was not to be altered by a biography of an
already dim historical figure. Before he had even finished the second
Frederick volume, his complete collected works began appearing, volumes that were duly praised or damned, and his career summed up as
if it were over. According to Kaplan, one critic called him a "fait
accompli." Yet he went ahead anyway. The drive was still in him,
partly the Calvinist work-drive and partly his old ideological drive to
assert sound authority, strong essences.

He called the work history rather than biography, since, by his
gospel, world history and great-man biography were of a piece, and
Frederick had clearly dominated a whole phase of European history.
Frederick he called "the last of the Kings," and he justified going
backward to a lost essence by asking—and not answering—what part
of the "exploded past" might be "reshaped, transformed, re-adapted,
that . . . it [might] enrich and nourish us again." Frederick, who had
"vanished into the inane," was not a promising subject for someone on
the lookout for *living* essences, but Carlyle was lucky in having among
his sources much material about Frederick's childhood, a childhood
that had psychic affinities to his own. From the distance of more than
a century it now seems fair to say that the childhood findings redeemed the whole venture, as biography at least.

His chief early source was the private journal of Frederick's sister
Wilhelmina. He had not faced up seriously to child development in
the genre except with Sterling, and Sterling was a nonhero. In *Sartor
Resartus*, it is true, he had described some experiences of his own
childhood, but only fictionally, deviously. In skimming the early lives
of Luther, Cromwell, and company he had often gone along with
mere legends illustrative of the mature hero's character, but he had
been quick to criticize their doubtful authenticity, and while racing
through the childhood of Cromwell he had positively raged against

biographical reconstructions of early lives, pointing out how little was truly known. So the challenge of showing at length, and accurately, Frederick's childhood and adolescence was essentially new to him. For the first time in his writing life, he now spent his best energies—the first two volumes—on the facts of his hero's pre-leader life.

Interestingly, such an expenditure was in the large new to biography too. He became an innovator despite himself, and his first two volumes were much the best.

Aside from the valuable data he found in the tonnage, he had on his hands a child whose background and upbringing resembled his own. Frederick also was the son of a stern, religious patriarch, and it did not greatly matter that the patriarch was of a different culture and epoch, or that he was a king rather than a stonemason. What mattered was that the patriarch had firm notions about bringing up children and regulating lives and that he was, like James Carlyle, relatively unlettered. The German culture around 1720—before Goethe, Schiller, and the other idealist greats—was like the Scotch culture before Knox. It was filled with "grim hirsute Hyperborean figures . . . growling in guttural Teutsch what little articulate meaning they had," and spending their inarticulate hours drinking beer. Amenities for child princes were supplied by French governesses, and young Frederick knew French before he knew German. His German father did not approve, however, of frenchification—it was effeminate—and put Frederick at age eight in the hands of German males. He also prescribed, in writing, that Frederick should be taught arithmetic, mathematics, artillery, and economy ("economy to the very bottom"); that he should quickly move to fortification; that he should not learn Latin; and that he should learn to reverence God but no papist God. Before the child was ten, the father had him marching around in uniform, leading a true military company of other little ones through constant drills, and becoming "a miniature image of Papa . . . resembling him as a sixpence does a half-crown." Carlyle had not had to do all that for his father, but correspondences must have been easy to imagine.

Then came adolescence and the predictable resistance to the father's thumb. Frederick had no pocket money. He had to go on great hunts. He was provided by Papa with a daily schedule, mixing prayers and military maps. He began to despise hunts and despise the schedule, liking "verses, stories, flute-playing better." The father, worrying lest he become a French fop, had his hair cut short, while Carlyle

watched the son's resentment build with some satisfaction, saying that
Frederick's "Course of Education did on the whole prosper, in spite of
every drawback," producing in the long run a leader "equipped with
knowledge, true in essentials . . . upon all manner of practical and
speculative things." And in the short run it even produced, to Carlyle's
delight, a great runaway episode.

Seventeen-year-old Frederick had made a friend of a certain foppish
Lieutenant Katte. When the royal father brought Frederick and Katte
along on a warlike mission to Berlin, the two quietly left the entourage
and were to be found nowhere. The father took their act to be
outright military desertion, tracked them down in Potsdam, shouted
and swore around the palace, knocked Frederick's sister unconscious
for defending Frederick, and had Katte executed. Carlyle took the
episode through fifty pages, bringing the son up to the point of
composing a letter to his "All-Serenest and All-Gracious Father," con-
fessing his fault and announcing his total, instant reform. (The father
was also considering executing *him*.)

It was a comic letter, if the occasion was not, and in Carlyle's
hands it was also a revealing letter, showing the drift of Frederick's
mind at that point to necessary deceit, which Carlyle then detailed
for another fifty pages. Frederick had to walk warily, to wear "among
his fellow creatures a cloak of darkness, . . . to look cheerily . . . and
yet continue intrinsically invisible to them." He had to "regain favor
with Papa" by eating crow, dutifully learning the management of
"domains" and agreeing to marry a "blockhead." Carlyle at the same
time made perfectly clear that, though Frederick had not just become
a good little boy, he had not become a villainous Machiavel either.
Instead he had begun to like his ferocious Papa even as he tried to
maneuver around him. He was finished with his "apprenticeship" and
ready to be Papa—but better at it.

So what Carlyle had uncovered and described, by the end of
volume 2, was a fine, complicated, psychic mixture in his hero, a quite
different essence from the earlier divine essences he had sought out
and preached. In effect he had put together his own brand of psychobiography, with roots in his own childhood traumas. The biographer
had moved close to the biography.

I don't know of any comparably thorough treatment of the human
maturing process in biography up to this time, especially the exploring
of the father-son relationship. The classical tradition of biography had
in general denied its relevance, the assumption being that there was

always a little fellow who came to be, in a straight line, the big fellow. Plutarch's Cato was the type. Early in life, Plutarch reported, Cato showed "an affection for steady and inflexible justice." Do children ever, early, show that? By 1860 the explorations of self in autobiography and in fiction had begun to be detailed, but biographers had not for the most part acknowledged their connection with such matters, since the adult *public* being was still thought to be their proper province. Carlyle, struggling with his last Great Man, moved in on the prehero province with remarkable prescience.

Of course, he then struggled with six more volumes about Frederick *as* great man. For the future of biography they were not needed.

◦ ◦

That is, they were not needed if the purpose of biographical study is that of finding "the figure in the carpet." That motive has been asserted in our time by Leon Edel—quoting his own biographee James—and by many others as the final motive for biography, but Carlyle, writing of Frederick in the 1860s, found the figure as if by chance in Frederick's childhood—a chance certainly encouraged by his lifetime's researches into his own childhood. Helped by that figure he was able to revise, for example, his early assumptions about divine intervention as the final cause behind the mystery of Great Men learning to "take hold," as in the case of Luther and the thunderstorm. (More of Luther later while discussing Erik Erikson.) The theory of maturing he had expressed in his hero-worship volume had been that of natural, essential leaders living a life of psychic calm until, in maturity, they were somehow suddenly stirred up to cosmic needs for rebellion against the status quo. That was a romantic theory indeed, and Carlyle pretty well destroyed it while dealing with Frederick. In doing so he joined the moderns.

Then, when he was seventy and at last finished with Frederick, came the death of Jane. Carlyle felt like no hero but only a miserable, erring human when he undertook a short biography of her. He began it with an account of Jane's life written by Geraldine Jewsbury, which detailed not only Jane's talents and strength of character ("very few women so truly great," Jewsbury concluded, "come into the world at all") but also her long sufferance as helpmeet of a finicky genius. Jewsbury was a great admirer of George Sand, and apparently a lesbian. There has been speculation about her relations with Jane, but Kaplan's considerate account suggests that the advances were hers and that Jane rejected them. Probably some enterprising biographer will

come along, if he has not already, and carry Frank Harris's caricature
of Carlyle as a weepy penitent about his impotence one step further,
by proposing that both Thomas and Jane were promiscuously homo-
sexual. But my sense of them is that, instead, they were both sexually
repressed, and that Carlyle himself addressed his problem by letting
loose in his prose. In any event, after including the Jewsbury account
he acknowledged and thanked Jewsbury for her truths, and proceeded
with his own encomium of Jane, which was touchingly, devotedly
sentimental. If he was doing penance, so be it. It was worthy penance.

Of course he had always wanted to be worthy of her by being one
of his own Great Men, and even at the end his ego was still at work
in him in ways that future biographers would find inappropriate in
biography. In America, particularly, the demonstrative narrators who
were influenced by him did not take to biography at all, but to
autobiographical fiction, poetry, and meditations, most notably *Walden*, *Song of Myself*, *Moby Dick*, and *Bartleby the Scrivener*. For it was in
other genres than biography that a great ego could be itself without
being a threat to others. Carlyle, in his memoir of Jane, accepted with
surprising humility that he had been a threat to her, but he did serve
his penitent self as the same time.

All in all, despite that memoir, his crusty authoritarianism does
not seem ever to have left him. As a result, apologies were being made
for him, as a breeder of tyrants, long before German idealism had
become National Socialism. In 1886 even Leslie Stephen made apologies in the *Dictionary of National Biography*, asserting that Carlyle's
kind of arrogant prescience might well confuse a Cromwell with a
Napoleon, and adding sharply that his merits as a preacher were to
be estimated by his stimulus to thought rather than by the soundness
of his conclusions.

But now we are at least far enough away from him, and from
Hitler, to understand him as of a quite different historical era from
that which bred Hitler, and to let at least some of his views rest quietly
with, say, Mill's utilitarianism, as instances of a kind of social hypoth-
esizing now suspect but not thereby originally malignant.

And we can as well, I think, now understand his eccentric, intense
approach to biography as of the same order. The essence he preached
may have been a confused essence, a transitional essence, an historical
phenomenon, and his intensity about it as he preached it now seems,
to say the least, generically misplaced, so badly so that there will
probably never be another biographer so wrapped up in his own

schemes as he, or so conspicuously his own subject (though I will come to the problem of Norman Mailer). Yet we can at least say of him that he was eloquently wrapped up. He was a great writer who was tyrannical about every sentence he ever wrote. Here are two samples of Carlylean verbal tyranny, one early and one late.

> ... History can note with satisfaction, on the ruins of the Bastille, a Statue of Nature; gigantic, spouting water from her two mammals. Not a dream this, but a fact, palpable, visible. There she spouts, great Nature; dim, before daybreak. But as the coming Sun ruddies the East, come countless Multitudes, regulated and unregulated; come Departmental Deputies, come Mother Society and Daughters; come National Convention, led on by handsome Herault; soft wild music breathing note of expectation. Lo, as great Sol scatters his first fire-handful, tipping the chimneys and chimney-heads with gold, Herault is at Nature's feet (she is plaster of paris merely); Herault lifts, in an iron saucer, water spouted from the sacred breasts; drinks of it, with an eloquent Pagan Prayer, beginning 'O Nature!' and all the Department Deputies drink, each with what best suitable ejaculation or prophetic-utterance is in him. *(The French Revolution)*

> His Majesty is in a flaming height. He arrests, punishes and banishes, where there is trace of cooperation or connection with Deserter Fritz and his schemes. The Bulows, brother in the King's service, sister in Wilhelmina's respectable goldstick people, originally of Hanover, are hurled out to Lithuania and the world's end: let them live in Memel, and repent as they can. Minister Knyphausen, always of English tendencies he, with his Wife, to whom it is specially hard, while General Schwerin, gallant, witty Kurt, once of Meckleburg stays behind—is ordered to disappear, and follow his private rural business far off; no minister, ever more. *(Frederick, vol. 2)*

II

Leslie Stephen's *DNB* and the Woolf Rejoinders

L eslie Stephen (1832–1904) was the first editor of the *Dictionary of National Biography*, and he also wrote the *DNB*'s biography of Carlyle. It is a model biography for the *DNB* project, but it is also a kind of biography that Carlyle would not have wished to write.

Stephen knew Carlyle's works well, and would not have wished to write *them*. He described Carlyle's style as the worst possible model and encouraged in his own biographers an alternative approach to the genre that was conspicuously anti-Carlylean. Also, though his own brother, James Fitzjames Stephen, was a Carlyle intimate and became Carlyle's executor,* Leslie found Carlyle personally difficult and thought Carlyle did not like him. But from a distance he much admired the man. When his daughter, Virginia, was fifteen, he gave her a reading list of fifteen books, of which four were by Carlyle and one was Froude's biography of Carlyle. He knew him as a man to be reckoned with.

Both Stephen and John Stuart Mill saw powers in Carlyle that they did not themselves have and an approach to essences that they could not themselves take. The words *poet* and *mystic* come to mind—for neither Mill nor Stephen thought of themselves as either—but words are not sufficient here, especially since Carlyle himself frowned on most poets after Goethe. Let me dwell instead upon essences, move

---

*James Stephen did, though, review Carlyle's *Collected Works* with some of Leslie's reservations, saying that Carlyle was "a real and great genius" but an "unreliable moralist and politician." (Kaplan, *Carlyle*, 143.)

away from Carlyle for a moment, and consider, as a fine essence, the white whale.

It was thoughtful of Herman Melville to make the white whale accessible to us. The whale was not accessible to Ahab. He had to sail the oceans to find it, and when he found it, he had to reckon with the biggest fact about it, that it was just not an accessible whale. But now, as a result of Melville's labors and all the scholars who have labored after him, anybody can row out to it, row around it, and then row safely back to shore, perhaps taking notes about it. It is at anchor off the town wharf, the mere relic of an untamed essence.

We should remember it in its untamed days, though if we do it is hard to see its resemblance to the psychic essence I mentioned earlier. Psyche was a beautiful human female in Apuleius's first-century fable who was admitted to the essence known as heaven because Cupid loved her. Heaven was not far away then. It was a domestic place, and Cupid himself, though a god, had a domestic body with a natural affinity for Psyche. The nineteenth century, perhaps helped by "German Philosophy" but more by a whole new world of knowledge and enterprise, translated their affair into one with an earthly essence, bringing about the stirrings we have seen in Carlyle, himself an Ahab. (Could Melville have had Carlyle in mind as Ahab? I do not quite jest, though I think it more likely that Melville had Melville in mind.) When Carlyle walked about in Edinburgh, then London, as a young historian, political thinker, Calvinist *manqué*, and Man of Letters, he was looking for *his* white whale.

The Man-of-Letters role was the one suiting Carlyle's Ahabian need best. Goethe and others had shown him that the Man of Letters was the new age's form of hero, "our most important modern person," even though he sat "in his squalid garret in his rusty coat." He was important, beyond all other persons, because he was concerned with essences. He was after big game.

And negatively Carlyle was, like Melville's squalid Bartleby, one who made much of what he preferred *not* to do. He preferred not to concern himself with small game, not to be a clerk or Professor Dryasdust. He was after "the Reality which lies at the bottom of all appearance," and in that role he played guide to others with less lofty aims. Though he was not, then, as great as Goethe, or Johnson, or Burns, or Rousseau, he still imagined himself as a "wild Ishmaelite" of a Man of Letters, like Ahab's own narrator. His proper ambition was not to continue to walk "unrecognized, unregulated" among us, but to "step forth one day with palpably articulated, universally visible power."

The essence productive of such power was potentially of whale dimensions, and since Ishmael-Carlyle was a biographer, the genre made unlimited demands on him. Each biographee had to be the white whale, even before Melville invented him.

Melville's debt to the transcendentalists is not my point here, though the debt is large, goes beyond Melville, and continues in American fiction and poetry right into the twentieth century. My point is that the debt has not carried over into biography. Neither in England nor America have the biographers been attracted to large essences. Led by Leslie, they have steadily been ready to scuttle biographical Ahabism. Perhaps Stephen's objection to it was, as he implied in his constant depreciation of his own talent, that he was not personally up to whaling, or perhaps it was that he really doubted the white whale's existence. Either way, he denied the whale, and the result was the *DNB*.

His attraction to Carlyle may have proceeded from his being, like Carlyle, both Scotch and Evangelical, but the Scotch in him was two generations back, and the Evangelical in him was within the Church of England. Stephen's grandfather had become a prominent English importer and member of the House of Commons. His father, for some years colonial undersecretary for Great Britain, had become a professor of modern history at Cambridge and also a biographer, a turgid scholar whose prose style went against his own preaching of the virtue of simplicity. The father produced a two-volume study of ecclesiastical biography in which he said that while he was reading his predecessors, his ear ached "for a few plain words quietly taking their proper places," but his own words left ears aching. Leslie may have been driven into clarity and brevity in reaction.

The father brought the children up in London, though when young Leslie was, regularly, sick, he took them all, regularly, to Bath. In being an unpleasured utilitarian the father resembled John Stuart Mill's father. He was a severe, hard-working puritan, subject to great depressions, who did not abandon Christianity dogmatically—as James Mill had—but managed to display enough disaffection from it, in his Cambridge lecturing, to be much criticized. Unlike James Mill he did not himself educate his sons—indeed he kept his distance from them, as well as from everyone else—but he must at least have planted agnostic seeds in them. He sent them both to Eton, which they despised, and then Cambridge, where they were bred up with only nominal Christian faith. Leslie by his own account took orders at Cambridge only to become a don and defray his father's college expenses for him. He then gave up the church appointment, after deciding, he said, that he did not believe in Noah's Flood. Whether the Flood was involved, or merely a change in the financing of his appointment, his account is strikingly casual, with no suggestion of spiritual conversion. He seemed to move out of the ministry into Life as if changing offices in Fleet Street.

There remains the likelihood, though, that his casual air concealed unmentionable stresses. Carlyle too had unmentionable stresses—it was Victorian to have them—but while he couldn't mention them, he exuded them anyway with his urgent manner. Stephen neither spoke them nor showed them, except in the following odd passage, addressed privately to his children much later (and published, as *The Mausoleum Book*, a safe seventy years after his death):

> My mental and moral development followed a quiet and commonplace course enough. I do, indeed, remember certain facts about myself. I could give a history of some struggles through which I had to pass— successfully or otherwise; but I have a certain sense of satisfaction in reflecting that I shall take that knowledge with me to the grave. There was nothing unusual or remarkable about my inner life; although I may say that without a knowledge of the facts to which I have referred, nobody could write a history of my life. As the knowledge is confined to me, and will never be imparted by me to others, it follows that no adequate history of my life can ever be written. The world will lose little by that.

Now *there* is a logical swamp, and Stephen then swamped the passage further with a little footnote:

> The only living person who could say anything to the purpose at present would be F. W. Maitland. He as I always feel understands me, and I have explained my view upon this subject to him. But even he could only write a short article or 'appreciation.' . . . No 'life' in the ordinary sense is possible.

These remarks manage to declare, simultaneously, the importance and unimportance of the inner life, a whale that Stephen could not face yet wished to characterize as a minnow. Certainly he did not wish the world to face it, so broadly proposed its indispensable existence to any biographer.

It follows that F. W. Maitland, one of England's greatest historians but also a relative of Stephen's, did undertake the impossible biography and did little with Stephen's inner life. The Victorian climate for biography favored protecting near and dear ones, and helping them carry the inner life to the grave. At the same time it was a climate full of the new scientism, with its earnest truth-protestations. In other words it was a complicated, changeable English upper-middle-class climate, to which Carlyle came late and uneasily, but in which Stephen grew up.

As his modern biographer Noel Annan has noted, Stephen's family ties were to a large political-spiritual clan, the Clapham Sect, of important persons who "did not belong to either the High and Dry or the Low and Slow parties in the Church" of England, and were commonly to be found working for reforms the ruling class was resisting. They possessed security, however, in the form of big-business connections and an in-group consensus about values that made them Establishment even when they were resisting Establishment. Certainly they were above "grinding economy, seediness and niggling," and possessed of a "natural ease of manner"—persons with names such as Wilberforce, Macaulay, Trevelyan, Bradley, Symonds, Duckworth, Strachey, Wedgwood, and Russell. They could not have produced a Carlyle, though in Stephen they produced a sensibility capable of appreciating him, and they were restrained, by breeding, from emulating him. The breeding made literary whaling bad form.

Cambridge developed his proprieties forcefully, transforming a sickly adolescent into a strong oarsman, hiker, and mountain climber, a "muscular Christian" who became a rowing coach, the president of a walking club, and for a time, something of an anti-intellectual. Cambridge also developed in him a spirit of scientific caution and skepticism. Biographer Annan put it that a Cambridge man of the period, unlike an Oxford man, was suspicious of prophets, preferring "to take on studies which were precise and yield[ed] tangible results." The Cambridge man did not go along with the likes of Oxford's Professor Jowett, who was Stephen's bane. From the point of view of the Cambridge mind, Jowett was "an intellectual harlot masquerading beneath the bombazine of a high-minded ethic," hence "the antithesis of the Cambridge mind." Of course Annan was himself a Cambridge mind, which was "a mind in firm control of the heart," and so was aware of what such control could eliminate from life. His biographical intimacy with Stephen kept revealing to him how Stephen had struggled against the controls, but revealing also how effectively the controls dominated the career. His biography shows the balance handsomely.

Stephen set out in the world, after the ministry, as a political journalist, writing several columns a week for such periodicals as the *Saturday Review* (where his brother was a prominent contributor) and the *Pall Mall Gazette*. Then in his early forties he switched to loftier expression, trying his hand as an historian of ideas. During the 1870s he wrote the two-volume *History of English Thought in the Eighteenth Century*, which he later, too modestly, described as superficial, while at the same time he undertook a book on Alpine climbing, as well as articles for the anthology *Peaks, Passes, and Glaciers*. Also at that time he became editor of the *Cornhill Magazine*, which was bourgeois rather than lofty. In short, up to middle age he was a gentlemanly liberal with miscellaneously aimed energy. He did not change his spots when he turned the energy on biography, and his life, unlike Carlyle's, does not seem to have been marked by any significant spiritual conversion.

Annan described the *Cornhill* as "a family magazine . . . designed for drawing-room tables of the upper-middle class," in which Stephen was careful not to offend Victorian Christianity and prudery. He even had to caution Matthew Arnold against questioning miracles and tell Thomas Hardy "that the heroine in *The Trumpet Major* married the wrong man." Hardy replied that "they mostly did," and Stephen said, "not in magazines." He thought of himself as a free thinker, but was careful, unlike Carlyle, to be inoffensively so.

Despite his caution the magazine did not thrive financially, but the owner, George Smith, was impressed by him anyway and in 1882–83 launched the *DNB* with Stephen at the helm. George Smith seems to have been a businessman-saint who, having made a sufficient fortune in table water to do something capitalistically else, turned to publishing and became the benefactor of many good writers. He undertook the *DNB* with the expectation of losing £50,000, actually lost £70,000, and could afford not to mind. As the publisher of Thackeray he watched forty-year-old Stephen become enamored of, and wedded to, Thackeray's daughter Minnie (whose sister Annie, a novelist, then moved in with them), and must have seen Stephen as much socially as in his office-study. For his long association with Stephen he was rewarded posthumously by Stephen's ambiguous description of him as "a fine generous fellow . . . as liberal and honest as a publisher can be." Certainly Stephen depended on him, for all those years, for a straight salary, with all the personal complications that such a friendship produces. Smith seems to have let Stephen run the *DNB* show and become the primary shaper of its biographical formula. There is, though, no way of telling what direction Stephen's career might have taken if he had remained a bachelor don, and had not met Smith. My guess is that he might not have gone into biography at all.

I say this, thinking of his history of eighteenth-century thought. The history developed his talent for rendering abstractions precisely and clearly, a talent that might, under different conditions, have gone whaling. He must have found an intellectual challenge in writing the history that editing the *Cornhill* did not offer him, since in the history he was thoroughly at home. There, in survey fashion, he described the ideological positions of the best and most complicated eighteenth-century minds he could find—Descartes, Locke, Berkeley, Hume, and the rest—and showed himself to be a better expositor than they. I am an outsider to the history of philosophy, and do not know a better place to go than to Leslie Stephen's work to understand, for instance, Berkeley's "direct and immediate demonstration of God's existence." (Berkeley himself I have opened without enlightenment.) Stephen both knew the material well and enjoyed it, so that for him to move into the dryasdust of dictionary work was an intellectual comedown. In the *DNB* it was not appropriate—or so he conceived the dictionary's function—to focus on what a biographee *thought*.

His decision to take on the *DNB*, and to limit its biographical intent, must have been based partly on his constant need for money, and partly on his own observations about the tenuousness of relations between thoughts and lives, or thoughts and the world around thoughts. In formulating the *DNB*'s premises he saw himself as of an age that did not deal happily with abstract thought-whales. He also saw *himself* as easily too abstract, and put his own problem well as he described Hume's blindness to the connections between philosophic truth and history. Hume's method "confined him to the examination of the individual *mind*" (my italics), isolating him from "the faculties of the individual [that had] been built up by the past experiences of the race." Hume's search for truth was, then, like Ahab's ocean quest, in that it proceeded independently of the world around him. Stephen's surroundings and obligations made him fear Ahabian obsessions, and he thought biography should fear them too.

If his familial and educational past made him a conformist, so, though painfully, did marriage. In fact, marriage, coming into his life at age thirty-five, probably kept him from becoming an old-maid don who, in Annan's words, "gyrated in orbits of ever wilder eccentricity." Marrying Minnie Thackeray in 1867, he was brought into the Thackeray social circle, and then was brought into parenthood by the birth of Laura, a retarded child who was not recognized as retarded until nearly grown. Following the sudden death of Minnie in 1875, Stephen was brought into deeper family waters by marrying the widowed Julia Duckworth (nee Jackson). Julia had two children of her own, and she and Leslie then had four more, further discouraging Ahabism.

So though Stephen was like childless Carlyle in his demands for privacy and silence, he could not readily make the demands stick, and may not have wanted to. His daughter Virginia said of him that he was really three people: the sociable father, the writer father, and the tyrant father. The father she remembered best was the tyrant father— presumably the father Carlyle would have been—and when he was *that* father, "it was like being shut up in the same cage with some wild beast":

> Suppose I, at age 15, was a nervous, gibbering, little monkey, always spitting or cracking a nut and shying the shells about, and mopping and mowing, and leaping into dark corners, and then swinging in raptures across the cage, he was the pacing, dangerous, morose lion; a lion who was sulky and angry and injured; and suddenly ferocious, and then very humble, and then majestic; and then lying dusty and fly pestered in a corner of the cage.

Naturally, at fifteen she would have remembered that father best— and he is the unpleasant father who appears, mostly, in *To the Lighthouse*—but there were the other fathers too: the writer father who presumably engendered the tyrant father, and the sociable father who had to escape being either. The sociable father was a family father, a sentimentalist, and a great storer-up of miscellaneous familial detail, of which *The Mausoleum Book* is full. If Stephen had been only a tyrant father, he might have been able, like Carlyle, to chase a great whale; but with these other identities to fill, the *DNB* was a good project for him, as well as for the age.

He was sensitive, though, about the lowbrow character of dictionary-making, and kept complaining like Carlyle about dryasdust detail. He could even sound like Carlyle occasionally, though he was mostly just "dusty and fly pestered." In a late essay on the whole subject of national biography he joked about a certain worthy Simon Browne who "had received a terrible shock," with the result that "his mind became affected" and "he fancied that his 'spiritual substance' had been annihilated." He was, therefore, "a mere empty shell, a body without a soul." What could he do? "Under these circumstances . . . he took to an employment which did not require a soul: he became a dictionary-maker." After telling the joke Leslie went on to defend the *DNB*, but his defense—there and in other writings, especially *The Mausoleum Book*—was excessively modest. He *had* hoped for more of himself. He *had* hoped to be mentioned in other than "small type and footnotes" when "the history of English thought in the 19th century" was written.

It was at age fifty, with his fourth child Virginia just born, that he took on the dread *DNB*. Doing so was neither a No nor a Yes for him. It was an enormous Job. He personally wrote 378 of the accounts in the first twenty volumes, gravitating to big authors like Coleridge, Dickens, Fielding, Johnson, Milton, and, yes, Thackeray. Each of the big subjects extracted from him between five and ten thousand words, but he led the *DNB*'s coverage into "the second-rate people" too, a procedure for which there were plenty of antiquarian precedents. He was by no means the originator of national biography—and Annan describes him as in a race, in the 1880s, against a number of similar enterprises on the Continent—but he personally supervised and put together the first *DNB* volumes, setting their focus, format, guidelines, and tone. In an age of democratic pluralism and scientific encyclopedism they set a remarkably high standard for dictionary biography.

Yet if they had contained a biography of the White Whale, it would have begun by describing him as "a large, warm-blooded, fishlike mammal" and then would have contained, as the main body of the text, a detailed chronological account of his travels through the seven seas, concluding with a brief evaluation of his performance in comparison with one or two of his whale contemporaries. And omitting any mention of an Essence behind the mask.

Blame the omission perhaps, on Cambridge, where objectivity and attention to facts prevailed. Other Cambridge desiderata: detachment and attention to method and structure. With these objectives in mind the word *science* of course also enters the mind, as it certainly entered Stephen's mind and the minds of the Cambridge editors of the *Encyclopedia Britannica* of the period. Suddenly all classifiable objects, including selves, were approached scientifically. Stephen was conven-

tional in his scientism except when he poor-mouthed the results, one
of his interesting habits.

Yes, after the *Dictionary* had been in progress three years, he told
Julia, "When I am by myself I always begin thinking what poor stuff
all my writing is. . . . the practical moral is that I may as well do
Dictionary work as anything else." In saying that he was saying what
Carlyle might have said of him, and of the *DNB*, but he was also
acknowledging what had become for better or worse, his *virtù*.

• •

In late life Stephen described the function of the *DNB* as primarily
that of codification. He professed to think that the longish biographies
in *DNB*, such as those he took on himself, were not priority items in
the project, since the big names were known and attended to elsewhere. Doing well by the "second-rate people" was the main job,
though by doing well with them he did not, he said, mean quite what
his editor-successor Sidney Lee meant when he proposed that the
great function of the *DNB* was commemorative. No, there had to be
a plan, somehow and somewhere, for separating the sheep from the
goats. To use his metaphor, the *DNB* had to be a "causeway" through
the "morass of antiquarian accumulation."

In arguing for his causeway he referred directly to Carlyle and to
Carlyle's rages against the "vast dust-heaps accumulated by Dryasdust
and his fellows." He wanted to save scholars, like Carlyle and himself,
from the dust-heaps—and of course he might well have added wanting
to save the librarians. He was speaking in 1898, speaking the complaint
now endemic in academia, and his irony was heavy. He doubted that
the accumulation was an "unmixed benefit." He said that to walk
through a library was to feel the wilderness springing up about one
"with tropical luxuriance." He did not, however, give an answer to his
sensible question of how to reduce a biographical dictionary's size
from, say, 300,000 to 30,000 names, and he concluded by proposing,
with fine British humanism, only "a rule of thumb."

He was more specific with his program for handling those who
were in fact chosen. The first rule was condensation, "the virtue to
which all others [had to be] sacrificed," and he gave several sentences
over to describing what was *not* to be included: "I used rigidly to excise
the sentence, 'Nothing is known of his birth or parentage,' which
tended to appear in half the lives, because where nothing is known it
seems simpler that nothing should be said; and yet a man might have

to consult a whole series of books before discovering even that negative fact." He then added that the biographer should, again in the interests of condensation, "often make the sacrifice of keeping his most important reflections to himself." But at this point he inserted a vital qualification, saying that the important reflections of the biographer, though not expressed, should nonetheless "be in his mind," for if they were in his mind they would govern the condensing: "The difference may be enormous between the writer who sees what are the really cardinal facts and the writer to whom any and every fact is of the same importance; and yet both narratives may appear at first sight to be equally dry and barren."

This was sound advice for any biographical scholar, and also a way of characterizing the meaning of "rule of thumb," with the thumb only to be exercised by someone with an *experienced* thumb. Unfortunately, it was also advice that could only finally distance biographer from biographee, even if the biographer was as thorough and conscientious as Stephen himself. Carlyle could not have lived with it.

This matter of the biographer's tie to his subject interested Stephen greatly, it being a point that went far beyond *DNB* requirements, and perhaps his own talents. While still ostensibly discussing the *DNB*, he took several pages to meditate on what would have happened if Boswell had not been the one who had written Johnson's biography, but it had instead been written by "a most detestable fellow," Sir John Hawkins, whom Johnson had happened to like. Hawkins, Stephen said, would have presented Johnson as an impressive but grotesque figure who went to parties at the Devils Tavern and shocked Hawkins slightly, though only drinking lemonade. Hawkins, an "unusually dull, censorious and self-righteous specimen of the British middle class of his time," could not even see that Johnson had a sense of humor, whereas a true biographer, like Boswell, could be depended on to become a full partner in the biographical proceedings. In other words a biography, to be successful, required both a good subject and a biographer up to the demands of the subject.

Yes, indeed. But could the true biographer be both a good *Cambridgean* and a full partner? There was Stephen's dilemma, the one that made him a moody lion, since tied to his procedures for biography was a psychological impediment to full partnership. He could admire from a distance the extended commitments of Boswell and Carlyle, but he could not himself take on such burdens. He liked to have his subjects nicely boxed before he started, did not like the

unknown. If he had been Ahab, he would have arranged in advance
to encounter the White Whale at a particular spot south of the
Marquesas on a Thursday morning, and he would have brought along
modern weapons. As he put it (with yet another metaphor), for him
it was a matter of "laying bricks, not blowing futile soap bubbles."

The result was a great dictionary and an important—if not always
wisely important—influence upon modern biography generally. He
endlessly purified the biographer's role by excision and in the process
brought a kind of order to the least orderly genre we have. If we put
aside for a moment his own reservations about the process, we can
build a strong case for the *DNB* formula as an admirable one for the
genre generally. At the level of the "second-rate people" it gives us, in
a paragraph or two, all we need or want to know about such persons
as "MacFarlane, Mrs., murderess," who, having married John Mac-
Farlane, met a certain John Cayley, and when Captain Cayley called
on her on 29 December 1716, she, "for reasons known only to herself
and him, fired two shots at him, one of them pierced his heart," then
went and hid somewhere so successfully that she later became a figure
in a story by Sir Walter Scott. Finis. And at the level of the longer
biographies it gives us in a few pages what takes hundreds in the
hands of dryasdusts.

Furthermore, the longer biographies, especially those written by
Stephen himself, are models of how to take a pat biographical format
and make it personable. Stephen's scientism did not extend to his
sense of what constitutes a readable, human text. His biography of
Carlyle is his prize, and still, I think, the best place for a scholar to
begin in studying any part of the Carlyle saga. He left out no significant relationship or event in the life (though he was understandably
weak on the Emerson connection, where Mark Van Doren, later, in
the *Dictionary of American Biography*, was strong), and he illuminated
each detail with the right references for further study. He put forth
the beginnings, and trials, of each of Carlyle's significant works, together with their reception. He dealt chastely but helpfully with Carlyle's life with Jane, and had many knowledgeable observations to
make about Carlyle's temperament. He expressed, as well, many strong
and provocative opinions about both the man and the work—for
neutrality of judgment was not part of his scientism—and he did so
with the kind of authoritative modesty that will catch a student
plagiarist almost every time. Thus the good student will see—and the
bad will not—that to write of Carlyle that he "judged by intuition

rather than calculation" and that "conventionality was for him the deadly sin" is to copy something that needs attribution. Leslie Stephen was always present, inconspicuously.

Yet he was, as he pointed out, also holding himself in. He was leaving to the reader—whom he pictured as more intelligent than a plagiarizing student—the job of putting "the dots over the *i*'s" and deciding on the significance of biographical facts provided. Furthermore, he was not disposed to provide the reader with what might be called ideological facts. A student, good or bad, looking to Stephen's Carlyle biography for a quick way into transcendentalism, should be advised to go to almost any other reference book.

The ideological omissions are also evident and striking in his dictionary biographies of Locke and Hobbes, whose philosophies he had well described in separate, short volumes for the English Men of Letters series. Writing of Locke for the *DNB* he crammed almost every possibly useful fact about the man's family, education, and career into ten pages, and dealt with the publication and reception of each work, but managed to say nothing at all, directly, of what Locke's *Essay on Human Understanding* was "about." In fact, he was so referential about that central work that a reader can find the full title of it only at the end of the piece; elsewhere it is referred to as "the Essay." Here is a characteristic passage, in which, please note, he shows no interest whatsoever in describing Kantian doctrines or "innate ideas":

> Locke's authority as a philosopher was unrivalled in England during the first half of the 18th century, and retained great weight until the spread of Kantian doctrines. . . . His spiritual descendant, J. S. Mill, indicates his main achievement by calling him the unquestioned founder of the analytical philosophy of mind. . . . His famous attack upon 'innate ideas' expressed his most characteristic tendency . . . but critics have not agreed as to what is precisely meant by innate ideas.

Stephen could defend his omissions on the ground that the *DNB* was not the place for ideas, innate or other, but for facts; and he must have felt that he personally knew too much about the ideas to summarize them roughly for future misuse, so he saved his words about them for his English Men of Letters biography of Locke. Still, other editors of encyclopedias have not felt equally rigorous, and the editors of the *American Dictionary of Biography* are among them. The *ADM*, which began in the 1930s, was modelled in most ways upon the *DNB*, but has deviated in its handling of the basic beliefs, tenets, and doctrines of its biographees. A fine example is its biography of Mary Baker Eddy, written by one of the editors of *ADB*, Allen Johnson. Johnson's account has an excellent summary of Eddy's faith and philosophy, and while her thoughts may be easier for a biographer to summarize than Locke's or Hobbes', she obviously can be misrepresented too. The problem is not one of scholarship, in the biographer or his reader, but of simple codification. How far beyond vital statistics should a dictionary biographer go? For not very clear reasons Stephen usually decided not to be a thinker while he was being a dictionary biographer, though he allowed himself unlimited incidental opinions.

As an aside about the presenting of opinion it should be said that Stephen's successor on the *DNB*, Sidney Lee, was of the same eccentric school, with the result that the *DNB*'s final, sixty-three-volume immensity (not counting supplements) is remarkably uniform, for a reference work, in *not* being uniform. Lee was a vital statistics man too, but he was also a Victorian prude who enjoyed expressing his prudery and tended to complain about his biographees' morals rather than ignore them. He spoke as a clergyman, for instance, when he took on Laurence Sterne, managing to disapprove of both his private conduct and his literary foolery. At the outset Lee was not even disposed to label Sterne a writer or a divine, but only a humourist and sentimentalist, two terms precise but insufficient and derogatory. And he harped censoriously on Sterne's "light-hearted indifference [to his] sacred function," his wife-enraging "visit to London on an adulterous errand," and his "compromising relations with a maid-servant," bringing about, according to Lee's account, "an attack of insanity in the wife."* Of the genius of Sterne he made only brief acknowledgment at the end, yet his account remains an excellent preliminary source of information on Sterne. That the *DNB* could encompass such diversions as Lee's, yet do its dictionary business, is a tribute to its underlying humanity—no modern dictionary is so tolerant of personal intrusion.

The intrusions, though, were usually of a certain kind for both Lee and Stephen. Both of them were committed to displaying *moral* character, which meant that they liked to comment on proper and

---

*In contrast to the Lee account, A. Alvarez introduces the Penguin edition of Sterne's *Sentimental Journey* by sympathizing with Sterne's unfortunate predicament, holed up in a Yorkshire parsonage "with a half-mad wife." (Alvarez, Introduction to *A Sentimental Journey* [New York: Penguin, 1968], x.)

improper social conduct. With such an emphasis they could be immensely inhibited about mentioning inner lives, the main subject of most modern biography. The inhibition is most evident in Stephen's EML biographies of Locke and Hobbes, where, under no pressure to be concise, he bottled himself up anyway. He carefully walled the lives away from the thoughts, by devoting the first quarter of each volume exclusively to the life and the last three-quarters exclusively to the thoughts. (In the thoughts section he was wholly abstract, seldom even mentioning the thinker.) And he also restricted his observations about character to the qualities of his subjects visible in a parlor at tea. Both Hobbes and Locke had been, like most of England's intellectuals in the seventeenth century, in political hot water at one time or another and had been driven abroad by the officialdom in power, but while Stephen was attracted to the ins and outs of the countercultural politics and was conscientious in tracing the miles of his subjects' travels, he had no time for their personal traumas. Instead, he was anxious to show that Hobbes, celebrated for his ferocity in print, was really very *nice.* "It would be altogether unjust," he observed, possibly thinking of himself, "to set down Hobbes as a man of cold nature. . . . Everything goes to show that he was a man of kindly, if not ardent affections." He went so far as to defend Hobbes for being something of a "cold bath" (as Minnie and Annie Thackeray sometimes described Stephen himself): "A man who is above all to be a cool reasoner and to shrink from no conclusion forced upon him by logic, is a very valuable person, and may be forgiven if his spiritual temperature does not rise to the boiling point and obscure his clearness of vision." So much for "character." There was no reason to go further.

But when it came to the thoughts of biographees he could be spacious—in the proper place; the proper place was simply not the *DNB.* He had scholarly justification for avoiding ideological simplification right out of Locke himself, for whose approach to thought he had great sympathy. Early in his Locke account he pointed to Locke's "lifelong dislike of priestly authority," and made clear that his anti-authoritarianism was intellectual as well as political; one didn't just establish the meaning of "innate ideas" by fiat. Our excellent modern *Catholic Encyclopedia,* in handling Locke, rushes right into specificity of definition at this point, by enumerating three specific kinds of innate ideas, and there the ideas sit, in any public library, ready to be abused by a sophomore. Neither Locke nor Stephen would have approved of the *CE*'s procedure, and the *DNB* under Stephen was not allowed to approve either. As the confused utopian Axel Heyst kept saying in Conrad's novel *Victory*, "It's facts that I want, facts." If there was anything that the *DNB* taught Stephen, it was that biography began with facts.

Of course he knew well that there were other ingredients to the genre than facts, but working for eight years at the *DNB* made it hard for him to think of them. At the *DNB* he had to think facts, and he had to think small. He had to think in terms of deadlines and in terms of the surface life of a subject, the vital statistics, the visible accomplishments. He had to think hard-headedly, in the way that has become the mark of the professional journalist-biographers of our time, who can turn out lives by the yard.

But did Stephen come to think that biography in the large had also to be like the *DNB* procedurally? The end of his career suggests that he did, while regretting that he did and lacerating himself with the contradiction.

With puritan intensity he struggled with the *DNB* alone for eight years, and "a very worrying piece of work" it was. Then he went on with the help of Lee for another three before resigning. By the time he resigned, twenty-six volumes had appeared (they came out quarterly, starting in 1885), and he had made himself seriously ill with them. A good professional should have known better than to do this, but at bottom he was not a good professional; he was a troubled man *trying* to be a good professional while believing that he was, somehow, above mere professionalism. "I fancied," he said, "that I was completely well but in 1888 I had a serious attack. Julia one night found me in a state of unconsciousness." He had further attacks. He also had trouble sleeping, would "sometimes awake in a fit of horrors," and suffered periods of deep depression that he felt obliged to apologize for to his children (in *The Mausoleum Book*). His point for the apology was that in those periods he had treated Julia badly, as he presumably had. He protested that he was not the tyrant that Carlyle had been, but of course he had Carlyle in mind as he did so. The high model was always Carlyle, even in guilt. "If I felt," he said, "that I had a burden upon my conscience like that which tortured poor Carlyle (in his treatment of Jane), I think I should be tempted to commit suicide." Biographer Annan uses, cautiously, the word "manic" about him, noting not only his depressions but also his compensations for them, notably overwork. A good professional writing machine cannot be temperamentally like that, for long.

He did not like to admit that he could not be like that, did not like to admit his own problems, except in wild bursts, but instead preferred to find the manic strain in others, notably the Thackeray family. Except when "hideous fancies haunted him," he tended to agree with his family that he was a cold bath. Yet there he was, *en famille*, with all his Carlylean intensities, intensities that he simply kept out of his biographies. He had a study nearly as isolated as Carlyle's, and he sat in it in an enormous rocker in such a way that his feet never even touched the floor, sat there with his own great and forbidding self, and self alone, being objective until dinner time.

Recovering physically from the *DNB* in the mid-nineties, he proceeded to live another ten productive years, despite Julia's death in 1895. He wrote a biography of his brother and one of a Cambridge friend, Henry Fawcett, but these, not being properly objective, were not properly biographies either; they were reminiscences. And as further distractions from biography proper he took on his contributions to the English Men of Letters series. In the latter he could be chatty and discursive about the lives of his subjects for the first fifty pages, and then methodically shift over to his subjects' thoughts for the rest, putting the lives quite out of mind and talking of the thoughts as if they could have been anybody's. The EML volumes were old-man productions. By this time he had such fixed notions of what was proper in the genre, and in what place, that he was constantly wanting to escape it entirely, escape into genres for which he hadn't fixed the boundaries. Shortly before his death he sat in his rocking chair completing another philosophic work—modelled on his early work about eighteenth-century thought—on the English Utilitarians.

But the late work showing best his need to escape his own biographical jail was *The Mausoleum Book*. It was his place for coping with the psyche. It was informal autobiography, dripping with sentiment though also containing growls from the fly-pestered lion. In it he was thoroughly *subjective* for 110 pages.

The occasion for the book was Julia's death and his own consequent need for sympathy and attention from others than Julia. He seems to have felt obliged to blame himself and defend himself at the same time. He described his cold-bathness (and at the same time the warm feelings he thought lay underneath) and described his doubts about his own talents (with at the same time his respect for his talent). Above all, he tried to describe his contradictory feelings about his wives. His handling of the wives, though decorous, was more revealing of him than his handling of himself. He was full of the need to assert his devotion to them, but he also had to let the spigots of truth flow. He would flatter and console them, and then his conscience would attack him and he would attack them. He was especially ready to criticize Minnie, along with her sister Annie.

Minnie was not a great beauty, he wrote, but she had beautiful blue-gray eyes and was much better looking than Annie, whose "face was always ill-drawn or clumsy, though singularly amiable and intelligent." Annie had a trace of her father's genius (she was a popular novelist in her own right), as Minnie did not, but she was "oddly unmethodical," having never been educated systematically. Minnie was dependent upon Annie, having "far less intellectual power than Annie," but she had—and this Stephen asserted as her great attraction— "the very soul of a sweet child": "She was pure minded as happily many women are pure minded, in the ordinary sense of the word— free from the very slightest taint of any coarseness of feelings . . . free from the alloy of self-consciousness, conceit or desire for meaner things which destroys the true thing of natural affections."

So Minnie was something of a fool in the way that, in his private opinion, most women were. He could not hold her condition against her (though he did), but he could make his dissatisfaction evident indirectly by suggesting that the condition of their one child, the retarded Laura, had a Thackeray source. Annan points out what several psychobiographers have also tried to develop in Stephen, that he was not equally ready to recognize his own family's history of mental instability.

In Julia he found an intellectual equal, and he lavished praise upon her intelligence as well as her temperament, while managing to suggest that her very superiority had been a problem for him. Like him, she was a sharer in marital tragedy (her first husband, Duckworth, had died suddenly when she was only twenty-four), and like him, she had been obliged to learn to live with such tragedy—though unlike Leslie, she had loved her first mate more than her second. Leslie felt that she never really did recover from her life with the first, and he devoted about a page to saying that she owed "her purest happiness to another man"; but he balanced this complaint with gratitude for her tenderness. She was a "sister of mercy" to all. She was "a woman of intense and exalted feeling," and "when she expressed what she felt, one was inclined to say, 'that strain I heard was of a higher mood.'" In other words she was, in his estimation, a full-grown adult as well as a saint.

His words suggested that with Julia, unlike Minnie, his dominating, patriarchical role was not secure.

Certainly it was Julia to whom the children went, just as Leslie himself had gone to his mother rather than his father. It was Julia who maintained "extended" family relations, Julia who managed the money, and Julia, "the best of nurses," who took care of Leslie! Apparently, though, she paid little attention to his work, and Annan discovered somewhere that she "loathed the Dictionary." Otherwise she was wholly the good wife, and Leslie was near to maudlin in describing her virtue. He therefore, as Annan put it, "luxuriated in the pain" of her death and then "expected his family to minister to him as Julia had done." And in *The Mausoleum Book* all or most of these qualities in himself— some admirable and some not—are made visible. Biography as he practiced it never was intended to perform such a function.

At Julia's death he seems to have tried to regain his patriarchal role and to pass on the duties performed by Julia to his stepdaughter Stella. Stella, however, died suddenly of appendicitis, and the other daughters were resistant, with good reason. In old age he became impossible, and his demands always emerged in front of the weaker vessel, woman. Unstable Virginia, taking care of him at the end (she was twenty-three), wrote in her diary after his death from cancer, that had he lived longer "his life would have entirely ended mine." She was perhaps overreacting, as he tended to, but we can be grateful for that, since her disposition to react had so much to do with what made her the writer she became. Stephen's influence, like that of most fathers, went more than one way.

◆ ◆

Naturally, the influence upon Virginia Woolf's view of biography went far beyond her father's work in his rocking chair. She came to live, as he did not, with modernity around her, biographically in the form of Lytton Strachey, and psychologically in the form of Freud and his followers, of whom there were many in Bloomsbury. When she thought of biography, she thought of fiction rather than the genre proper, and she thought of isolated psyches rather than large public figures on platforms, thought of them looking out at the world of their psyches as if from a cave. Surrounded by her own cave and her own genera-tion's literary lore, she did not have to go back to her adolescent memories of her father's dictionary labors at all; yet the books that have now been written about her, as well as her own books about herself, show that she went back a great deal. And in the three of her own works that can be called biography (two of which are parodies, of sorts), the evidence is that she went back to her father's handling of the genre as a rebel looking for targets.

The first is *Orlando: A Biography* (1928). In its opening chapter, she goes to work satirically on the genealogical snobbery cluttering up the genre. Orlando's forefathers, she begins, "had been noble since they had been at all. They came out of the mists wearing coronets on their heads." She also hastens to mock the heroic promise to be seen, conventionally, in a highborn infant from the moment of birth: "Happy the mother who bears, happier still the biographer who records the life of such a one! Never need she vex herself, nor he invoke the help of novelist or poet. From deed to deed, from glory to glory, from office to office he must go, his scribe following after, till they reach whatever seat it may be that is the height of their desire." In this way she quickly makes her Orlando ready for the pages of her father's *DNB*. She finds him ready not only because of his noble heritage, but also because he is destined by that heritage to be worthy of it. She traces his worthiness right back to the beginning of England as a nation, and makes him a composite hero, keeping him alive for 350 years. (At that age he looks exactly like Woolf's intimate, Vita Sackville-West, a picture of whom as Orlando appears in the volume.)

But he is not just heroic. He is a black sheep too. His features, though properly candid and sullen for a respectably dense hero, reveal a "confusion of the passions and emotions which every good biographer detests." Thus, when still a child, "sights disturbed him, like that of his mother, a very beautiful lady in green walking out to greet the peacocks with Twitchett, her maid, behind her; sights exalted him—the birds and the trees; and made him in love with death."

So equipped, Orlando rapidly achieves adolescence and is courted by the queen herself, who falls in love with him, especially his legs, and confers quick honors and estates upon him. He in turn falls in love with a Russian princess, who instantly betrays him, so that by the end of the first chapter he has become a very poor candidate for biographical study, having determined (like Virginia Woolf) to have a private life.

No matter. The biographer must go on. He must "fulfill the first duty of a biographer, which is to plod, without looking to the right or left, in the indelible footprints of truth; unenticed by flowers, regardless of shade; on and on methodically until we fall plump into the grave and write *finis* on the tombstone above our heads."

That is a fine passage, telling us that Woolf did *not* think that sheer plod makes plough down sillion shine, and it has also to be a passage about her factual father in his armchair. An Annan comment applies:

> The image of writer-father was stamped (in her mind) on a steel engraving captioned "Cambridge intellectual." The plate remained unbroken throughout her life; she knew the likeness all too well, G. M. Trevelyan and Charles Sanger were struck from it. She measured others against them, the more brittle of second-generation Bloomsbury, and often found them wanting. But respect that engraving as she did, she found it too literal and exact for her liking.

I have to accept Annan's judgment that she did respect the engraving, but remain more convinced than he that she found it far too literal and exact. Literalness and excessive exactness were the qualities in the father that she seems to have resisted hardest as she matured. Annan quotes, for instance, a passage by her about his literalness that seems to me simply vicious, from the same unpublished manuscript in which she described his three character roles (as writer, tyrant, and sociable being):

> There are no crannies, or corners to catch my imagination; nothing dangles a spray at me. . . . I find not a subtle mind; not a imaginative mind; not a suggestive mind. But a strong mind; a healthy out of door striding mind; an impatient, limited mind; a conventional mind accepting his own standard of what is honest, what is moral, without a doubt accepting this is a good man; that is a good woman . . . obvious thing to be destroyed—headed humbug; obvious things to be preserved—headed domestic virtues.

For such a mind the character of Orlando became, by the beginning of chapter 3, disgraceful biographical material. Orlando had been betrayed by a poet as well as by a princess. He had permitted another female to enter his life and give him lustful dreams in the form of a Bird of Paradise that was more like a vulture and "flopped, foully and disgustingly, upon his shoulders." He had become a public man despite himself and had found himself incapacitated by his public roles. He was *not* conventional. He was *always* troubled by easy acceptance of what was good and bad. He was *riddled* with "crannies."

Furthermore, as he entered upon the time of life when he was expected to be serious about having a career, he made trouble for any potential Cambridge biographer by allowing a great lack of data suddenly to surround him. A revolution broke out, and a fire destroyed vital documents. "Often the paper was scorched a deep brown in the middle of important sentences," so that the dutiful biographer, should he have appeared, would have been obliged "to piece out a meagre summary from the charred fragments, . . . to speculate, to surmise, and even to make use of the imagination."

So, uncooperatively, Orlando in subsequent chapters grew up with England. He was made ambassador to Turkey and given the title of duke. He lived in great luxury in Constantinople for as long as he could stand it, and then, during a ceremony in his honor, betrayed his heroic trust by having a low love affair. He sank into a coma and arose, some days later, a woman, at which time the three goddesses Purity, Chastity, and Modesty strongly objected to biographical reportage of the conversion. Eventually Truth triumphed, the sex change was acknowledged, and by the beginning of chapter 4 he (now she) had lived through a stressful period among gypsies and was back in England on his (now her) estate with all its attendant comforts and obligations. No one on the estate even noticed the switch, since "one (Orlando) was as well favored as the other (Orlando); they were as like as two peaches on one branch."

The time, though, was now no longer Elizabethan, nor even the Restoration, but the eighteenth century of Swift, Addison, and Pope. In this era Orlando learned from Lord Chesterfield that "women are but children of larger growth," and Pope sat in a carriage with her and presented her with a certain famous line from his "Characters of Women" (presumably, that women have no character at all), while the gallant lords of the period kept talking with her of exciting social matters of which, later, she could not remember a syllable. Their empty ambience drove her swiftly into the Victorian Age, where she again discovered that no males ever said anything intelligent to a woman. Luckily, the emptiness put her on her mettle, so that by the time she married a certain Marmaduke Bonthrop Shelmerdine, Esquire (who was always rushing off to Cape Horn and sailing through the stormy Straits), she had learned to *interpret* what he meant when he said nothing. When he said, for instance, that the biscuits had given out around Cape Horn, she knew he meant that "negresses are seductive."

Within that lonely marital context she slowly resumed her old love, writing. (I forgot to mention that she had been writing an epic called *The Oak Tree* since 1588.) In doing so she discovered that she could resume a role for herself that she had almost forgotten, that of being herself (or Virginia perhaps, or Sackville-West). Yet when she did so, she found it hard for her to catch, at the same time, the spirit of her Age. The age now was the twentieth century and all she could say in her writing about it—so long as her writing did not have her *thoughts* in it—was that the month was November, that December was near, and then January:

> This method of writing biography, though it has its merits, is a little bare. . . . Life, it has been agreed by everyone whose opinion is worth consulting, is the only fit subject for novelist or biographer: life, the same authorities have decided, has nothing to do with sitting still in a chair and thinking. Thought and life are as the poles asunder. There-fore—since sitting in a chair and thinking is precisely what Orlando is doing now—there is nothing for it but to recite the calendar, tell one's beads, blow one's nose, stir the fire, look out the window until she has done. Orlando sat so still that you could have heard a pin drop. Would indeed that a pin had dropped!

Thus Orlando arrived in the twentieth century as a human chowder of many characters and ages, but there at last discovered herself and became one person, one whole. She thereupon went out under the heavens and flung herself on the ground beside the oak tree that had been her refuge since 1588. What to do next? She decided to bury her epic then and there.

Actually, though, she could not really bury it because it was already in its seventh edition, but at least she was finally content with her life. Why? A useful explanation is that Orlando had managed to do with herself what the editor of the *DNB* had not been able to do with himself. She had managed to move beyond the chronological and the factual in her understanding of herself and others. This explanation is even documented; Orlando is allowed to mention the *DNB* specifically while she is beside her tree, thinking of these matters: "The true length of a person's life, whatever the *Dictionary of National Biography* may say, is always a matter of dispute. Indeed it is a difficult business—this time-keeping; nothing more quickly disorders it than contact with the arts."

So Orlando the artist finally triumphed over father the dictionary man. At least, to read *Orlando* with the conflict between father and daughter in mind is to understand it in those terms. That understanding vibrates throughout the book with the feelings that Woolf put down explicitly about twelve years later, in reminiscences ("A Sketch of the Past") that she thought inadvisable to have published in her lifetime. The reminiscences constantly confirm that Orlando's fantasy life had a direct autobiographical source and that Orlando's troubles with the various English establishments around him, from 1588 on, had their thickest roots in Leslie Stephen's character, opinions, and life habits. The connection is so firm that a biographer of Woolf has to push hard to say that there was love for the father mixed in with the antagonism.

Yet Quentin Bell, who is certainly the greatest authority here, says that there was "a special" bond between them that overrode the differences. And a more recent biographer, Lyndall Gordon, quotes her as in maturity seeing her father "from two angles at once—as a child condemning; as a woman of 58 understanding." What do I do with such opinions when I hear Virginia describing, in maturity, her father's view of character as "so crude, so elementary, so conventional, that a child with a box of colored chalks [would be] as subtle a portrait painter as he." Love there must have been between them, but a vast intellectual chasm lay between them too.

Predictably, Virginia's mother was the one to whom Virginia looked for the qualities missing in the father. The mother, said Virginia, could see and pass on a vision of the "panoply of life," since for the mother (and Virginia, and Orlando) a personality was not to be summed up by a series of events and dates. It was *at all times* present, itself, a gestalt. If we can believe Virginia, the mother disliked the *DNB* as much as Virginia did. At any rate Virginia did pick up her mother's sense of character as a wholeness, an entity not penetrable by orderly sequences.

One of Woolf's images for that entity came from a moment in her childhood that she recalled with pictorial clarity, the kind of clarity she thought her father could not achieve. She was standing in the garden at their summer place at the shore in Cornwall: "I was looking at the flower bed by the front door; 'That is the whole,' I said. I was looking at a spread of leaves; that a ring enclosed what was the flower; and that was the real flower; part earth; part flower. . . . I felt that I had made a discovery. I felt that I had put away in my mind something that I should go back to, to turn over and explore." She then compared that illumined moment with another moment, one of an incomprehensible, pointless childish action that left her feeling hopeless and sad. She added that her mature writing impulse was to *make* things whole, and that when she felt she could do so she was happy. She felt that her father had no conception of such wholes.

Her mature view of her father was, however, so heavily tainted by her mother's death and her memories of the father's self-indulgent sorrow at that time—and of his having "no idea of what other people felt"—that she probably should be looked at as an unreliable witness. *Orlando* has all these feelings as background and is therefore also suspect; yet as a statement of Woolf's own view of biography it remains central.

Furthermore the view is not just Woolf's, but a replica of dozens of other artist-views out of which modern art and literature rebelliously sprang. What is fascinating about Virginia's personal rebellion is that it should have been so often focussed on a genre not usually tied to the modernist revolution at all.

• •

Woolf's next biography was *Flush: A Biography* (1933). It was a lesser work than *Orlando* and is sometimes looked at as a potboiler because it sold well, but it had serious moments and was definitely another piece aimed at ridiculing her father's pedagogy. Flush was Elizabeth Barrett Browning's real red cocker spaniel, a thoroughgoing anti-Victorian dog though from Wimpole Street. His lineage, like Orlando's, was absurdly great, going back into Spanish history "when the Carthaginians landed in Spain [and] the common soldiers shouted with one accord 'Span! Span!' [since] the land abounded in rabbits and Span in the Carthaginian tongue signifies Rabbit." Spain became Hispania, or Rabbit-land, and "the dogs, which were instantly perceived as in full pursuit of the rabbits, [came to be] called Spaniels or rabbit dogs." At least that was one explanation, though the biographer, to show her scholarship, proposed two others before moving forward to describe how the spaniel soon became the dog of kings, and then the dog of lesser luminaries like the Howards, the Cavendishes and the Russells, being slowly purified (in ways, the biographer noted, that man had signally failed to purify his own species) to the specifications of the Spaniel Club. In the modern era the Spaniel Club had prescribed what constituted the vices and the virtues of a spaniel. The vices were light eyes and curled ears. The virtues were complex:

His head must be smooth, rising without a too-decided stoop from the muzzle; the skull must be comparatively rounded and well developed with plenty of room for brain power; the eyes must be full but not gozzled; the expression must be one of intelligence and gentleness. . . . The spaniel that exhibits these points is encouraged and bred from, [whereas] the spaniel who persists in perpetuating topknots and light noses is cut off from the privileges and emoluments of his kind.

The biographer then pointed out how confused, in comparison, were human specifications for virtue, even among the royal houses of Bourbon, Hapsburg, and Hohenzollern, and went on to consider the particular lineage of Flush, his birth, and his first rather humble months of life (his owners had "fallen on evil days"), together with his first love affair: "Before he was well out of puppyhood, Flush was a father. Such conduct in a man, in the year 1842, would have called for some excuse from a biographer; in a woman no excuse would have availed." And so, relentlessly through the life of Flush, Woolf pushed the parallel between her chore in writing of Flush and the chore of a biographer of humans. (The biographer of humans, she kept noting, was *more* concerned with rank, breeding, and propriety than she had to be.) Relentlessly also she pushed the connection between Ms. Barrett and Flush. Dog and dog's mistress shared the inhibitions imposed on them by a patriarchal Victorian father resembling Virginia's own. Mr. Barrett was "the most formidable of elderly men, demanding obedience of his daughter," and sending "shivers of terror and horror . . . down Flush's spine. So a savage couched in flowers shudders when the thunder growls and he hears the voice of God." Fortunately, Mr. Barrett was extremely stupid, and when Robert Browning was paying court to Elizabeth "he noticed nothing. He suspected nothing." He left Flush "aghast at his obtuseness."

More parallels between Virginia Woolf and Elizabeth Barrett (and Flush) can be drawn, such as the escape from Victorianism represented by Elizabeth's elopement with Browning and Virginia's own marriage. But such overlap is less important to mention here than the biographical procedures that Woolf ridiculed as she progressed with *Flush*. She converted the whole book into a flip demonstration of what a biographer should *do* with facts. She carried the demonstration right into the footnotes and bibliography, where, to show thoroughness, she provided a long list of letters from Barretts, Brownings, and Mary Russell Mitford (Flush had descended from a line of Mitford spaniels), as well as a collection of poems about Flush by Elizabeth, one of which she quoted in its entirety. Further, in the footnotes she professed to great scrupulosity in her use of sources, explaining in one instance that Flush's ransom, when he was stolen away from Wimpole Street by villains, was not six guineas—as she had asserted in the text—but twenty pounds (and for three dognappings, not one). She made additional scholarly fuss about a peripheral matter having nothing to do with the story of Flush at all, that is, the background of Elizabeth Barrett's servant, Lily Wilson. "No human figure in the Browning letters, save the principals," she said broadly, "more excites our curiosity and baffles it. Her Christian name was Lily, her surname Wilson. That is all we know of her birth and upbringing." She then speculated for five footnote-pages about Lily—a happy parody of scholarly irrelevance. Her intent was of course to suggest that the biographer was *not* to bog down in the problem of six guineas or twenty pounds. He was to use his imagination in reconstructing the life.

An instance of her own Flush-reconstruction began with a direct quotation, presumably real, from Elizabeth Barrett in which Elizabeth Barrett briefly conjured up the thoughts passing through Flush's mind as he, looking bored, watched a liberty parade in Florence. Woolf felt licensed to add several pages to those thoughts, providing Flush's view of the parade, Florence, Italians, the human universe. It was an exercise for her in how a biographer might *participate* in his biographee's life. As she explored Flush's doggy sensibility—imagining, for instance, what Flush deduced from the odors of Florence rising up to him—I was reminded of Jack London and his projections of superdog Buck's thoughts in *The Call of the Wild*. Of course, Woolf was being frivolous in providing Flush with human thoughts, but she was also being, oddly, more serious than London about the integrity of her procedure. After all, London had merely taken on a doggy evolutionary romance, while Woolf had biography, real biography, on her hands and was lecturing about it.

Yet Quentin Bell in discussing *Flush* has described it as a novel, adding that the model for Flush himself was really Leonard and Virginia Woolf's own cocker spaniel, and that the Barrett-Browning connection was just a spoof. I can hardly claim that Bell's view of Woolf's motives is narrow—his own biography of her is one of the spacious biographies of our time—but I do think that in his attention to her primary genre, the novel, he underestimates her commitment to biography. (He is equally inattentive to *Orlando* as what its title proclaims it: a biography.) If Woolf had heard Bell classifying *Flush* as a novel, she might well have said, "Yes, it is a novel *too*." The overlapping of genres was essential to her way of literature. Hers was the gestalt principle; the reality of a flower was in its being "part earth, part flower."

The principle was comically set forth at the end of *Flush*, when Flush met none other than Thomas Carlyle on the deck of a rolling Channel steamer: " 'Mr. Carlyle!' he heard Mrs. Browning exclaim; whereupon—the crossing, it must be remembered, was a bad one—Flush was violently sick. Sailors came running with pails and mops." Here was no place for analysis of the great complex of Flush's feelings. What was simple and clear was that Flush's whole being was unable, at that moment, to cope with Mr. Carlyle.

◆ ◆

Finally, there was Woolf's *Roger Fry: A Biography* (1940). Fry was real, a contemporary, and a close friend. Virginia could not make of his life an exercise, a parody. And as further handicap she took on the project at a bad time for free imaginative construction, for the world as well as herself. The world was moving to World War II. Her husband and her friends were deep in the national feud between activists and pacifists. Meanwhile, her own literary life was stalled in the middle of what would become her last novel, *The Years*. The novel was a great trial, and she found herself, she said, slipping casually into the Fry biography just to escape it. (A bit later she slipped over into "A Sketch of the Past," to escape *Fry*.) Should she have taken on the biography at all? Bell reports that her friends, and Roger's, were divided on the point. Fry's own sister encouraged her to go ahead, and so did Fry's mistress, Helen Anrep, who later "took credit for the result." On the other side was, notably, Virginia's husband, Leonard, who said she should not have tried it at all, since she always had to be "writing against the grain [in it], continually repressing something which was natural and necessary to her peculiar genius." In my own opinion Leonard was exactly right. The book did go against the grain, not only of her genius but of her announced ideals for the genre. It was a conventional biography and featured the conventions she had opposed; that is, it was (a) relentlessly chronological, committed to full and orderly coverage of events, and (b) uniformly impersonal. She adopted a remote, third-person manner throughout and never allowed herself even to appear to be reminiscing about her old friend. In these omissions she outdid father Leslie himself, who had at least had a cubbyhole in his orderly mind for reminiscence. Obviously she felt that she had to do what she did, but the effort remained an anomaly for her. As she wrote, she fulfilled what she ridiculed in *Orlando* as the first duty of a biographer: "to plod, without looking to the right or the left," to the "finis on the tombstone."

So she did plod, and suffered from plod, just as her father had suffered in his rocking chair, and Carlyle had suffered in his sound-proof room. She went so far as to say, while plodding, just the sort of thing that they had said while plodding: "The drudgery of making a coherent life of Roger has . . . become intolerable."

And when she had finished the book and was reading proof, she did what she did soon after with *The Years*. She dumped it into a wastebasket, retrieving it (as authors tend to do) a bit later.

As a conventional biography *Roger Fry* has the merit of giving a complete rundown of the public life and thought of an important figure in twentieth-century art. It shows Fry growing away from Victorianism in art and morals via Cambridge (which receives oddly high marks). It shows him moving uncertainly out on his own, and finding himself obliged to be, simultaneously, artist, art entrepreneur, and art critic–journalist. It shows him groping for his artistic identity as the Post-Impressionists come into his life, and it records the mixed public reception of his activities as a new radical. It shows him failing to impress British academia, which would not hire him until he was over sixty, and failing also at an art enterprise known as Omega, a badly timed Good Idea in art sales that left him broke and thoroughly cynical about the public taste. It also sums up at some length—as Leslie Stephen probably would not have done—his shifty aesthetic. I do not personally know enough about Fry to affirm that for students of Fry the Woolf biography is the place to go, but my guess is that it is. Yet as biography—biography of the kind Woolf herself wished biography to be—it is not.

The trouble with the book is that Woolf could not let the reader in on what she knew and felt about Fry, beyond the data and the art criticism. She said as much to friends, on a number of occasions, acknowledging omissions but defending them on the usual grounds of not wishing to offend. She who had been advocate of the biographer's participation in his subject's life had found herself faced with writing about a man whose wife, like Virginia herself, had been put in an institution soon after marriage, and about a man who had had an affair with her own sister. She had also been faced with writing for an audience familiar with such matter and possessed of an emotional stake in it. So she was driven back on propriety, on discretion, on all the properties of Victorian biography that she had so long resisted. The result—aside from omissions of the dubiously scandalous, to be found fully aired, now, in Bell's biography and elsewhere—was a feel-ingless performance. It was feelingless even when she was discussing public matters like Fry's aesthetic. With the aesthetic she *sounded* like an art critic.

Bell himself must have been thinking she sounded like an art critic when he excused her for having had to cope with a "a side of Roger's life which needed to be described by an artist or an art historian." Bell added that it was the kind of "study for which Virginia had not, and did not pretend to have, the equipment." Actually though, she did have the equipment, having learned a good deal about art from Roger himself. What she did not have, apparently, was the feeling for it that would have brought forth her own language in describing it. If she had been dealing with the character of Roger that she knew personally—the character behind the brittle art jargon that he devel-oped—she might have have been able to mediate between the jargon and the person. Unfortunately she was disabled from dealing with that Roger, and left with the jargon.* Here is a typical passage, in which she, not Roger, is trying to describe his amalgam of the analyt-ical and the artistic. I ask, rhetorically, if it sounds like Woolf.

> But though the scientific method seemed to him more and more the only method that could reduce the human tumult to order, there was always art. In painting, in music, in literature lay the enduring reality.

*An instructive analysis of Woolf's attitude toward her Fry biography is supplied by Panthea Reid Broughton in an essay entitled "Virginia is Anal: Speculations on Virginia Woolf's Writing *Roger Fry* and Reading Sigmund Freud," *Journal of Modern Literature* 14 (Summer 1987):151. Broughton tells us that Woolf twice described the Fry volume as anal, and then traces Woolf's concern about its character back to Fry himself, who had, in a "facetious remark" to Woolf's sister Vanessa, said, "Virginia's anal and you're erotic." Ms. Broughton goes through a revision of the Fry manuscript that occurred after Woolf's reading of old letters between Fry and Vanessa, and also describes Woolf's sudden, concurrent interest in Freud (apparently she went to him to read about anal eroticism) as she was making her revisions. Broughton describes the Fry biography as Woolf's only biography, however, and does not deal with the difference between it and the two fictional biographies described here.

And though in the 'twenties he noted with dismay the return to mysticism in religion, and the return to nationalism in politics, by one of those paradoxes that were forever upsetting the theorist [in him] he was forced by the evidence of his own eyes to believe that, far from perishing, art was more vigorous than ever.

One of the remarks about modern biography that comes to mind, ironically, when one is thinking of Virginia Woolf's career in it is Leon Edel's. He said, in *Writing Lives*: "Biography has been the wayward child of individual talents. It has suffered, through three centuries, from a lack of definition, a lack of method." If Edel was saying that until modern biographers came along, the genre was not fixed in its ways, the remark does not fit the Woolf experience at all. Woolf as a modern biographer *was* a wayward child, and as a wayward child she suffered, through all of her hero Orlando's three centuries, from too much definition, too much method. Edel's remark was essentially prefatory to asserting a new methodology in biography, to be discussed in the next essay. But in the context of this one, it definitely misses the biographical climate into which Virginia Woolf was born, a climate so full of method as to *produce* her rebelliousness, and lead her into the larger revolution that was modernism.

An uncautious word about that larger revolution seems in order now. It was indeed a reaction to the methodical and convention-restricted ways of thought and life that Leslie Stephen—and many many other late-nineteenth-century intellectuals—offered up as their legacy to the future. We have labelled their offering Victorianism, even in America, and in our century we have seen Virginia Woolf's reaction to it repeated throughout art and literature. We have not, however, seen much of its mark on biography except in connection with Freud, and the reason that biography has been largely spared the non-Freudian aspects of modernism would seem to be that biography has—despite Edel's complaint—an inherent natural order built into our expectations of it, an order that goes beyond changing cultural conventions and certainly militates against its being a "wayward child."

For there is, after all, justice of sorts in a biographer's plodding, without looking to the right or the left, from the birth to the grave of a biographee. There is nothing arbitrary and artificial about beginning with the genealogy of a biographee, moving to the birth, childhood, and education, and then on to the career—the successes, failure, honors, decline. This pattern has the shape of every human's life solidly behind it, unlike the fourteen lines of a sonnet. And so Woolf's reaction to the traditional chronological properties of biography is somewhat less defensible than the same reaction to chronology in, say, fiction. The novel was, and would remain, more open than biography to the artist's, as opposed to pedant's, dominance.

Another way of putting Woolf's problem is to say that she was further out on a limb in attacking biography and her biographical father than she would have been if she had gone after her novelist-relative Thackeray. Her father had, despite his narrowness, a generic point or two in his favor.

III

Sigmund Freud and His Disciples

W e must also take hold of biography," Sigmund Freud wrote to
his opponent-to-be, Carl Jung, in 1909, the year he took on
his biography of Leonardo da Vinci.* He could well have written the
same thing in the 1890s to his earlier friend, Wilhelm Fliess, since it
was then that he was first attracted to Leonardo, and also then that
he was, as he was later with Jung, reaching for a collaborator in
carrying forward his sexual studies. With Fliess he found that collaboration could not go far, since Fliess was a physiologist all the way and
Freud a hopeful metapsychologist.† Freud and Fliess broke up deci-
sively—Freud never adjusted well to "we"—yet the remark about taking
hold of biography lingers on.

   After all, the practice of what is now called psychobiography has
stirred up the whole genre, its focus, its underlying traditional intent.
Before Freud there had been plenty of students of the psyches of the
great—particularly of how those psyches caught or failed to catch the
spirit of their times and peoples—but no one before Freud had thought
to deal with an individual psyche as deeply unpublic. Now nearly all
biographers do so in some measure, since now it is conventional for a

---

*This chapter has been revised several times, and in a shorter version printed
in *Delos* 1, no. 1 (1988), I incorrectly identified the opening quotation—"We must
take hold"—as Freud writing to Fliess rather than, somewhat later, to Jung. The
point would be trivial if the remark were not an important part of my theme
here.

   †Freud had been experimenting at large—with hypnotism and electrother-
apy—in the treatment of hysteria and other neural diseases.

biographer to assume that he must show his biographee to be not what he publicly seemed to be. If a biographer in our time has not secrets to tell, what good is he?

So the question arises of whether Freud, in moving to take hold of biography, had in mind what focusing upon private lives would do to the recording of public lives, or was just casting about for cases. Probably at first it was just cases. Of course he knew that the practice of biography was essentially literary, and though he was himself literary he was, in his early years, modestly so. He spoke of artistic matters defensively, as if in disturbing them he was somehow encroaching. He was studying the sexual past of his patients, and it seems most unlikely that he also wished to repudiate biography's traditional purposes—though if a new purpose crops up, can repudiation of an old one be far behind?

He was greatly intense, and as he later remarked in his autobiography, he had developed "an inclination to concentrate [his] work exclusively on a single subject or problem," surely a great understatement. So he was ready and anxious to *use* biography, or anything else, to help him toward his coming-into-focus goal. Biography looked promising because it was a traditional procedure for looking at people. What he needed to do with it was to make it more a procedure for probing than one just for looking, make it an analytical procedure, make it a *mechanism* for looking.

But what he also needed to do was to make it into a mechanism that looked at that at which it was forbidden to look. The hidden, the secret, was not hidden idly. By the 1890s Freud had already experienced several years of resentment from medical colleagues for his interest in sexuality and had broken up with an earlier collaborator, Josef Breuer, largely because he wished to concentrate their collaborative studies of hysteria upon sexuality to the exclusion of other "excitation." Breuer would not go along with him here, and exploring the forbidden slowly became Freud's passion.

It became so for reasons deep in Freud's own past, but the only reason he dwelt on twenty years later in his autobiography was not sexual. It was his Jewishness. To his being a Jew he attributed his familiarity "with the fate of being in the Opposition and of being put under the ban of the 'compact majority' "; and he proceeded to make the presence of the Opposition a recurrent theme (now central to psychobiography) throughout the account.

He began the account, though, not in childhood but at the university, where in his medical studies he said he was "expected to feel [himself] inferior, an alien because [he] was a Jew." He then traced the Opposition's role in his career, as it excluded him from an academic laboratory (for bringing the news, from Paris, that hysteria was not exclusively a female disease), encouraged his withdrawal from academic medical life entirely and, after his separation from Breuer, left him "completely isolated" for ten years. "In Vienna I was shunned; abroad no notice was taken of me. My *Interpretation of Dreams*, published in 1900, was scarcely reviewed in the technical journals."

The depth of his sense of the Opposition permeates this account, which is on the one hand a clear history of his ideological development (the autobiography was a limited assignment: to write an account of his medical career only) and on the other a bitter history of the defectors from his camp as he developed his theories. Breuer he was kindly but patronizing toward, Fliess he could not bring himself to mention, Janet he wrote a short polemic about, and Jung and Adler he described as "secessionists" who in their different ways escaped the "repellent findings" of psychoanalysis. He did not attribute their defections to anything other than prudery and ideological differences, but his certainties in the face of such Opposition show the hardening of his resistance to the Opposition's authority. He was learning to rid himself of their authority and assert his own.

In that process he began, with Breuer, studying hysteria as a particular and isolatable nervous disorder. Breuer and he produced a book together that "laid stress upon the significance of the life of the emotions" and introduced a "dynamic factor" by proposing that a "damming up" of emotional energy could send energy off in the wrong direction. They then suggested a method of cure, which Breuer described as cathartic, that involved turning the energy back into its "normal path." So far so good, but the theory said nothing about sexuality. More important, it insisted on the abnormality of the damming up. At that point Freud began to "suspect the existence of an interplay of forces and the operation of intentions and purposes such as are to be observed in normal life"; and with that suspicion working in his head he was ready for a radical shift in focus that would come to include the study of normal lives, even model lives, as "cases." So he was ready for biography, and also ready for literature, drama, anthropology, history, what-all. He was ready to go on the attack against the Opposition, or to join it on his own terms.

In biography, he noted, the Opposition had been inclined to present the world "with a cold, strange, ideal figure" instead of with a human being to whom we might find ourselves distantly related." It had therefore sacrificed "truth to an illusion" and abandoned the "opportunity of penetrating the most fascinating secrets of human nature." His observation was just, being directed at the one-sided commemorative tradition in biography, and it indicated as well that he now knew where he wanted to combat the "illusion." The time was 1910. He was fifty-two. He now knew that he wanted to "penetrate" human figures of stature, wanted to translate the ideal ones down.

As I mention that wicked verb, *to translate*, in connection with making ideal models human, I am also thinking of the opposite motion, the motion upward, a process frequently described in classical and early Christian literature. There a great leader, secular or saintly, was said at death to have been "translated" to a higher sphere or condition, i.e., heaven. Freud in effect was setting out to reverse that translation process (and his successors would soon labor to make the reversal stick), though in later years he frequently denied that when he penetrated famous persons he *was* translating them downward. He claimed that he was not treating them as patients,* yet the process he went through with the ideal figures was the same as that for the patients. In both cases a transfer was effected from one sphere of understanding—what he came to call the manifest content of a life, or work, or dream—to another—what he came to call the real content. Such a translation was obviously a comedown for the models, and to the degree that the models were psychologically the Opposition for him, his translations of them were also triumphs over them. A new role for biographers.

I should add here—lest I seem to have forgotten the usual meaning for *translation*—that Freud in his early years had already tried his hand at conventional translation—from English to German—and had there proceeded with unusual freedom. His disciple Ernest Jones described him as "specially gifted as a translator," adding that "instead of laboriously translating from the foreign language, idioms and all, he would read a passage, close the book, and consider how a German writer would have clothed the same thoughts." Whom did he so translate? John Stuart Mill and also, apparently, Carlyle. I have not located the

---

*His psychobiographic successors have issued similar denials. For example, Leon Edel, who in his *Writing Lives*, said, "A biographical subject is not a patient, and not in need of therapy" (28).

German results so cannot comment on the magnitude of their freedoms, or on the direction that those freedoms took, but I certainly see
the freedoms elsewhere in his handling of texts. Professional translators in our time have not often recommended closing the book, but
Freud started doing so early with actual printed texts, and then
graduated to the free translating of lives themselves, lives of the great,
where he also closed books, doing so for his own thematic purposes.
In Richard Ellmann's words, he was "not inhibited by the scarcity of
documents."

His first, and also most extended, biographical study was of Leonardo da Vinci.* Leonardo was comfortably far away, and Freud was
able to pick up his most useful information about him—aside from a
short passage in Leonardo's notebooks, and of course the paintings—
from a *novel* about Leonardo current at the time by Dmitri Segeyevich
Merezhovsky. In other words, he let himself go. In a rare unprofessional moment later, he said of the finished work that it was the "only
truly beautiful thing" he had ever written, a remark that seems to jar
badly with his utilitarian remark about taking hold, unless it be
surmised that he was by now trying to meet the Opposition on other
than medical grounds. But such an expansion of his activity was
clearly the case. He wanted to go *beyond* analyzing the Mona Lisa
smile psychoanalytically, though the smile was a lovely professional
topic. He had on his agenda the equally interesting challenge of
dealing with the great in terms that the great deserved and that
admirers of the great would acknowledge. Leonardo was not a patient.
Leonardo did not need help. His paintings were, Freud reported, the
"highest realization of a conception of the world that left his epoch far
behind it." In pulling out all the stops he wished to make clear that he
was not only not questioning Leonardo's greatness, but was also
communing with it.

But communing is a complicated psychic business, and the relationship between Leonardo the great artist and Freud the communer is
itself worthy of analysis. Freud did not to my knowledge do such an
analysis of himself, but he did analyze his tie to another great art
object, the Parthenon, in a tedious essay, "A Disturbance of Memory,"
written at age eighty. In it he recalled visiting Athens for the first time,

Leonardo da Vinci and a Memory of Childhood (1910). Freud's much later study
of Woodrow Wilson was long, but it was a collaborative work, with William C.
Bullitt.

at age forty-eight, with his brother—this was five years before writing the *Leonardo*—and having mixed feelings of pleasure and guilt as they stood looking at the Acropolis. His father had not been financially able to do so. The father, "under the limitations and poverty" of his and his children's "conditions of life," had made the Acropolis seem so remote to the children as to be unreal. So when Freud actually stood looking up at the Parthenon he might, he observed, have said to his brother with pleasure, "We really have gone a long way," if he had not at the same time sensed another layer of feeling in him moderating the pleasure. On the one hand "the essence of success" was "to have got further than one's father," but on the other hand, "to excel one's father" was "still something forbidden." Then,

> as an addition to his generally valid motive there was a special factor present in our particular case. The very theme of Athens and the Acropolis in itself contained evidence of the son's superiority. Our father had been in business, he had no secondary education, and Athens could not have meant much to him. Thus what interfered with our enjoyment of the journey to Athens was a feeling of piety.

So the beauty of the Athens scene bred feelings in him about other matters than its beauty, complicated and forbidden feelings that made him think of father-son relations and their ties to the Opposition, of whom the father was a major, though ambivalent, psychic member.*

Now with these feelings of his in mind, think back to his remark about the beauty of his *Leonardo*. It was made to a woman by name of Lou Andreas-Salome, who had been an intimate of Nietzsche and Rilke, among others. She was, whatever else, a distinguished intellectual. She was also far outside the familial world of Freud's own past, and the world into which, as a patriarch by traditional inclination, he customarily thrust females.† Ernest Jones describes their relationship

---

*Note that he also had cultural guilt feelings about the *Leonardo* book itself, similar to those when standing in front of the Parthenon—guilt about damaging Leonardo's paintings in the book by conducting the "business" of analysis in their presence.

†He put Martha Bernays, for instance, into the patriarchal niche for females even before their marriage, when she read his translation of Mill and earned his disapproval by expressing admiration for Mill's advocacy of equality between the sexes. Freud advised her of Mill's inveterate naivete, said that women had a function of their own in the world, and added, "Am I to think of my sweet, delicate girl as a competitor?" (Freud, *Letters*, 76.)

as simply mutual admiration, with Freud thinking that her "ideals . . . far transcended his own." There may have been more in his thoughts than idealism, since her absence at one of his lectures—as he said in an early letter to her—caused him "to fix [his] gaze as if spellbound on her empty seat," but their correspondence was not romantic, and shows them talking intimately only about other people's intimacies. It is probable that for her benefit he was thinking of his *Leonardo* as intellectually beautiful. He always put on his best cultural airs with her, as she did with him, and in their letters they also babbled comfortably of medical and psychological matters. Andreas-Salome seems to have been a happy form of the Opposition for him. She understood his "repellent findings" about the role of sexuality in life. They met as equals.

In contrast, the woman he married, Martha Bernays, is reported to have said that psychoanalysis was a kind of pornography.

Beautiful or not, the *Leonardo* is a curious document, not perhaps a major work but a major development, and preceded by a truly major work, *The Interpretation of Dreams* (1900), that greatly influenced it. Of the dream book Freud said later: "It contains, even according to my present-day judgment, the most valuable of all the discoveries it has been my good fortune to make. Insight such as this falls to one's lot but once in a lifetime." He was right about the book, which came into being partly because he had recently divorced himself from both Breuer and Fliess, and was left with his own insight. He was alone at last, but precariously, as he located the land of the unconscious. We now accept the subconscious as if it were a remote but solid continent like Antarctica, but in 1900 it had no such solidity.

When he began to explore it, he did so with a fine awareness of how remote it seemed to the world. *The Interpretation of Dreams* emerged as the result of much imaginative research (for "interpretation" one might substitute "close-the-book translation"), but it was also a demonstration by a master salesman with a product to sell. It was a big step along the way to taking hold of biography and much else.

Yet even his own dreams in the book were not presented in such a way as to be illuminating about himself. They were put forth as illustrative, typical dreams, dreams that he felt displayed the configuration of dream work in general. In presenting them he did not even follow his own rule of psychoanalysis, that of allowing free association to prevail as they were recounted. No, he rigorously excluded portions of each dream that did not suit his thematic purposes. He cut and chopped the dreams, and admitted doing so. His announced purpose was not to plumb any individual case, especially not his own, but to describe the dynamics of all dreams.

His organization for fulfilling that purpose was to establish dream categories, to shift methodically from the surface of the categorized dream patterns to their depths, from simple conclusions to complicated ones, and especially from obvious and inoffensive dream work to its alarming forbidden elements.

Such preliminary self-analysis as he indulged in before writing the book must have told him much about himself, but in the book he did not let it surface. He supplied fragmentary detail, yes, but essences, no. Thus, he would briefly place each of his own dreams in a context, such as an academic squabble about promotion, a vacation in the mountains, or a trip on the train with no readily accessible toilet. Then he would give the "manifest content" of the dream, or that part of it he thought relevant to the dream category he was describing, and would follow the description with commentary on some of its lurking immediacies of other content. He would *not*, though, take his commentary back to the hidden treasure of sexual content at which the book was ultimately aimed. For example, one of his most suggestive remarks about himself had to do with the complex alignment of his friends and enemies in the very first dream of the book, the now professionally well-known dream of "Irma's injection." He noted the manner in which the friends and enemies were cloaked and confused by the dream's workings, but then he did not follow through with his remarks in order to tie them to his recurrent, lifelong sensitivity about the Opposition in general. Nor did he try to root the dream in his infancy, to his complicated relations with his father. *The Interpretation of Dreams* was not, he had decided, the place for such analyses.

Was there a place? Later, in his autobiography, he not only found that the autobiography was not the place, but he also sourly remarked that he had "already been more open and frank in some of his writings than people usually are who describe their lives for their contemporaries or for posterity," and had "had small thanks for it." He may have been right in saying he had gone farther than others, but he had not gone as far as his "system" proposed, or as he went in his seminal *Leonardo.*

Alan Tyson, translator of the standard Norton edition of the *Leonardo,* points to three German experiments at the same time as Freud's (1908–9) in the "application of methods of clinical psychoanalysis to the lives of historical figures in the past," but none earlier. He describes the *Leonardo* as Freud's only "large-scale excursion" in biography, yet the book is only a ninety-page excursion. What is large-scale about it?

It is large-scale in how much it sets out to explain. It is also large-scale in its formal mode of explanation, since it performs its revelation of the real Leonardo by eliminating a life's worth of Leonardian chaff and finding the secret, *singular* base for that reality. Freud's narrow focus on just one "reminiscence" is surely the source of the *Leonardo*'s weakness as biography, but it is also the probable source of the beauty he found in it, a compressed, structural, artful beauty.

Unfortunately, the Opposition has not, since then, seen the beauty for the weakness. The beauty has been neglected in favor of sometimes bitter arguments about Freud's apparent misreading, in translation, of the single "vulture" passage in Leonardo's notebooks that provoked his whole analysis. Leonardo wrote it while he was discussing the characteristics of bird flight, and all he said was, "It seems that I was always destined to be deeply concerned with vultures; for I recall as one of my earliest memories that while I was in the cradle a vulture came down to me and opened my mouth with its tail, and struck me many times with its tail against my lips." That was enough for Freud. (He must then have closed the book!) And later, when the vulture turned out to have been, in Italian, not a vulture at all, but a kite, he said what most bird-identification amateurs might have said, that it did not really matter. At that point in his life, though, he was famous, or perhaps infamous, and the anti-Freudians around him quickly became bird experts (and translation literalists). They declared that it did matter, and their point was that much of his thesis depended on its being a vulture, not a kite.

They were right, but in their rightness they managed to ignore the fact that Freud's psychic translation of the bird's meaning was a milestone anyway, a milestone in biographical procedure. Who before Freud would have hung a biography on a childhood vulture *or* kite? Even Freud did not come out and say that there was the beauty. Yet there it was.

The vulture was so important to the whole that he saved it for chapter 2. In chapter 1 he set the stage for it. He rambled through various early accounts of Leonardo's life—particularly those by Giorgio Vasari and Edmondo Solmi—and then he moved to the Merezhovsky psychological novel, *The Romance of Leonardo da Vinci*. He was chiefly interested in the different hypotheses he found for explaining Leonardo's trouble completing a painting. He discarded Vasari's theory that Leonardo was slow because he was a perfectionist, but accepted with caution the Solmi theory that he was slow because distracted from his art by the scientific ramifications of the art. He proposed that science simply came to *replace* art in Leonardo's psyche, and having put his biographer predecessors—except for Merezhovsky—in their place, he set out to look into Leonardo's childhood, noting at the end of the chapter that practically nothing at all was known about the childhood—except by Merezhovsky. In just one paragraph he then summarized the known, and was ready to devote much of the rest of his account to the vulture item.

He looked at the vulture speculatively, as if he were Sherlock Holmes or Hercule Poirot on a case. He called his aim investigative, but he soon became discursive also, doubting that Leonardo's reminiscence was a reminiscence at all. It must instead have been, he thought, an early fantasy, and that thought led him to compare it to the memories in history itself, as written "among the people of antiquity." He said that the materials emerging as history in ancient times were fantasies of history, but real anyway. They cloaked the real history, and the cloak was itself a part of the reality.

Note the heavy weight of pedagogy here. Freud was not just dealing with Leonardo but also explaining and selling his approach to Leonardo. He found himself four pages into his eleven-page second chapter before he could deal with the vulture itself and present the now predictable Freudian translation of such an image, that the vulture's tail was a "substitutive expression" for the "male organ," and that the tail's "beating about . . . corresponded to the idea of an act of fellatio." He added then that the fantasy resembled "certain dreams found in women or passive intellectuals," and paused for more pedagogy, warning the reader against allowing "a surge of indignation to prevent his following psychoanalysis any further." *Then* he was ready again for Leonardo, and what else the vulture cloaked. It cloaked "a reminiscence of suckling—or being suckled—at his mother's breast, a scene of human beauty that he, like so many other artists, undertook with his brush, in the guise of the mother of God and her child."

Note that Freud did not apologize at this point for having jumped to the Madonna and Child. He was in full flight, ready to ask where the vulture came from in the development of the human psyche collectively—a Jungian slip?—and his now anthropological translating took him to Egypt, where, in ancient hieroglyphics, the vulture represented the Mother Goddess (Mut). He needed two paragraphs to explore the Egyptian connection, saying that vultures in ancient Egyptian lore were thought to be always female and to be impregnated by the wind. The connection was fragile, but Freud liked it more and more as he worked on it. Was not Leonardo a wide reader of ancient lore? And even if he had not been, would he not have heard of the female-vulture lore from the fathers of the church? After all, the church fathers, Freud had been informed by a "learned editor and commentator on Horapello," took the lore as "a proof drawn from natural history" of the validity of the Immaculate Conception. The fathers decided that "if vultures were described in the best account of antiquity as depending on the wind for impregnation, why should not the same thing have happened on one occasion with a human female?"

So it was now definite. Leonardo must have known about the motherliness of vultures, and Freud was ready to translate the manifest content of Leonardo's reminiscence into its real psychic content. The vulture was really a mother substitute, and its appearance meant—because the Egyptian goddess was androgynous and had a penis—"that the child had become aware of the father's absence, and found himself alone with the mother."

Freud was not unmindful that Leonardo would have been surprised to hear all this. He repetitively admitted that real content had a way of *seeming* absurd, and insisted that its absurdity was an essential part of the psyche's defensive, cloaking mechanism. He had no qualms about dealing with the remote ties of the Leonardo fragment to the Egyptian Mut as if Mut had been a part of Leonardo's own dream-infancy. He added up his miscellany and produced—with the help of questionable data from Dmitri Merezhovsky's novel—an image of little Leonardo being brought up by his real mother for five crucial years, then being taken over by his father and a stepmother, and being as a consequence permanently, as it were, Mut-ed. In that "decisive time," and at "so tender an age," Leonardo "became a researcher, tormented as he was by the great question of where babies come from, and what fathers have to do with their origin." Soon it even became evident that the vulture fantasy was what first stirred Leonardo's curiosity about the flight of birds, and therefore caused its mention in the notebooks. End of chapter 2.

It was a busy chapter, discursive enough to have impressed Tristram Shandy, yet its underlyingly simple structure, put with chapter 1, was the source of its "beauty." Freud was a kind of minimalist. In chapter 1 he had proposed to trace Leonardo's delay problem to an infantile sexual development. In chapter 2 he had located the difficulty in one reminiscent sentence in the notebooks. Then he had moved out from the sentence to a succession of related hypotheses explaining Leonardo's homosexuality. The shape of the two chapters was of a V closing to its point and then radiating from its point. The shape was an elemental shape, comparable to a simple equation like $E = mc^2$.

Chapters 1 and 2 contained his basic shaping for the whole study. Of the four chapters that followed, three were additions to the reopened V, and the last one was an affirmation and summary of the real content and its relation to the Leonardo life. A diagram of the complete translation structure can reasonably look like this:

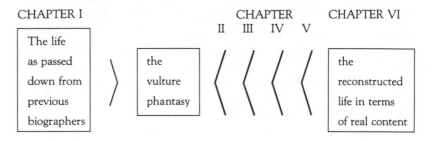

CHAPTER I   CHAPTER   CHAPTER VI
                                    II   III   IV   V

| The life as passed down from previous biographers | the vulture phantasy | | the reconstructed life in terms of real content |

Now this arrangement is essentially thematic and has no chronological base except in its movement back and forth between childhood and maturity. It is an arrangement that is insisted on, yet put aside during discursive flights. At the beginning of chapter 3 Freud seems for a time to have abandoned any designs at all upon biography, for his mind turns to homosexuals in general, and many other matters in general, before returning, in the last four pages, to Leonardo. In chapter 4 he again switches out of the life extensively, in order to examine the paintings and discover that their real content is also mother-based. In chapter 5 he moves to the father, largely on data from the Merezhovsky novel, and is largely diverted by the subject of fathers. It is only in the final chapter that he minds his p's and q's chronologically with Leonardo's life. There he makes, in three pages, an excellent reconstruction of Leonardo's whole psychic life—excellent if one accepts Freudian premises—and puts the life before us as a triumph, if flawed, of the sublimation principle. It is a triumph because Leonardo was able to sublimate his sexual instinct into his art and then "into the general urge to know," and had, as a symptom of his underlying sexual problem, only the relatively minor psychic handicap of not being able to finish his works to his own satisfaction.

This reconstruction presents Leonardo's development in about ten stages, and the stages are so neatly and logically presented—with one aesthetically crucial gap—that they can be looked at as a model of the discipline that a Freudian approach is able to impose on biography. I will simply summarize them.

As an infant he was "kissed into precocious sexual maturity" by his mother's "tender seductions." He accordingly "researched and gave emphasis to the erotogenic zone of the mouth," an emphasis he "never after surrendered," though he later also "behaved in the contrary direction," with sometimes "exaggerated sympathy for animals." Repression set in as he matured, but the "excitations of puberty" did not "make him ill by forcing him to develop substitutive structures of a costly and harmful kind," since he sublimated his sexual instinct into a "general urge to know." A small part of his libido still devoted itself to "sexual aims" in the form of an ideal, as opposed to active, love for boys, and he emerged from puberty "as an artist, a painter and a sculptor," though it is not possible (here is the aesthetic gap) "to give an account of the way in which artistic activity derives from the primal instincts of the mind." Then repression set in, signalled by his inability to finish *The Last Supper*, repression that can be "compared to the regressions in neurotics." He was led to sublimate this repression not in art but in scientific investigation. At last he met "the woman who awakened his memory of his mother's happy smile of sensual rapture," and recovered his artistic drive.

The amount of archetypal sexual data that Freud himself imposed on the Leonardo life is hard to measure because he borrowed so much from Merezhovsky, but it is certainly heavy. Also, the aesthetic gap in the middle of the sequence—that between explaining the artist's drive and explaining the great results—is not the demonstration of modesty that it first appears, since he was strongly proposing that artistic achievements would not have been hurried on their way without the erotic underground stimulating them, and he was at the same time *explicating* their complex appearance. Given Freud's intensities, one can speculate that he did indeed think, though he did not say, that he was giving an account not only of the operations of neurotics, but of genius itself.

Richard Ellmann in an excellent essay on Freud as biographer in the *American Scholar* (1984) remarked that Freud "*acknowledged* that the comprehension of genius was beyond his powers" (my italics). I agree that Freud *protested* much about his powerlessness—about three pages' worth in the *Leonardo*—denying that Leonardo should be looked at "as a neurotic or a 'nerve case,' as the awkward phrase goes," declaring that "pathography [did] not in the least aim at making the great man's achievement intelligible," and quoting Jacob Burckhardt that Leonardo was a universal genius "whose outlines can only be surmised, never defined." Yet the defining and making intelligible occupied him for more pages than that; he busied himself at it throughout.

And in any event the *simplicity* of the underlying causative drive in Leonardo that he uncovered is, I believe, at the heart of what he found beautiful in the work. He saw it as aesthetically beautiful, with a logic, balance, and economy that he must have believed the sophisticated Andreas-Salome would admire. Best of all, it was a beauty he had himself created.

Also, he must have seen the form as *biographically* economical, since he had derived so much about the life and the work from so little. In his minimalist fashion he must have believed that his reductions to such real content offered hope for escape from tons and tons of biographical waste matter in the world's libraries. He was purifying the translation process—making the translator a summarizer, an eliminator of chaff, a what-you-meant-to-say reporter.

What he may not have noted about his processing is that though the *Leonardo* displayed the virtues of an uncluttered, basic form, it also had an aura about it not of form but of formula, and that it took hold of its neatness at such a distance from known data about the biographee that the biographer's role was like that of a bombardier locating his targets—in the shape of texts, paintings, life—through clouds, by instruments, from 40,000 feet. Though he had done a bit of homework on Leonardo and had looked hard at some of the paintings, he had ended with a theorist's vision of the man. Whether he knew how abstruse he was or not, it is not surprising that he found Merezhovsky his most profitable source. It was Merezhovsky who not only gave him most of what he surmised about Leonardo's parents, but also put him onto the bad translation of the vulture. If some Dryasdust were now to discover that the Caterina of Merezhovsky's novel had not after all been Leonardo's mother, the vulture error would be compounded, yet the theoretical structure—given Freud's overriding preoccupations—would remain. There had been a bird any-

way, and there had been a mother anyway.* What more was needed
for translating manifest content into real content? Sometimes Freud's
thinking seems to have been as minimalist as that.

The little vulture passage produced, then, Freud's most ambitious
foray into biography itself, but for the last thirty years of his life he
remained constantly attracted to the genre's possibilities. Freud biographer Clark reports, for instance, that Freud had much to say about the
international significance of Kaiser Wilhelm's withered arm, and that
he once informally advised Thomas Mann that Napoleon's "rash, poorly
prepared campaign against Russia . . . was like a self-punishment for his
disloyalty to Josephine," and went on to explicate an odd connection
between Napoleon's feelings for Josephine and his feelings toward his
own elder brother. (Clark observes, "It might have been wiser if Freud
had admitted that military and political motives were not insignificant.")
Then there were, of course, his many investigations of fictional characters and their relations to their great authors. His famous remark about
Hamlet's Oedipus complex appeared first as a footnote in the first
edition of *The Interpretation of Dreams* (1900), but later, in *Totem and
Taboo* (1913), he found an Oedipus complex everywhere he looked. And
even in his autobiography (1925) he talked assuredly of the connection
between Hamlet's problems and Shakespeare's own.†

In his defense it should be said that he did not always close off

---

*Merezhovsky's own source for an extended and rather sexual description of
Leonardo's relations with his mother seems to have been one obscure reference in
Leonardo's notebooks to a visit made by Leonardo, in adolescence, to a certain
Caterina. Otherwise nothing is known except that Leonardo was taken away from
the unwed mother, whoever she was, early, and brought up by the father's parents.

†In the famous footnote he declared that Hamlet was really in love with his
mother and had himself therefore wanted to kill his own father and replace him,
as Claudius had, in the mother's bed. Then he added: "It can of course only be
the poet's own mind which confronts us in Hamlet; and in a work on Shakespeare
by George Brandes [1896] I find the statement that the drama was composed
immediately after the death of Shakespeare's father [1601]—that is to say, when he
was still mourning his loss, and during a revival, we may safely assume, of his own
childish feelings in respect to his father. It is known too that Shakespeare's son,
who died in childbirth, bore the name of Hamnet (identical with Hamlet)." (Freud,
Interpretation of Dreams, 164.) In old age, though, surrounded by controversy about
the notion, he felt obliged to withdraw the biographical connection, saying, "I
have particular reasons for no longer wishing to lay emphasis on the point." Then
he did not provide the reasons! The note was in a later edition of the autobiography, added in 1935, and now printed in the Norton edition.

manifest content and rush to real content so swiftly. His analysis of Michelangelo's sculpture of the seated Moses holding the Tables of the Law (published in 1914) is a case in which he was thoroughly inductive and did not resort to evidence beyond the work itself. He described the work in great detail, with emphasis upon the position of the hands and beard and facial expression, before moving to interpret. And during the interpretative process he did not attempt, like later Freudians, an explanation of Michelangelo's relationship to the work's meaning. The work therefore seemed to be his exclusive focus, except that the *occasion* for troubling to interpret the work at all surfaced slowly as he proceeded. The occasion proved to be not mere delight in the work itself, or even in explaining it. The occasion was one for refuting other critics—the never-absent Opposition—who had neglected to reconstruct the psychological condition of Moses at the sculptured moment.

Rebutting other critics was one of Freud's abiding professional missions. With Leonardo he was only incidentally biographical. With Michelangelo's Moses he was only incidentally art-critical. In both cases his own underlying motive took him away from his ostensible subjects to his larger cause, psychoanalysis, and its superior validity as a probing instrument. His final emphasis was always upon the instrument, a fact that is of moment here—though the subject is biography, not instruments—since Freud has been, easily, the greatest single influence upon biography's modern drift into social and professional instrumentalism, a drift making it serve matters beyond its always apparently insufficient self. In the old days biography commonly served as a moral instrument, with the lives of saints and villains being served up as illustrations of proper and improper human conduct. In our time its products have drifted into the realm of psychological and sociological case studies, in which the particular lives studied are, again, converted to illustration. Freud led the way, and two instances from his later career are illustrative.

The first is his handling of a long Danish short story, *Gradiva*, by William Jensen, which he undertook not out of an interest in assessing either the story or its author, but because he wanted to assert a connection between dreams in stories and dreams in heads. While reading *Gradiva* he became convinced that it was autobiographical and that Jensen's description of a dream in it—one involving a trip to Pompeii during which a person out of the narrator's childhood suddenly emerges from the ruins—was closely related to Freud's own discoveries about dreams in analysis. He felt that Jensen's fictional act of tracing the dream was sustenance for his own theory and practice, but only if Jensen had not been influenced by Freud's writings before he wrote the story. He corresponded with Jensen and was delighted to learn that Jensen had never heard of Freud.

The second study is the odd case of the "wolf man," an actual patient of Freud's, beginning in 1910, someone not ostensibly worthy of conversion to biography but useful in describing modes of psychiatric therapy. In 1915 Freud wrote a case history of the man's problem; and much later, other psychoanalysts, and the patient himself, undertook to fill out the history and in effect *make* a biography of it—a complete book of 350 pages. It remained, however, essentially a case history, perhaps best described as something setting a precedent for some of the prominent later features of psychobiography.

As with the *Leonardo* and other accounts I have mentioned, Freud began the wolf-man study with procedural remarks, but in this case his procedural commitments were disturbed by the emerging, deep-seated differences between Freud and Jung and Adler about what was relevant in psychoanalysis. At the time Freud was determined to be restrictive and stick to childhood sexual matters; in a footnote to the complete edition he even suggested that when he first wrote the case down he had not been *sufficiently* restrictive, having then been "still freshly under the impression of the twisted re-interpretations which C. G. Jung and Alfred Adler were endeavoring to give to the findings of psychoanalysis."

Twisted or not, his opening "general survey" of the patient was hardly a survey at all. Both the patient and his parents were presented as dim, desocialized figures badly needing grass under their feet. They were given a social milieu consisting only of a nurse ("an uneducated old woman of peasant birth"), an English governess, and the patient's sister. Descriptions of the patient's childhood were limited to notations about friction between the nurse and the governess, sexual episodes between the patient and sister, sudden rages in the patient, and eventually the revelation of a "primal scene." And descriptions of the patient's adolescence were limited to the information that the patient's "health had broken down in his 18th year after a gonorrheal infection," and that he had become "entirely incapacitated and completely dependent upon other people when he began his psychoanalytical treatment several years later." Before the infection "he had lived an approximately normal life," but what had been the normal life? The patient

himself was left to describe that in a 30-page autobiography, his account producing fascinating scraps badly in need of supplement. He
was upper class. His mother had Titian red hair and a sense of humor,
calling the patient's siblings the brothers Karamazov. His father was
"one of the richest landowners in Southern Russia," but also melan-
cholic and a student of that disease. Particularly striking was the
patient's news that as he was about to enter the University of St.
Petersburg, he was examined by a doctor in Moscow for his "neuras-
thenia" and then given instant admission to a new neurological insti-
tute in St. Petersburg that specialized in hypnosis. The institution was,
it seems, one that the father had expressed interest in supporting.

Here was someone, Freud advised, who had come to be known as
the wolf-man because of a childhood animal phobia, a condition
causing him, before the age of eight, to scream at the sight of wolves
and such like. Yet the pictures of him reproduced in the volume
showed him as, first, a rather nice looking little fellow and, second, a
rather commonplace looking big one. Before World War I he had
travelled to and from German sanatoria as if they were ski resorts,
with an entourage that included his own private doctor to play chess
with on trains. (From the doctor he also learned the art of gambling.)
After the war he had found himself a penniless emigré from his
homeland. So: he was a man who had lived with both the survival
handicaps of the very rich and the survival demands of the lost and
disinherited. He was thus presented with all the phobias and fragments
of his complicated life, but what of his talents, his manners, his way
of thinking, speaking, living day by day? What of his accomplishments,
if any?

And, heavens, what of his feelings about the Russian Revolution?
He reported that the revolution had left him on the Austrian border
with just enough money to buy lunch, yet in his account the revolution existed only as a personal inconvenience.

Nor did the patient's reminiscences about Freud help much. He
praised Freud at all points and described what he had learned from
him about psychoanalysis in general (sometimes making Freud appear
to be more lecturer than psychoanalyst), but he said practically nothing about himself *as* analysand. It was here in the last essay in the
volume, that his later analyst, Ruth Mack Brunswick, proved to be
more helpful. A sensitive observer, she had the job of coping with a
late-life recurrence of the patient's obsessional neurosis in a new form,
an obsession about an injury to his nose.

She dealt with the nose at length, using Freud's case history as her starting point, and she also dealt at length with underground matters, such as the primal scene; but beyond all this she, at long last, stepped in to describe what had been missing from the earlier accounts in the volume: the man she saw before her.

He was, it turned out, a man in his late forties who, aside from being a useful *case*, was a run-down gambler with an "odd, indulgent little laugh" (especially when he talked of Freud), someone who looked in the mirror a lot, let his wife buy his clothes and manage his finances, lied a good bit, and was committed to "petty deceptions."

In other words Dr. Brunswick saw, and described, a person whom Freud never revealed that he saw. What she described was disconcerting biographically—since to the degree that the wolf-man was not just a case but a person, he was a pretty dull person, more a wolf-boy than wolf-man—yet the humanity in her account is a rewarding moment in the wolf-man volume because it suggests something about the development of modern biography that Freud himself had in mind when he first "took hold" of the genre, yet managed later to forget in his concentration upon psychoanalytical procedures. In the *Leonardo* volume he had been quick to point out that traditional biographers tended to present their subjects as ideal figures, thus neglecting their common humanity, yet his absorption in his own cases *as* cases came to make him neglectful too. Dr. Brunswick's account helped restore the wolf-man to the human race, and incidentally to point up the broadening scope of psychoanalytical studies as the influence of Freud became a settled twentieth-century phenomenon.

But in passing, before going on to the broader scope, I must mention his late-life collaborative study of Woodrow Wilson in which he broadened his scope without acknowledging that he was doing so. The work was called *Thomas Woodrow Wilson: A Psychological Study*, but it was a good deal more, and the more was, to say the least, unprofessional and unscientific. As Richard Ellmann analyzed the book, it "originated in what might be called counterfixation, an active dislike," and the polemical result brought forth an actively negative review from historian Barbara Tuchman, who said, "The Freudian method can do much—on one condition; let it for God's sake be applied by a responsible historian."

The collaboration was with William C. Bullitt, a journalist turned diplomat who had been at the peace negotiations in Paris with Wilson, and had left in disgust. Its title was meant to inform the reader of the limited biographical aims of the authors, but it did not inform that reader that both Freud and Bullitt had a massive political axe to grind with their subject. Their insistence inside the book that their axe did not influence their analysis had a most hollow sound, since their annoyance with the public Wilson, the man who in their joint opinion wrecked the Treaty of Versailles, is evident throughout, evident despite the psychoanalytical facade.

The origins of the book are interesting but murky. Bullitt in his foreword reported that he and Freud had been friends for some years,* and that Freud was the one who proposed the study. Bullitt had been working on a book about the treaty in which he had allotted one chapter to Wilson and his malevolent influence on the treaty. As for Freud, he had been living in Vienna for a decade with some of the consequences of the treaty, and in 1930 was about to live with more. As he put it in his introduction, he was one of the many who had "suffered from the consequences of [Wilson's] intrusion into our destiny." They met. Bullitt put aside his Wilson chapter in favor of book-length collaboration on the man, collected great masses of matter about him for Freud to read, and the two of them then struggled together for perhaps two years to reconcile their divergent styles and thought patterns.

Freud's first biographer, Ernest Jones, read the result in manuscript and seems to have liked it, though he acknowledged that it was easy to tell who wrote what in it. Apparently the authors themselves were less pleased. Bullitt in his foreword said that "the more [they] worked together the closer friends [they] became," but added that when the manuscript "was ready to be typed in final form, Freud made textual changes and wrote a number of new passages to which [Bullitt] objected." Biographer Clark quotes a franker Bullitt comment that the manuscript was "the result of much combat. Both Freud and I were extremely pig-headed." Whatever the feelings, Bullitt did not agree to Freud's last-minute changes, and the work languished in drawers for several years of developing Naziism. At the end of the 1930s Bullitt was stationed in Paris as the American ambassador, and the eighty-year-old Freud was still in Vienna, about to be threatened with arrest. With the help of Bullitt and a few others, such as President Roosevelt, Prime Minister Neville Chamberlain, and the archbishop of Canter-

*According to Freud's biographer Ronald Clark, Bullitt's second wife had been a patient of Freud's.

bury, Freud was in 1938 granted a permit to leave Vienna with much of his family. His wife, his daughter Anna, two maids, and a doctor then boarded a train with him to Paris, where he was met by Bullitt and other officials. Paris was only an episode in his trip—since he was to continue to England, and die there the following year—but for the Wilson book it was important. Bullitt's account tells us that Freud there "agreed to eliminate the additions" that had caused their rift, though for a number of other reasons the volume did not appear in print until 1967.

In format the book is divided into a background section that is not to be thought of as a psychological study and a long, jointly written section that is. But the sectioning is not as distinct as announced; background merges with analysis, analysis with background, and the collaborating is chunky throughout. For example, the first two chapters of the study proper are billed as joint ventures, but they are actually out-and-out Freudian pedagogy in which Wilson is not even mentioned. And the long Bullitt background section has a title that could only have been Freud's: "Digest of Data on the Childhood and Youth of Thomas Woodrow Wilson." Thus was Bullitt himself translated into the clinic.

Furthermore, the disagreement between the two men does not seem to have been substantive, for at no point in the text did they express doubt about treating Wilson as if he were in the clinic. They looked at him as a patient throughout, and a pretty sick one at that. Bullitt's contribution was a racy English that mixed exposition and editorial comment boldly. Freud asserted himself with a show of scientific caution that served to clinicize the proceedings without softening the polemic. Their joint approach contrasts strikingly with other accounts of Wilson's life, of which the one written for the *Dictionary of American Biography* by a non-Freudian and nonjournalist, Charles Seymour, may be taken as a solid instance.

Seymour was a professional historian who, long before he became president of Yale, accompanied Wilson to Paris—as had Bullitt—for the treaty negotiations out of which the dark side of Wilson's character was to emerge. Seymour's own biographer in the *DAB* reported that Seymour "became increasingly frustrated and disillusioned as the conference progressed [and] deplored Wilson's failure to stand by the principles enunciated in the Fourteen Points." Furthermore, Seymour's reputation as an historian eventually rested on his editing of the *Intimate Papers of Colonel House*, a prime source of information about the weaknesses of the Wilson presidency. Yet Seymour himself, in writing of Wilson for the *DAB*, did not insert his own sense of frustration and disillusionment in Paris. He came at his biographical function in the accepted manner of biographical dictionaries generally. He mixed praise and criticism, but let both praise and criticism be largely from other mouths than his own. Also, he was at all times decorous. Bullitt's and Freud's procedure was to throw bricks. Here are a few examples from both accounts, in which the issue is not the accuracy of either.

• •

Of Wilson's parents. Bullitt reported that Wilson's father "was everything that the son wished to be and was not," and that the son "modelled himself so completely on the father that he too looked like a Presbyterian minister." (Elsewhere, both Bullitt and Freud relentlessly pushed the psychic connection between the pious father-God and the Wilson who in maturity took over the role of God from the father.) As for Wilson's mother, she coddled him devotedly. Together the parents so "guarded" him that he grew up "sickly, spectacled, shy," and "never had a fist fight in his life." On the other hand Seymour reported politely, of Wilson's early years, that they "were colored by an atmosphere of academic interest and intense piety," and that Wilson "took keen delight in the personal and intellectual relationship of the father."

Of Civil War memories. Bullitt said that while the war "left scars in the souls of almost all Southerners of his generation," it "left no scar in [Wilson]." Said Seymour, "The impressions of horror produced upon him by the Civil War were indelible." (How could this difference have come about?)

Of Wilson's Princeton years. According to Bullitt, Wilson entered Princeton "badly prepared [and] especially deficient in Greek and mathematics [but] determined to make himself the leader that his God expected him to be." Then he took to oratory, deciding to "conquer the world by his moral earnestness and his choice of words and gestures." According to Seymour, Wilson had "serious intellectual interests [that] did not lead him to seek high marks in his classes," but he led in debating and wrote an "outstanding essay" on cabinet government in the United States that he later made into his Ph.D. thesis at Johns Hopkins. (Bullitt constantly sneered at Wilson's "literary inclinations," while Seymour went about admiring them.)

Of his marriage to Ellen Axson. Said Bullitt, "He could rest on her shoulder with as complete confidence as ever he had as an infant sleeping on the breast of his mother." Said Seymour, Ellen was Wilson's "most important single influence, a woman capable of enduring the economic hardships that go with the life of a young teacher, appreciative of his capacity, and profoundly sympathetic with his ideals."

◆ ◆

Neither Bullitt nor Freud made any bones about their dislike of the man, and the dislike conveniently focused on what Seymour regarded as the strong points of Wilson's character, points without which Wilson could indeed have been thought a prig and escapist. His strong points were his mind (the conscious, rational part) and his capacity to assert a powerful and pleasing public presence. Bullitt and Freud were always ready to pooh-pooh the mind as dreamy and idealistic, and to undermine the public presence by calling it narcissistic. Their main line was expressed—surely by Freud himself—in these words:

> In this psychological study of Wilson we have devoted little attention to the conscious portion of the mind, and we have no apology to offer for our concentration on his deeper mental mechanisms. The more important portion of the mind, like the more important portion of an iceberg, lies below the surface. The unconscious of a neurotic employs the conscious portion of the mind as a tool to achieve its wishes. The convictions of a neurotic are excuses invented by reason to justify the desires of the libido. The principles of a neurotic are costumes employed to embellish and conceal the nakedness of unconscious desires.

A reader does not have to be for or against the study of the real content of icebergs to note the omission, in the Freud-Bullitt volume, of the *manifest* content of neurotic Wilson's Ph.D. thesis on constitutional government, the manifest content of his dispute about educational principles with Dean West at Princeton, the manifest content of his politics as governor of New Jersey and then president of the United States, or the manifest content of the first five of Wilson's famous Fourteen Points. The Freud-Bullitt study strongly proposed that Wilson's whole career, from Princeton to the White House to Paris, was meaningful merely as a case history of personal aggrandizement amidst a variety of political bosses. The study declared that Wilson's concern was always with his own reputation, not the institutions and principles he professed to serve. In fact, the study kept insisting that institutions and principles were never real content anyway, an insistence that in this extreme case could only backfire, since any skeptic—and there were many—could with justice declare that the institution of psychoanalysis with *its* principles was not real either, not nearly as real as the analysts' malice and opportunism.

Perhaps Freud should be excused for his ideological fervor because of his age, but Bullitt's performance (he was thirty years younger) seems odd indeed. How readily the clinic and the modern American newsroom seem to have met in him. For clinician Freud the real Wilson motives were to be understood as unconscious. For journalist Bullitt they were to be understood as a mixture of the unconscious and of the consciously venal. Their different professional interests therefore managed to merge at the level of disbelief in their subject's moral convictions, his rationality, and his literary, historical, and political credentials. As a result, *both* their professions had succeeded in Taking Hold. They had beaten down an Opposition. They had translated Wilson into a patient, but at the cost of their own credibility. So at least the party of indignation has responded to *Thomas Woodrow Wilson: A Psychological Study*.

But Freud's *Leonardo* was another matter, and as far as the genre of biography is concerned, the difference is probably best understood by looking at the relations between biographer and biographee. The Wilson case was one of coping with an Opposition; the *Leonardo* was an act of communion. Hence, to the extent that the tradition of biography as an act of commemoration is to be thought central to biography's existence, the *Leonardo* was both spiritually and psychologically sound as a venture, the Wilson not.

◆ ◆

Now to pass beyond Freud himself and suggest the breadth of the Freudian phenomenon historically, I know no better way—though it may seem diversionary—than to begin with one of W. H. Auden's best short poems. Auden was a Freudian in his own way when he wrote the poem, in the late thirties.

Who's Who

A Shilling life will give you all the facts:
How Father beat him, how he ran away,
What were the struggles of his youth, what acts
Made him the greatest figure of his day:

Of how he fought, fished, hunted, worked all night,
Though giddy, climbed new mountains, named a sea;
Some of the last researchers even write
Love made him weep his pints like you and me.

With all his honors on, he sighed for one
Who, say astonished critics, lived at home;
Did little jobs around the house with skill
And nothing else; could whistle; would sit still
Or potter round the garden; answered some
Of his long marvelous letters but kept none.

It is a great poem all by itself, without consequential messages attached to it, but the messages are there. It is a little lesson in modern biography, proposing a possible new kind of value model for the genre, not someone who is "the greatest figure of his day" (or, it goes without saying, someone who makes a great case study). From the poem's title to its descriptions of the insensitive life-researchers it questions a basic assumption of the genre itself. The anonymous quiet person of the sestet is an alternative to heroes. He is presented as wise and as contented, in comparison with the astonished critics as well as the hero himself. All the persons in the poem *except* the quiet one are imperceptive and shallow, unaware that there may be forms of success other than naming seas, climbing mountains. Auden is nudging the who's who world to recognize the virtues of puttering.

But am I not imposing upon Auden's intent in the poem by making it a piece of pedagogy? The quiet one is so sketchily described that we are not even sure of his sex, and may suspect that he is merely the hero's alter ego, the figure the hero would like to be, late at night, when his back aches from climbing mountains. Yet, sketchy though he is, he is better off in important ways than the worldly ones around him, and better off also than the Wolf-Man, since he is in control of himself, has no apparent problems, is in no jams, and does not appear to have ever been a patient.

He is, it is true, some sort of minimalist being, but what is wrong with that? He has escaped the clutches of world *and* medico, and is put before us as someone to admire.

I grant that Auden does not name a publisher who would contract for a biography of him, but just to admire that life is to go a step farther than Freud toward the setting up of a noncelebrity model. Admiring was not part of Freud's professional interest after his early rounds with Leonardo and Shakespeare. What would he have done, for instance, with the quiet one's lack of interest in analysis? Unlike Freud, the quiet one recognized and quietly coped with the pitfalls of self intensity by whistling. He might, of course, have then been diagnosed as full of repressions, but Auden's description of him does not point that way. He is presented as simply living at home without "symptoms." Ridiculous.

Yet in 1939 or 1949 Auden wrote an elegy to Freud ("In Memory of Sigmund Freud") in which he put aside the argument against case studies of self-intensity implicit in "Who's Who" in order to say the good things about Freud that needed to be said, especially in an elegy. He wrote, "All he did was to remember / Like the old, and be honest, like children." As a result, he said, "the proud can still be proud but find it / A little harder." He went so far as to assert that though "the household of Impulse" mourned Freud, he had also been a rational voice, a point that needs constantly to be made about Freud's legacy even though Freud's own remarks frequently undercut it. And in an essay in the 1930s before Freud's death, Auden had pushed Freud's rationalism even harder, quoting an unusual remark *by* Freud. It is a statement that nicely balances the urgencies of Freud's usual campaigning: "The voice of the intellect is soft and low, but it is persistent and continues until it has secured a hearing. After what may be countless repetitions it does get a hearing. This is one of the few facts which may make us rather more hopeful about the future of mankind." In that statement Freud could well have been the quiet one of "Who's Who" speaking. That side of Freud was quiet indeed in biography, since he was customarily busy "taking hold," yet it needs to be remembered about the man, and about his influence too.

◆ ◆

Two classic instances of psychobiography actively built upon the base that Freud provided are Lytton Strachey's *Eminent Victorians* (a book that in many respects is not so much psychobiography as social history) and Erik Erikson's *Young Man Luther*. Both volumes speak, each in its own way, to the relationship of psychoanalysis and biography, a subject that Freud mostly avoided. Freud was the great innovator, but the principles with which he wished to take hold of the genre are probably best illustrated in the extended works of his followers.

Not that his principles were all new. In asserting, for instance, the presence of a reality core in the subconscious, he was also pointing, if inadvertently, to biography with purposeful limits, monograph biographies, biographies written in the context of clearly defined values. From Plutarch's *Lives of the Noble Grecians and Romans* to Samuel Johnson's *Lives of the Poets*, the biography ritual had been largely one of identifying biographees with groups, and attaching relevant group standards to the lives. In the nineteenth century the genre had begun to move away from such ideas of relevance and to assert, with Edmund Gosse, Leslie Stephen, and others, that group views should not apply to biography. Freud, by fitting his cases to the context of archetypal subconscious feelings, supplied a new group context even as he narrowed the biographer's focus in other respects.

And his procedure had, aside from its merits as therapy, the merit of asserting that biography could have other than chronological shape. Lytton Strachey was one of his early biographer disciples who could see this formal virtue embedded in the "case" principle.

Strachey's knowledge of Freud's work seems to have begun with Freud's *Psychopathy of Everyday Life* (1914), since at about that time he composed a comical conversation—called "According to Freud"—between a sophisticated woman who had read Freud and an ignorant man who had not. Strachey's younger brother James was to become, in the 1920s, Freud's chief translator into English, as well as the editor of Freud's collected works in English; yet biographically Lytton's development was not, at first, via the subconscious. At Cambridge he was a talented radical who became a member of an exotic secret club, The Apostles, and composed little shockers for delivery at their regular soirees—on the virtues of homosexuality, on the importance of "the class of the Bawdy" in art, and so on. From such papers he moved to reviews of biographies and collections of letters. Thus in 1907, while still frequenting Cambridge (but about to move to Bloomsbury and to propose, by mail and unsuccessfully, to Virginia Woolf), he commented upon *Lady Mary Wortley Montagu and Her Times*, by George Paston, that the book, "with its slipshod writing, its uninstructed outlook, its utter lack of taste and purpose, is a fair specimen of the kind of biographical work which seems to give so much satisfaction to large numbers of our reading public," then adding his own succinct, well-shaped summary of Lady Montagu's life. Between his Cambridge days and his death in 1932 he published some thirty-five "biographical essays" in which his steady intent was to dispose of biographical chaff and be, simply, "accurate" and "interesting."

Strachey used those two words in a biographical essay on John

Aubrey, whose *Brief Lives* was surely a model for some of his own. He praised Aubrey's "natural gift of style," saying that *Brief Lives* was "one of the most readable of books." His conclusion: "A biography should either be as long as Boswell's or as short as Aubrey's. The method of enormous and elaborate accretion which produced *The Life of Johnson* is excellent, no doubt; but, failing that, let us have no half-measures; let us have the pure essentials—a vivid image, on a page or two, without explanations, transitions, commentaries or padding." When he wrote that in 1928, he had completed three half-measure books— *Eminent Victorians* (1918), *Queen Victoria* (1921), and *Elizabeth and Essex* (1928)—and presumably had decided that they were not vivid enough. If so, he was right about the last two: they are not tediously long, but they are not incisive either. Nor do they have a clearly operative principle informing them. A recent biographer of Virginia Woolf, Lyndall Gordon, has observed that Strachey was more attracted to "pomp and flourish" than to "the hidden fact at the center of character," especially when dealing with women, and she quotes Woolf as saying of his style that it was "metallic and conventionally brilliant," meaning, I assume, that what he had to say was superficial. Perhaps it was, but if Strachey had substance in his works to reckon with, it was largely in his short biographical essays and in the first of his three extended works, *Eminent Victorians*. In those he was at his Cambridge-intellectual best—that is, he was full of large historical-sociological theory—and could begin a metallic brevity by saying, for example, that "the visit of Voltaire to England marks a turning point in the history of civilization." The editor of *The Really Interesting Question, and Other Papers* points out—quite rightly, I think—that Strachey was much more attracted to "social questions" than he is usually given credit for. And particularly at the time of the writing of *Eminent Victorians* he was deep in all the issues of World War I. His correspondence with his brother James concerning how most effectively to combat conscription laws showed one side of his radicalism, and his steady complaining about Victorian manners and morals showed another. The issues to which he addressed himself in *Eminent Victorians* were perhaps superficial, in the sense of being more thoroughly matters of public conduct than a psychobiographer is expected to bother about, but they were at least issues that made him question the public motives of his biographees constantly, made him search for their hidden agendas and self-deceptions. So though his approach to them was more social than psychic, the result was still Freudian in its probing for "real content." His basic strategy in *Eminent Victorians* did not take him back to primal scenes in their lives, but it did entail his giving his readers an untechnical, semi-Freudian account of each subject's underground. The result was a version of Freud's double-life motif that gave each of his biographees a little drama of internal conflict.

The four persons he chose were Cardinal Manning, Florence Nightingale, Thomas Arnold of Rugby, and General Gordon of Khartoum fame. Their conflicts were alike in all being of the familiar ego-id variety. Cardinal Manning was professionally saintly but inwardly entrepreneurial, a grasper for power, and was presented as having struggled, as he grasped, with his conscience almost as much as with his clerical opponents. Similarly, Florence Nightingale's medical saintliness amid the dying was set against her inner demon (Strachey remarked that "demons, whatever else they may be, are full of interest") and found to be ruthless, ravenous, and much else. Dr. Arnold's saintliness was much less conspicuously opposed within him than Manning's and Nightingale's, but as he struggled to make Rugby over, he revealed an inner sense of his own grandeur that deceived him into thinking he was a new Moses bringing the laws of God to his chosen people; and he was so wrapped up in his mission that he thought he was producing godly Christians and English gentlemen, while really his students were emerging as worshippers of athletics and "good form." And last, General Gordon was a successful military Victorian (he had done great things in China) who hid within himself not a demon or an angel but something possibly worse, an excess of simple Englishness. Thrust into the mess at Khartoum in 1884, he was so narrowly committed to his national and military-professional ideals that he made a military fool of himself, providing England with one of its great disasters. (My guess is that in writing of Gordon's Khartoum failure in the middle of World War I, Strachey had in mind the bumblings of the "Colonel Blimps" of that time, who were a sort of Victorian table scrap.)

Here then, in all four cases, was biography with a point, a nub. It was not the nub that Freud might have chosen, but it was related to Freud's nubs. What Strachey was doing was suggested on the very first page of his Manning biography, where he tied Manning's "psychological problems" to "the spirit of his age." He said in effect that the psychological problems of Manning were the problems of Victorianism itself, and he proposed that Victorians as a whole lived in a mist of high ethical thought, as Manning did, while constantly distinguishing themselves (as other civilizations continue to do!) for greedy, self-centered, worldly accomplishment and pride. In short, Victorianism hid its "real content." Manning and the others, he was proposing, might have benefitted from a bit of self-analysis, and so might have all proper Victorians.

Strachey's procedure here was to put the public and private lives sharply up against each other, as a dramatist might, by including what was relevant to the conflict he had settled on and rejecting what was not. In the process he was reductive with subjects' lives, though not as severely as Freud. He was more respectful of the traditions of biography than Freud but remained dependent upon Freud's preachings. I know of no better short biographies in English than these of Strachey, but their thematic pointedness remains a dangerous model.

Their pointedness has also kept them from being admired by stern scholars. Thus, Paul Levy begins his introduction to *The Really Interesting Question* by remarking that "the four biographical sketches [in *Eminent Victorians*] are too short to convey much information to the serious student." Information is the watchword in scholarly biography now, and Strachey was not an author of reference books.

◆ ◆

Erik Erikson's *Young Man Luther* (published in 1958) is not a reference book either. It is readable. But like *Eminent Victorians*, it does move out and away from the biographee's psychological problems to the problems of his age, doing so with greater thoroughness than Strachey. It is also more intensively and professionally Freudian than Strachey's volume. Erikson notes that he began thinking of his Luther study as only "a chapter in a book on emotional crises in late adolescence and early adulthood," but then the subject of Luther grew into a "historical book" with the subtitle "A Study in Psychoanalysis and History." The process by which he moved into the genre was, then, like Freud's, in that he began with his psychiatric specialty, at first resorting to biography as only illustratively useful. For Freud the focus was early childhood; for Erikson it was late adolescence and its problems of identity.

What Erikson at that point did, however, to enlarge his biographical commitment was to place his biographee in the milieu of modern American social science. This placement led him to contend with all sorts of large cultural-historical problems, a big advance in contextual breadth over Freud's customary confinement to neurotics.

Yet Freud and Erikson would have made close colleagues, I think. Erikson is a true disciple, despite his disagreement with the master, and in relation to biography his discipleship has meant that he has simply extended the "we" of Freud's early remark to Jung—"We must also take hold of biography"—to the whole modern community of psychoanalysis, a community now influential in all fields, so influential that Erikson is defensive about its range even as he insists upon it.

He says, for instance, that "we . . . have learned more about the infantile adult than was ever before known," and that with such knowledge "we have prepared an ethical reorientation in human life which centers on the preservation of those early energies which man, in the service of higher values, is apt to suppress, exploit or waste." Unfortunately, he continues, "we" did not include "in our awareness" what "neurotic patients and panicky people in general" might make of it all, especially of "the minutest references to sexual symbolism." Accordingly, "we were dismayed when we saw the purpose of our enlightenment perverted into a widespread fatalism, according to which man is nothing but a multiplication of his parents' faults and an accumulation of his own earlier selves." The "we" here is obviously much larger than Freud's, but not all-inclusive. It does not, for instance, include such persons as nonclinical Strachey, or pre-Freudian students of the psyche like Carlyle. What it does include is a small army of professional psychoanalysts, whose knowledge is presented as extending far beyond the clinic to general, all-purpose knowledge of humanity.

If Freud were alive he might well enjoy the enlarged "we," and enjoy Erikson too; yet even Freud might well have qualms about the nature of the growth. For as Erikson himself points out, Freud was a loner. He soon even disposed of Fliess, Jung, and the others, becoming his own "we." He had no church, and early or late he was not ready, great salesman though he was, flatly to identify the lore of psychoanalysis with general human enlightenment. There is a difference between believing that one is right and believing that the world believes it.

Curiously, this difference bears directly upon Erikson's theme about Luther. Like Freud, Luther was a loner, and in his lifetime he was confronted with an Opposition loosely resembling Freud's. From childhood on he was separated, psychologically, from a number of potential we's in his universe, groups against which he steadily rebelled. He began in conflict with his parents, who "were hard, thrifty and superstitious, and beat their boy" (though the degree of strife is still much debated). Then, like the hero of Auden's "Who's Who," he ran away from their world—but not to climb mountains. He became a monk, and then rebelled against monkdom, and suffered trials of identity confusion before he was able to pin his at last discovered spiritual self to a church door in Wittenberg. The history of Freud was also like this. In Erikson's own words, Freud (and Darwin and Shaw and other creative souls with whom Erikson groups him) came upon his "most decisive contribution only after a change of direction." He came upon it "almost accidentally" after taking his medical degree late and delaying his "revolutionary creativity" with years of work in physiology. This pattern of Freud's development was, Erikson feels, a predictable one for a truly creative man, since a creative man in Erikson's book is almost sure to be a loner with identity problems like these:

> . . . A creative man has no choice. He may come across his supreme task almost accidentally. But once the issue is joined, his task proves to be at the same time intimately related to his most personal conflicts, to his superior selective perception, and to the stubbornness of his one-way will: he must court sickness, failure, or insanity, in order to test the alternative whether the established world will crush him, or whether he will disestablish a sector of this world's outworn fundament and make a place for a new one.

Needless to say the "we" with whom Erikson rather erratically identifies himself in his Luther study is not made up of such creative men. His "we," he keeps suggesting, is now in effect the whole significantly intellectual world. My guess is that Erikson actually thinks of himself as a loner—like Freud and Luther—and somehow distinct from that world.* Yet what he does with Luther is put him in the clinic and let the clinic world go after him.

Of course, the clinic is now a big clinic, and Erikson has had something to do with its new dimensions. His influential study of Luther makes two additions of consequence. First, it suggests that the biographer's aim, in or out of the clinic, is that of understanding and describing the whole man, in contrast to the aim of discovering, say, that the wolf-man had an obsessional neurosis. And second, it sets

---

*An interesting review of a later Erikson volume by another psychiatrist, Anthony Storr, points to Erikson's own life, and suggests that Erikson too had been psychologically a loner because of his mixed ethnic background and upbringing. (*Washington Post*, June 14, 1987.)

out to locate a moment in the whole man's life that is a conspicuously important *adult* moment, and thereby moves psychoanalysis beyond the bog of infant experiences with vultures. These two additions reinforced each other. *Young Man Luther* is a spacious biography in ways that Freud might or might not have approved, but would have been surprised by. It moves psychoanalytic study into *civilization* with its discontents to a degree that Freud was never able to.

Luther was an excellent choice for Erikson in his reaching for wholeness, but I must complain that he conspicuously fails to mention that Carlyle, a century earlier, had found Luther an excellent choice also, and had asserted Erikson's loner-conversion thesis about him in his best-known book. For Carlyle, Luther was one of the eleven inspired beings of his *Heroes and Hero-Worship* volume who did what he thought great heroes were destined to do. Luther's development as a great hero matched that of Carlyle's autobiographical-fictional Teufelsdröckh in *Sartor Resartus*, who was until adulthood a nothing, an aimless being surrounded by negative presences such as Puffery and Hypocrisy. Teufelsdröckh, and Luther also, then experienced a miraculous conversion, a second birth, and became positive spiritual presences in the world—in fact, leaders. Carlyle's interpretation of their conversion does not differ markedly from Erikson's except in being spiritually rather than psychologically focused, a distinction that both men would have probably wished to deny. In other words, both biographers took the legendary moments of decision in Luther's life as moments of *whole* truth, truth private and public, individual and universal, whether that truth was intuited or scientifically determined. They both located a great historical movement within the travails of a single psyche at a single point in history.

But Carlyle, for his pronouncement comes down to us as a mystic rather than a clinician, and his Ludditical drift may have underlain Erikson's ignoring him. As Mill said of him, he was a kind of seer, and clinician Erikson does not wish to be thought a seer. I have to say, though, that his role as seer does peep through.

He jumps from the small to the large in his book with the facility of a seer, and his large pronouncements, though academically qualified, frequently sound oracular anyway. What he does, in fitting his pronouncements to his clinic, is to impose the language of science upon his role of biographer and historian. He can announce scientifically, as Freud could not have done, that a primal event of childhood could have started the whole Reformation: "A clinician can and should make a connection between global occurrences and certain small town items recorded in the records of Mansfeld. Hans Luder had a brother in Mansfeld who was called Little Hans. The brothers had been baptized Gros-Hans and Klein-Hans, which paired them in a possibly significant way for Martin." The cautionary "possibly" represents the objective voice of science, but otherwise the passage is seerlike. The naming episode is presented to prepare us for Martin's fear of being like the Klein-Hans, and then for his developing a complex about being little in the presence of his big father and, eventually, of the pope himself. What is the clinical clincher?

> Every clinician has seen over and over again how a parent's fear that his child may turn out to be just like a particular uncle or aunt can drive the child in that very direction, especially if the warning parent himself is not an especially good model. Luther's father became a model citizen, but at home he seems to have indulged in a fateful two-facedness. He showed the greatest temper in his attempts to drive temper out of his children. Here, I think, is the origin of Martin's doubt that the father, when he punishes you, is really guided by love and justice rather than by arbitrariness and malice. This early doubt was projected later on the Father in heaven (later the Pope) with such violence that Martin's monastic teachers could not help noticing it.

I do not complain here, as I did in the case of Leonardo's vulture, about the paucity of biographical detail backing up the conclusions reached, though critics of the book do, pointing particularly to Erikson's handling of the child Luther; but I can mention with a frown the long and complicated causal chains upon which his proceedings frequently depend. (For want of a nail, the shoe was lost, and so on.) Freud quickly closed off his transactions with manifest content, so that he could move imaginatively to real content, and with Erikson the same process is at work. It is applied by hopping, as if on stones in a brook, from individual matters to global-historical matters or, in reverse, from global-historical matters to little Martin and his father.

Thus, Erikson has no trouble reconstructing Luther's father's thoughts about his son from the thoughts generally abroad in his country and age. It is "fair to assume," he tells us, that the father "wanted his son to serve princes and cities, merchants and guilds, not priests and bishoprics and papal finance," and that he therefore "wanted his son to be a lawyer, that is one who would understand and profit by the new secular laws which were replacing those of the Roman commonwealth." Also it is fair to assume, he continues, that "most of all [the father] wanted, as did millions of other ex-peasants and miners, to see his son employ his mind in higher matters . . . and to enjoy the wealth unearthed by others instead of dirtying his hands in shafts sunk into the earth." Such assumptions may be fair in a general sort of way, yet the last sentence of the paragraph quoted from moves suddenly away from assumptions entirely, to a flat statement of "fact." Following the phrase about shafts in the earth Erikson writes, "This, then, *was* what the history books call the 'peasant' father of the 'peasant' son" (my italics). How does Erikson move from the general assumptions to the particular, individually aimed "fact"? Such a shift is what brings great lawyers to their feet in great courts to cry, "I object!" and what causes scholars in their carrels to utter comparable cries, yet the shift has become a conventional device of social scientists' reportorial procedure.

Luckily, the result in *Young Man Luther* is not as unsettling as my now blooming polemic may suggest. At critical points in Luther's early life Erikson seems to me to be appropriately cautious. I cannot, for instance, go along with his severe critics, who accuse him of depending on suspicious data from malignant Catholic sources, and I even have trouble with the complaint of one of his most distinguished opponents, the ecclesiastical historian and biographer of Luther, Roland Bainton, that Erikson mistranslates some of Luther's own comments about his childhood in order to forward his theme of father-son strife. To my mind the volume moves into the caves of Luther lore in a reasonably neutral way and takes us through Luther's early years with properly academic attentiveness to ambiguities of detail—though I agree that Erikson could have placed more emphasis on Luther's own statements than he does. ("Why not," asks Bainton, "take Luther at his word?")*

Certainly, Erikson's handling of the celebrated thunderstorm episode is admirably thorough, far more complete historically than Freud's would have been. He begins by providing important background information: about Luther's unhappiness in his twenty-first year; about his going home from law school briefly (for disputed reasons); and

*Erikson's book (reinforced by later Erikson volumes, notably his biography of Gandhi) was sufficiently challenging to the professors of both history and religion to cause a stir. It was reviewed everywhere, and was so durable as a controversial event that it was the subject of a whole book of essays, in which Dr. Bainton's words appear, nearly twenty years later: *Psychohistory and Religion: The Case of "Young Man Luther,"* ed. Roger A. Johnson, (Philadelphia: Fortress Press, 1977). The Bainton question is on page 53.

about his talking with his father (according to some reports) about a marriage his father had been planning for him. Then Erikson proceeds to the thunderstorm itself, which Luther suddenly encountered on his way back to college. Luther was surprised by it, was nearly struck by lightning (perhaps knocked to the ground), possibly suffered a concussion, and then by his own account cried out (though no one was present to hear him), "Help me, St. Anne. . . . I want to become a monk." There it was, the great moment of truth, of decision, and Erikson sets it up fully in all its dubious historicity, before asking a good and relevant question, "Was this thunderstorm necessary?"

The question is good and relevant because it shows awareness of the slipperiness of moments of truth, and Erikson answers the question with care, first giving the answers of three biographers he has been following closely, and then providing his own preliminary answer. His own is that Luther badly needed *something* at just that crucial time, needed an appropriate occasion to make the great decision he was now ready to make—and the thunderstorm satisfied the need. So far so good; Erikson has cautiously adjudicated between Luther and history, and found the two waiting for each other. Nothing can be complained of in the Erikson account until one reads a few more pages and comes upon what might be called the Erikson fuller-explanation department.

It seems, Erikson tells us, that Luther's running counter "to his father's secular aspirations" managed to produce in him a "negative identity," that is, "an identity which he has been warned *not* to become." Such a creation, Erikson writes, "can serve high adventure" and the like, but it can also, "in malignant cases," produce persons who rush to psychotherapists. In Luther it served high adventure, since his negative identity later drove him to oppose church authority in the way that he had opposed his father; but though his case proved not to be malignant (unless perhaps judged by a Catholic therapist?), there it was, a case.

And as a case it now continues for the rest of *Young Man Luther.* For at this point Erikson takes Luther right out of history and plants him squarely in the clinic with the patients, and with the jargon that surrounds them. At this point, then, the difference between Freud's case-history procedure and Erikson's becomes much diminished. With all the modern prestige of the psychoanalytical trade at his elbow, Erikson proceeds to feed Luther, the whole of him, into the clinical machinery and grind him up.

I gather that for many years now he has taught the clinic's function—taught it, for instance, to his biographer and disciple, Robert Coles, a man I much respect who has carried the Erikson teaching into his own life and actions. This teaching is what largely occupies the last half of *Young Man Luther* and is summarized in the last chapter. There, we learn that the clinic's job (which is the biographer's job) is not to follow one soul from birth to death and then stop. It is not even to trace the connection between one soul and its historical milieu, and then stop. It is to determine and describe how each and every human life is tied to the process of mental and psychic growth that Erikson now labels "the metabolism of generations," and does not stop.

What the reader has suspected all along is now clearly affirmed. Erikson's biography of Luther is not at heart a biography at all, and not at heart about young man Luther. Its "real content" is a discourse on how a talented individual may "grow into the social process" and upon other cultural-psychological matters also more real than little Luther.

This discourse is impressively authoritative. It takes psychoanalysis into the business of assessing relationships of all kinds between human disciplines of all kinds, biography being just an incidental, contributory discipline along the way. With particular force it even deals with the ancient conflict between free will and determinism, though in a language of which the ancients knew naught:

> We say the tradition "molds" the individual, "channels" his drives. But the social process does not mold a new being merely to housebreak him; it molds generations in order to be remolded, to be reinvigorated, by them. Therefore, society can never afford merely to suppress drives or guide their sublimation. It must support the primary function of every individual ego, which is to transform instinctual energy into patterns of action, into character, into style—in short, into an identity with a core of integrity which is to be derived from and also contributed to the tradition.

So it is finally the clinical "we" that has made my polemic blossom. Even Erikson's steady assertion of the crucial role played by individuals—with their cores of integrity—reeks of the "we"; nothing is more apparent about his clinic's activities than that they are incurably group activities. A Freud or a Luther can no more escape than a John Doe.

Nor is there refuge from the patient groups in saying that after all a Freud or a Luther is a human being too, since the clinic is not now aiming at obvious points of groupiness. For entrepreneurial reasons it now needs the most conspicuously independent souls under its wing, needs them because they are the ones who, unlike John Doe, might somehow succeed in escaping the clinic and thereby diminish the clinic's operative realm. All individuals great and small must be ground up in the clinic machine, for the good of the cause.

The cause is the assertion of the clinic's view of "real content."

IV

American Biography

The public library in Hyattsville, Maryland, is a good small library, comfortable, well-run and reasonably quiet—except after school. It is also an excellent place in which to ponder on American biography. Its whole south wall on the main floor is laden with biography and autobiography, mostly American, shelved alphabetically beginning with Abelard and Heloise, and ending with Elmo Zumwalt. There are perhaps four thousand volumes on the wall, and they are of fairly recent vintage, since ancient tomes like Plutarch's *Lives of the Noble Grecians and Romans* and Franklin's *Autobiography*—of which there are few—are usually shelved elsewhere. The four thousand are a gaudy mixture of the journalistic, the literary, the political, the historical, the sociopsychological, and the Hollywoodal. As I write this I have been looking at the wall for some time, wondering whether to come at my task here alphabetically, or by the use of some loftier shaping plan. I know I need something, but I also know that no matter how I approach the wall, I have on my hands a miscellany that I can only sample. (And the whole wall is only a sample!)

The A's are heavy with Adamses, but infiltrated with Louisa May Alcott, Shana Alexander, Svetlana Alliluyeva, and King Arthur. There are only six Z's, six Y's, and one X (Malcolm X—six copies), but the W's are many, and have Mae West cheek-to-cheek with Edith Wharton, Simone Weil with *Big Julie of Vegas*, and Shelley Winters with Thomas Wolfe. I decide that I will not proceed alphabetically.

Should I begin where I know a little something, say with a literary biography? Should I begin where I have a deep and unshakable prejudice, say a Washington scandal-life? Or should I blindfold myself and simply reach out, as in *pin the tail on the donkey*? I look under "D" and am not excited. I roam up and down the wall aimlessly, arriving at "P." And there is what I have been looking for.

The book is *The World of Roger Tory Peterson*, an "authorized biography" by John C. Devlin and Grace Naismith, with a foreword by Elliott Richardson. I know Peterson, having carried a bird guide of his in the woods, and I am ever so slightly acquainted with Richardson, having met him once at a cocktail party. I am without prejudices about birds and have nothing worthwhile to say about them, despite Peterson. Birds and Peterson seem to be excellently neutral grounds, as does its publisher, New York Times Books. I sign the book out.

Roger Tory Peterson is a wonderful man (I discover quickly; the book reads quickly) and a friend of the authors. He lives in Old Lyme, Connecticut, partly because he likes the place and partly because it is "half way between his field-guide publishers, Houghton Mifflin, and the art centers of New York City." When he was young he was a "mischievous boy" in Jamestown, New York. His father beat him but also understood him, so he did not run away. With a friend he built and set up twenty bird-feeding stations in the woods, and the birds kept him, a neighbor said, from being "notoriously bad." He was more comfortable with the birds than with people because, for one thing, people in Jamestown, New York, did not like Swedes. "It is possible," the biographers wrote, "that the ridicule and insults whetted his almost fanatical desire to succeed, to prove himself, and to 'show them.' "

Roger's problem was not just Swedishness. His parents did not appreciate his being late for church because of his obligations to birds, and his biology teacher did not approve of his denying that the snowy egret was extinct, though it was not. Roger had trouble both at school and at home because he was simultaneously mischievous and dedicated. But his trouble was not deep-seated, and soon his bird future was hurried on its way by an Ernest Thompson Seton book that inspired his now famous bird-identification system. Soon he was moving in a straight line toward success; even at age seventeen he had two painting entries in an important bird-art exhibition.

The art exhibition led to art school in New York, where it was birds, birds, birds for him, plus a few nudes. He also learned there to imitate birds sounds, and successfully did so on a radio show. Then he landed a teaching job in Brookline, Massachusetts, where there were more birds and where Elliott Richardson, his best student, entered his life. One summer he took Richardson and Richardson's brother birding on Cape Cod, with the result that many years later Richardson could report that what Roger most effectively taught was observation.

Roger's chief early trouble was that he conducted himself as if he were an oaf. He did not dress well, did not care about such matters, and was much too sure of himself. Soon he was blackballed from an elegant Boston bird club, but the next year he was admitted to the club, and there met his future publisher. By the age of twenty-six he already had several books out in the big world and selling well. He was in Who's Who. He was educational director of the Audubon Society. And he had married into the New York Social Register. I pause. The biography is only ninety pages gone, but its mission seems already to have been declared and exploited to the degree that it is going to be. Is the story not to be one of the genteel success, with only minor hitches on the dedicated hero's road to the heights?

Yes, it is to be that. Roger went on many expeditions, held the record of bird-sightings "seen in one year in North America," and wrote many, many bird books (also flower books) that his second wife typed. He lectured everywhere on birds, went everywhere to bird congresses, and had troubles everywhere with his bird cameras. He became easily abstracted, drove erratically, had a way of leaving wives home to drink too much, and nearly drowned while birding off Patagonia. Yet nothing ever really went wrong except for the wives, who are described as very nice people. The awards, accomplishments, and years mounted up. As a bird authority Roger reached the top of the heap, and as an artist he learned, said one critic, to out-Audubon Audubon.* So I come to the end and read the authors' final sentence: "His field guides, his books, his teaching and lecturing, and now his gallery paintings further establish his permanence in the archives of great men."

I take in the message and decide, I hope not maliciously, that it is not just about Roger but also about a kind of biography. The message is that biography so constructed is rootedly quantitative in its assessment of human values. As in the profession of bird-sighting such biography measures its birds by the numbers, putting each sighting down methodically in the book.

---

*Another critic advised that many of his paintings achieved "fine art." The critic further explained that fine art "exists only for aesthetic reasons."

◆ ◆

So I return Roger Tory Peterson to the library, move to the south wall
again, and find myself staring at the I's. In 1984 Lee Iacocca, with the
help of William Novak and the thoroughly involved publishers (Bantam), put into national play a bestseller about himself, of which the
library has four copies.* I remove just one, and am soon deep in a
first-person account of American success. Unlike the Peterson bio, this
volume tries hard not to be genteel. From start to finish Iacocca
adopts—or is provided with?—a tough-guy manner that presumably
all those involved financially thought fitting for a story of entrepreneurial struggles in the American big-money jungle. Yet it is not a *very*
tough account, since the American jungle emerges as a friendly place
for hard-working souls like Iacocca. With the exception of a few unpleasant personages in the jungle like Henry Ford II, it is inhabited by
a "good gang" and is the land of opportunity it has been said to be. If
only we Americans as a whole would buckle our seat belts, reduce
labor's fringe benefits, raise our oil taxes, and give our basic industries
a break (meanwhile heeding what it is about Japanese management
that has made Japan a new industrial model), then we might become
collectively as wonderful as Iacocca. The secret for doing so is Iacocca's
own, though he had it from his parents: "I go back to what my parents
taught me. Apply yourself. Get all the education you can, but then,
by God, *do* something! Don't just stand there, make something happen. It isn't easy, but if you keep your nose to the grindstone and work
at it, it's amazing how in a free society you can become as great as you
want to be. And, of course, be grateful for whatever blessing God
bestows on you."

Iacocca then uses this little moral lesson, and others, as an introduction to a promotion of his Statue of Liberty restoration project. In
fact he ends with the Statue of Liberty. I sit quietly, read his self-
advertisement, and wonder if I am reading an autobiography or a
brochure.

But I worry about my cynicism. I take the book back to the library
thinking that I must be cautious and recall my own late 1930s maturing. Then it was conventional in my set to ridicule such preachings,
which were those of the likes of Dale Carnegie, and reached back to

*Four years later an unfriendly biography has, predictably, appeared. When
(and where) will it end?

John D. Rockefeller's remark that God gave him his money.* I tell myself that because of my past I am entirely too familiar with Lee Iacocca to read him objectively. His assumptions and those in the Peterson biography overlap (though Iacocca is fearful of being caught out as genteel), and I seem to have a conditioned scorn for the assumptions. Do I not approve of American success, and of biographers presenting models of such success for America to look up to? Watch it, I tell myself; these contributors to "my" genre are not to be dismissed lightly.

◆ ◆

So I go to "G," and there is Judy Garland, and right away I wonder if I will be more at home with Hollywood assumptions. I have been reading of Hollywood, and watching it, for about sixty years, and have been no fan of its success stories either. Or have I? Suddenly I remember *The Last Tycoon*, and then I think of other, related models, mostly in fiction. Somehow Hollywood has been different from Detroit and Old Lyme, Connecticut, and now I find that Anne Edwards's biography of Judy Garland is different too. Like the Peterson and Iacocca books it is a popular item, and one telling an excessively familiar American story, but the approach is different. Edwards does not appear to be *against* Hollywood, but she is hardly promoting it. She seems to be using it as a backdrop against which a societal crime is being committed, and finding that it is a natural backdrop for such crime. She is not, in any event, planning to impose a straight-line success story upon her heroine's life.

How many sociological studies have there been of Hollywood? Dozens and dozens. The pieties of Hollywood success have been so fervent for so long that they have created a whole complex of reactions and studies, some *impious*, to which we are now equally adjusted. Edwards's biography sits in between the pieties and impieties in just the way that amazing Hollywood has for decades encouraged intelligent writings about it to do. It has invited probes rather than, or in addition to, brochures. The probes can be slick or thoughtful—and Edwards's is thoughtful—but they have trouble being straight-line and

---

*During the presidential activities of 1988 I heard Republican candidate Robertson make Rockefeller's remark more directly political by saying, "Our property comes from Almighty God."

commonplace. Hollywood writers are seldom complacent, unless they are writing promotional material about the movies themselves. The movies regularly fare better than the performers, who are conventionally reported to have sifted down, as they aged, into a darkness deep and abiding. And so I begin reading of Judy.

Judy's infant entrance to Hollywood is so familiar and pat that Edwards can even quote Hedda Hopper without a qualm, though Hopper was one of the great Hollywood promoters of her day. Interestingly, Hopper was a reporter of darkness too, and in a passage that Edwards quotes, she describes Judy's mother as one of those obsessed parents who robbed their children "of every phase of childhood to keep the waves in their hair, the pleats in the dress, and pink polish on the nails." Edwards moves out from Hopper and shows the mother's obsession unsparingly, sometimes by quoting Judy herself on the subject. We see Judy as a lonely little mother-hater dreaming of being taken away from Hollywood by her less obsessed father; then as an unhappy but emerging performer; then as the traumatic recipient of news of her father's death; and then as a not-so-little recipient of kindness from Louis B. Mayer, who says to her (as he said to many), "I am your father, and whenever you have trouble, and whenever you need anything, come to me and I will help you." In any other popular source of biography in America than Hollywood, a father figure like Mayer is still apt to be a moral figure like Iacocca's father, but Hollywood has never been productive of moral uplift off screen. Its fragile celluloid connection to "real content" has given it a noisy skepticism about its own filmed values.

By page 40, therefore, Edwards has indoctrinated me with the shabbiness of Judy's success story, and I can see that the rest of the life will be crammed with ravenous mates and relatives, false friends, debts, subpoenas, alcohol, drugs, therapists, hospitals, and Olympian hotel suites.

And by page 130 I see that the story has been duly crammed, and that Judy is sick, betrayed, a goner.

And by page 150 I find that Judy has staged a comeback on Broadway.

And by 170 I find her a goner again. Then I meet the psychiatrists, who squabble cravenly over the responsibility for her latest near-demise, even while she is recovering in time to appear in Carnegie Hall.

And so on. During the last years of Judy's short life, biographer

Edwards is herself so dazzled by her heroine's pattern of success and misery that she does not know—who would?—what to do except proceed chronologically and quietly. She does, and when Judy dies, she cuts the book off quickly without background music. We are left with something alien in scope and purpose to the Peterson and Iacocca volumes. Something *without* success?

I think of Joseph Conrad's World War I novel, *Victory*, at the end of which Conrad's hero has somehow defeated the enemy but is now himself battered and is watching his own heroic and sacrificial loved one die in front of him. She "gloriously" whispers to him, "Who else could have done this for you?" And with "unconcealed despair" he replies, "No one in the world." Judy's success seems to have been a little like this, but what is biographer Edwards's intent? My estimate is that she wants us to admire Judy for her talent, but also wants us to note in passing what a fool Judy was and what a foolish world she lived in. Success? Somehow the essence of the book is not the patriotic, American-way-of-life success celebrated in Peterson and Iacocca. Yet it is not an anti–success-story book either. Is not its essence reportorial?

◆ ◆

To deal with that question, let me leave the south wall for a moment and go back to biographer Carlyle, his essences, and his influence on America. His influence was not primarily upon biography at all, though I am coming to one professed disciple, and not upon autobiography either, except autobiography of an odd kind like *Walden* and *Song of Myself*. It was an influence asserting the directorial presence of the biographer in biography, at a time when America was favoring biographers who wished to be anonymous, who did not wish to be mistaken for Carlyle—or for Emerson, Melville, Thoreau, or Whitman. I will describe some of the nineteenth-century results later, but the results are still around us now in American literary and historical biography, which is earnestly objective about itself. One American critic of this dispensation, Albert Britt, has put it that Carlyle "was in the modern sense no biographer, but a philosopher and a moralist." Another like-minded critic, Paul Murray Kendall, has declined even to mention Carlyle as a biographer, though he calls Carlyle's biographer Froude a biographer and though he quotes Carlyle amusingly saying, "How delicate, how decent is English biography, bless its mealymouth!" For Britt and Kendall a biographer is not, it seems, a man of letters at all in the sense in which Carlyle thought of a man of letters, but a personage like Carlyle's Professor Dryasdust. The true biographer provides the data-blessed truth and nothing but that truth. He avoids authorial comment and participation, and if he happens to show his authorial colors, he does so negatively, by opposing noisy writers like Carlyle.

In the late nineteenth century Carlyle had the same effect in England, though less emphatically, on Leslie Stephen and the *DNB*. Stephen commented that Carlyle's style was the worst possible model for a biographer, and he could readily have expanded the complaint to include Carlyle's whole personal, exhibitionistic approach to the genre; yet Stephen did, despite himself, admire Carlyle as a biographer; and partly as a result, biography is still frequently known in England by its authors rather than by its subjects. But who are the most famous American biographers? I think of Carl Sandburg, and after Sandburg—who is seldom thought of as a biographer at all—I slip rapidly down to the names of academic biographers (partly, of course, because of my own academic drift), noting that even the best-known of these, such as Ernest Samuels, Leon Edel, and Samuel Morison, are comparatively retiring. Who else is there to carry forward into the future the older, grander notion of the man of letters as biographer?

Norman Mailer?

◆ ◆

Yes, it is suddenly necessary to cope with Mailer's *Marilyn*, a much-reviewed picture book of the 1970s that had Mailer's aggressive stamp upon it. I rush to the south wall and find *Marilyn* among the missing. I go to the desk and am told that three other copies in the Prince George's County library system are also missing (since 1983). I go to the libraries of the University of Maryland, and find that their two copies are missing. I go to two bookstores of competence; it is not on sale. I go to *Books in Print*; it is not (though soon again will be) in print. There are other biographies of Marilyn Monroe now, including one by an opponent of Mailer, Gloria Steinem. What meaning is here? At any rate I must now still find Mailer and, having found him, compare him with Steinem. Biography is becoming complicated. I proceed to the Library of Congress.

In the Library of Congress there is just one card in the catalogue for *Marilyn*, though the card is stamped "copy #2," and the card declares that copy *#2* is in Rare Books. This bombshell makes me realize how far Mailer has come. Could any other modern writer have had published, within the last fifteen years, a bestseller, and have so succeeded with it that it is only to be found in Rare Books? I go to Rare Books, I fill out forms, I put all my belongings in a cabinet with a key so that I may enter the Sanctum harmless. At last *Marilyn* really comes, and as soon as I see it I remember it from its undusty dustjacket in bookstore windows. It *is* a rare book.

It is also a biography, and described on the jacket as Mailer's first. It contains "pictures by the world's foremost photographers," but it *is* a biography of sorts. Mailer himself tells us that it was begun as a preface to photographs only, and he apologizes for its being "a species of novel," that is, not a formal biography. "A formal biography," he adds, "can probably not be written in less than two years since it can take that long to collect the facts—princes have to be wooed and close friends of the subject disabused of paranoia." I decide he is saying that he could not himself write a formal biography because (*a*) he had to write *Marilyn* in a hurry, and (*b*) he would not be caught dead writing a formal biography.

Obviously I have come to the right place for further meditation about what Hollywood biography is and means (though even as I sit in the Sanctum the biographies by Mailer and Steinem are being reissued, and new biographies are expected). After a thousand words of Mailer's richest prose—in which he balances Marilyn's angel-of-sex image with her insecurity—he rises above Marilyn to quote Virginia Woolf: " 'A biography is considered complete if it merely accounts for six or seven selves, whereas a person may well have as many as a thousand.' " Thus does he show his intent not to underestimate the genre's problems, though he may not have time to face them.

Then he descends to biographers who have actually written about Marilyn, noting that they are the ones who are to provide him with facts. These burrowers turn out to have great limitations. One of them is a "feature writer heating up the old dishes of other feature writers." Another is extremely conscientious, and a fine source of information out of which a good biography *might* be written. A third, who was an early friend of Marilyn's, is not a burrower at all, but a great myth-maker. And a fourth, also a friend, is producing a definitive memoir that is sure to be right in all its details but has luckily not yet appeared.

And now, having put the competition in its place, Mailer considers the kind of biography he might himself have written of Marilyn, if only he had been, like Arthur Miller, married to her. He might have been able to produce a psychobiography with depth. But as he was not married to her and only knew even Miller slightly, he is at last ready to write what he knew he was going to write in the first place: a *Mailer* biography of Marilyn Monroe.

He does. He begins with the childhood and the traumas of child-hood (as reported in the other biographies) and his subject's resultant identity problems. Soon, he has put on display his own brand of psychobiography, containing all his theories about sex and America. Like a certain Viennese analyst, he has traced Marilyn's trouble back to her illegitimacy, the loss of her father, and other factors, and is ready, though she is still a child, to diagnose her adult problems. His diagnosis is not, though, Viennese in tone:

> We are all steeped in the notion that lonely people have a life of large inner fantasy. What may be ignored is the tendency to become a narcissist. . . . [But] since there is also a great tendency for every bastard to become a narcissist—the absence of one parent creating a sense of romantic mystery *within* oneself, within one of the two govern-ing senses of self, the future Marilyn Monroe was by illegitimate birth already in a royal line of narcissists. The orphanage [that she was sent to] would confirm this.

I am now beginning to have fantasies myself, and I see the face of the Viennese analyst merging with the face of an eccentric Scotch stylist. Here is another loner taking hold of biography his way.

In his forty years or so as a major literary phenomenon Mailer has made much capital out of being his own man, but while he has made us all know that he is unique, he has had models. Freud's influence upon him is obvious, but Carlyle's should not be ignored. After all, Carlyle was the great promoter in English of men of letters as cultural leaders, and he was also the most individual stylist of his age. Mailer would never think of writing a Carlylean sentence, but he has been his own eminent stylist, and he certainly thinks of himself as a man of letters who is also a cultural leader. With *Marilyn* he seems to have planted himself in biography as a searcher-out of the essence of great-ness. Like Carlyle.

But what is the essence that Mailer was looking for in the almost pitiable character of Marilyn? How could it be, as with Carlyle, an essence close to the greatness he has wished for himself? I watch him follow Marilyn through her sad marriages, her emergence as a great photographer's model and an uncertain actress, her sad years of fame with an entourage of the mighty, and I come to her sordid end, where, somehow, her greatness has also resided, for *all* her biographers. Mailer is at his absolute best here, as he puts her in the hospitals and watches the iron doors close. He contrives even to be sensuous about her decline and death, and to sum it up with a characteristically outrageous Mailer law. Note the "we" that he uses in it, and compare the size of the "we" with Freud's, even Erikson's: "If the law of passion is that we cannot begin to love again until we find a love greater than the last, the law of narcissism must be that we cannot continue to adore ourselves unless our display is [always continues to be?] more extraordinary than before."

Is Mailer himself part of this "we" or above it? One cannot be sure until, suddenly, he disposes of poor Marilyn, leaves her flat as *just* a child, just a little narcissist with fantasies, and concludes with a flip image of her in heaven, still dreaming. In his final sentence he suggests that she pay a call on Mr. Dickens up there, "for he, like many another literary man, is bound to adore you, fatherless child."

It seems quite the wrong ending, not doing justice to the woman he has evoked, yet it is definitely a Mailer ending, and probably that is its point. It reasserts Mailer. In it he patronizes not only Marilyn but also his competing biographers, who are, unlike himself, Dickensian and "bound to adore" such sentimental subjects as Marilyn. He seems to be saying that he is not an adorer, not one of the "we" either. He has removed himself, having finished his 90,000 words about her. She is now a case that he, the analyst, can dismiss. Her hour is up.

◆ ◆

Yet as I close the book and return it undamaged to the authorities, I wonder if I am reading Mailer right. I head out for Gloria Steinem in a quandary and find that Steinem's *Marilyn* (with "Norma Jean" superimposed upon "Marilyn" on the cover) is readily available everywhere. In format it is a direct steal from the Mailer volume. It also is half photographs. It also is glossy. It also is about nine inches by twelve, with a smiley, come-on picture—though a less sexual picture—on the dust jacket. But right away, inside, it reveals a separate mission of its own. It is clearly a set-the-record-straight book contending, though amicably, with other interpretations of Marilyn. It refers several times to Mailer, constantly to two heavily researched biographies, and sporadically to Marilyn's own memoirs as well as to a number of

interviews of Marilyn by Steinem's photographer-collaborator, George
Barris. Its revisionary purpose is well summed up in the double dedication to Marilyn at the beginning, where Steinem addresses the
volume "to the real Marilyn, and to the reality in us all," while Barris
inscribes it "to a gentle, fragile Marilyn, who will forever be in our
hearts."

In this volume, then, I am to understand that Marilyn is to be
real, gentle, and fragile, but most particularly real. The other biographers (Steinem declares there have been forty!) have somehow failed
to locate the real.

And Mailer is one of those failures, though, as will be seen, his
view of Marilyn is close to Steinem's. Steinem, like most feminists of
the last decade or so, has several problems with Mailer, and right at
the beginning she tells me something about him that I—a country boy
from Maryland who does not keep up with New York—did not know.
She tells me that Mailer wrote a "memory play" about Marilyn called
Strawberry, and cast his own daughter as Marilyn. "Oh," I say, "where
have I been?" I begin to see the worms in my interpretation of Mailer's
last paragraph, the one I quoted where he ostensibly dismisses Marilyn. Steinem in effect contradicts me, and describes Mailer as *obsessed*
with Marilyn; so I put that word on hold and go on reading.

The real Marilyn, she tells me, was Norma Jean.* The real Marilyn
was the "child within" Marilyn. She was a wholesome child (and the
photographs by Barris focus upon wholesomeness rather than allure).
She was a child who in maturity remained a child. She was not after
money and was constantly being cheated by money people. She was
"generous in a spontaneous way." She thought her lurid sex roles
stupid. In her relations with men she wanted to be loved, not kept.
She had, in John Huston's words, "no techniques. It was all truth. It
was only Marilyn." She liked *not* to be the famous Marilyn, but to
commune in private with working people and children. "If I am a star,"
she said, "the people made me a star," not the directors, photographers,
public relations men.

The difference between this Marilyn and Mailer's is at this point
emerging, but not clearly, for me. It seems more a matter of tone than
substance, but the tone is important. Both Steinem in her text and
Barris in his pictures are friendly in their approach to her because
they want to display a pleasantly childish, *warmly* real Marilyn, whereas

*Until the world found her, Marilyn's name was Norma Jean Baker.

Mailer, though also describing a childish Marilyn, is cold and Mailerly as he does so. He finds little warmth in her, sees her as having been frozen up by her past, a narcissist who has become "a queen of a castrator."

So the Steinem and Mailer views of her, though agreeing that she is a case, deviate with respect to how much of a case she was, how much was *left* to her in the way of warmth. Alas, finding warmth in a Hollywood star is not easy. The promoters of a star, who are never warm, are *creators* of warmth, and the job of distinguishing promoter warmth from real warmth is not for a sentimentalist. Photographer Barris, I note, is one. His pictures are aimed at catching Marilyn when she is not posing. They have the flavor of good snapshots. They seek out warmth as distinct from sultriness, but in the process they lose the mugger, the poseur-genius in Marilyn. As for Steinem, she wishes to avoid sentiment, yet her prose sometimes lapses into it.* Like Mailer she leans heavily toward the diagnostic, but her diagnoses are journalistic in tone. She finds her base not in Freud but in a volume called *Your Inner Child of the Past* by Dr. Hugh Missildine, a psychiatry popularizer, published a year after Marilyn's death.

Missildine was not writing about Marilyn at all, but Steinem thinks he could "almost" have been talking directly to her. He spoke, she says, "without the artificial language or gender-based theories of Freud," and he described how "the child we used to be lives on inside us," and how early neglect of that child—usually by "a father who somehow wasn't a father and a mother who somehow wasn't a mother"— affected the later life of the child. Then she reinforces her sense of Missildine's relevance to Marilyn by quoting two full pages of his book about neglected children, after which she addresses the reader, saying, "As you read and think about Marilyn, remember Norma Jean." The pages she quotes are indeed in a language foreign to Freud, but foreign in a way she does not mention or seem to recognize. Note particularly the "you" in the following passage, and how it make psychoanalysis sound like recipes in a cookbook:

> If you have difficulty in feeling close to others and in "belonging" to a group, drift in and out of relationships casually because people do not seem to mean much to you, if you feel you lack an identity of your own, suffer intensely from anxiety and loneliness, and yet keep people

*For example, her adjectives muddy her reporting when she describes Marilyn as "a beautiful adult woman, but one with the frail ego of a neglected child."

at a distance, you should suspect neglect as the trouble-making pathogenic factor in your childhood.

The "you" in the passage is its most instructive component. It is
not Steinem's "you" but the doctor's, yet it is a "you" of which Steinem
approves, declaring it aimed at the likes of Marilyn without "artificial
language." (But how about the phrase "pathogenic factor"?) In a cookbook the "you" would be given an explicit remedy for some kitchen
difficulty—"If your cake does not rise, and is burned to a crisp, try
cutting the heat down from 600"—but in the passage the remedy is
clear enough without being stated. It is, "Let's have a little less neglect
[from you] please." The trouble with this remedy is not in the remedy
itself, though it is kitsch (not kitchen) psychiatry, but in the impossi-
bility of its being proposed to anyone who has already been neglected.
The "you" can therefore not really be Marilyn, as Steinem proposes,
but has to be the great "you" of all the readers of the book who are,
perhaps at the moment of reading, in the process of neglecting
somebody.

So I see the passage as properly beginning, "Look here now, you
derelict fathers, mothers, and citizens," and then going on to warn all
of them of their responsibilities to their fellow men and children. The
passage is not clinically but socially prescriptive.

Naturally Freud's "artificial language" did not under any circumstances include such a "you," Freud having been a prescriber for
patients, not (overtly) societies. And Mailer's *Marilyn* is mostly in the
Freudian tradition, a tradition that Steinem has been trying to revise.
When she speaks prescriptively herself, she speaks, as did Missildine,
to the social cause of a psychic condition, rather than to a psychic
cause. Thus, she begins one of her chapters: "Children who are not
the focus of loving attention may come to feel that they are invisible.
They fight to be noticed to prove that they exist." These words are not
just diagnostic. They also point a finger at the nonproviders of loving
attention. They make the children not just cases but victims, and they
seek out the victimizers.

So I decided that the real Marilyn, for Steinem, is the child Marilyn
who survived, wounded, the assaults of a large social enemy composed
of characters extending from parents (both of them) up to all her
exploiters and adorers, including even two Kennedys. The enemy, she
is saying, surrounded Marilyn and kept wounding her, since the vulnerable child was always there to be wounded. In a rare complaint

about Mailer in the volume—mostly she leans over backward to appear to respect his opinions—she remarks that what he could not understand about Marilyn was her vulnerability, which Steinem felt to have been both real and very warm, very lovable. Thus Mailer could not understand, she felt, Marilyn's "refusal to marry for money." He thought of her as a castrator, when in fact she was a pawn in the games of a world (heavily male but not all male) she never made.

I think Steinem underestimates Mailer's sympathy for Marilyn's vulnerability, but the difference between Steinem and Mailer that now most impresses me is not that; it is one of professional perspective. Mailer's Marilyn is a literary psychoanalyst's Marilyn, with Mailer playing the detached analyst, and Steinem's Marilyn is a feminine social scientist's Marilyn, with Steinem playing the defender of vulnerable women. These two professional essences prove to be, on the page, close, yet they *are* primarily professional rather than personal essences, and their common professionalism reminds me again of Steinem's remark that Mailer was obsessed by Marilyn, the implication being that she, Steinem, was not. I think her wrong. I now think that neither Mailer (despite *Strawberry*) nor Steinem was obsessed by the poor woman. An obsession represents a lack of control, but both Mailer and Steinem had themselves well in hand as they wrote of her. They were both "taking hold" of their subject coolly for their respective professional purposes, for though Mailer had paraprofessional private purposes as well—he is the only modern biographer I have found who in any way resembles Carlyle—he certainly can be included among the taking-hold brethren of the genre.

◆ ◆

But the south wall is not to be understood as all Hollywood and clinic. Under "A" there are no less than seven statesmanlike Adamses present in force, plus Chancellor Adenauer, Prince Albert, Chester Arthur, and (as an antidote) Benedict Arnold. Under "B" there are Bismarck, Bolivar, Brezhnev, Begin, William Jennings Bryan. Under "C" there are Castro, Churchill, Chiang Kai-chek, Jimmy Carter. And on and on. These are leaders of countries, servants of the masses in the old way of service, the way upon which the genre of biography in classical times was built. On the south wall this tradition usually resides in new dust jackets, but it is present in great numbers. It is the matter upon which Sunday book review sections still rely more heavily than on any other category of biography. It is the national and inter-

national matter that Schlesingers and Kissingers regularly assess in
reviews, if they have not written the matter themselves.

And when reviewers assess such material, they concentrate, as do
the biographies themselves, upon the public lives of these figures, and
upon the decisions they made or failed to make that shook political
parties and capitals. The reviewers comment little upon such biographers except to point to what has been slighted or overplayed; they
think of the biographer's role as a passive one. And usually the
biographers of great leaders *are*, relatively, passive.

For such biographers and their reviewers are journalists mostly, and
political historians. Their professional commitments are to the recording
of big public moments. Their assessments, like Plutarch's two thousand
years ago, are of a leader's wisdom, courage, decisiveness. If a little
cheesecake should creep in, or if the leader should have been found
drunk in his bathtub on election night, so be it; the main subject
remains leadership in historic moments, not primal scenes in childhood.

Hence the biographer's job—if he is not just a dedicated muck-
raker—is seen as that of plodding through all the public documents
extant to find out who said what to whom in Washington or London
before the leader decided that yes, he *would* deploy the Seventh Regi-
ment in Patagonia or Pantellaria. The job is not seen as an occasion
for psychic probing except when probing may bear immediately upon
such actions.

For the psychobiographer, on the other hand, such biography is at
bottom simply "anecdotal," in that it does not face up to the "real
content" of a character's being, but only to his public facade. The
psychobiographer may or may not be right, but the great fact to be
noted about the south wall is that public biography, not psychobiography, is still the norm there, the main line.

Yet the south wall is reticent about the tradition on which the
norm rests. It is a modern wall with new titles largely, and looking at
it I realize that I must go to a university library to see where the
American roots for the genre are. I now do so and become submerged,
on the University of Maryland campus, in brittle, yellowing pages.
Days later I come up convinced that, yes, there were biographers of
public leaders in America in the nineteenth century too. I choose just
two, both of whom were admirers, from a great distance, of Carlyle.
One is highbrow Henry Adams (1838–1918), whom everyone still knows
though seldom as a biographer, and whom I cannot seem to avoid.
The other is lowbrow James Parton (1822–91), now passé. (In the

admittedly dreadful *Encyclopedia Americana* the only Parton is Dolly
Parton.) Let me start with Parton.

◆ ◆

James Parton was born in England; came to New York as an infant;
went to school in White Plains, where, according to his *DAB* biographer, George Genzer, "he acquired a taste for Homer and a distaste for
orthodox Christianity"; never attended college but taught school in
Philadelphia for four years; and moved in upon biography by being
an aggressive, do-it-yourself American, telling his printer-employer that
he could write a biography of Horace Greeley that would sell as well
as Benjamin Franklin's autobiography. The time was 1855; the employer
gave him $1,000 to write it. Parton finished off Greeley in eleven
months, and his book sold 30,000 copies, netting him another $2,000.
He went on to do Burr, Jackson, Jefferson, General Butler, John Jacob
Astor, and even Voltaire, as well as short biographies of "captains of
industry" and "daughters of genius," plus anthologies of verse and much
else. His *DAB* biographer reports that he became "one of the most
industrious, prolific, popular and well-paid writers in the U.S."

He could have been the same kind of success in our time. He had a
great sense of what would attract a large reading public in a democracy.
He had an easy, relaxed manner and a large capacity for storing up and
disgorging incidental detail. Psychobiographers would now fall over
themselves to call him anecdotal, but he used his detail efficiently in
supporting clear, constantly asserted themes. He did not trouble with
footnotes or bibliographies, but he made plentiful acknowledgments as
he went along. He liked to exaggerate, and not to qualify, but in a
journalistic sense he was thorough. Perhaps most important, he was, as
popular publishers always wish their writers to be, ideologically sound.

So I have been reading this Parton and trying to pick up from him
the nature of nineteenth-century American ideological soundness. After dipping in and out of five of his American volumes, I decide that
he had a perfect feel for it, from the very start, in his Greeley book,
which had the straight-line qualities of Roger Tory Peterson's biography.* Parton later chose a few less wholesome figures than Greeley,
but he never forgot the Greeley model.

*Parton's late-life two-volume biography of Voltaire is an anomaly in which
he confronted another culture and became pretty well lost. Like Carlyle and Leslie
Stephen, he there complained helplessly about the mass of matter to be mastered,
but he never mastered it.

For Parton the controlling fact about Greeley was the clarity of direction and purpose of his life. Even before Greeley was born, it was evident that a *hero* was to be born. His rightness began with his parents' pastoral background, and the background brought with it most of the other forms of nineteenth-century American ideological soundness, such as a respect for, rather than complexes about, parents, and an unwavering dedication to the democratic ideals floating in the American air. Greeley's character, we learn, was first molded by Scotch-Irish plain folk in a simple, boxy house (a picture was included) amid trees, mountain, snow, rain, sun, birds. Then there was a simple school and many books (Horace read every page with print on it in the neighborhood) and a small-town newspaper. Then there was the hero showing his mettle early by being conscientious and hard-working, by refusing to let troubles make him neurotic, and by demonstrating at every turn that life's hard knocks, not primal sex scenes, were at the heart of ideological soundness. The hard knocks came in a rush in chapter 4, for which the table-of-contents summary is more than adequate, though misleading:

His Father Ruined—Removal to Vermont
New Hampshire before the era of manufacturers—Causes of his father's failure—Rum in the olden time—An execution in the house—Flight of the father—Horace and the rum jug—Compromise with the creditors—Removal to another farm—Final ruin—Removal to Vermont—The winter journey—Scene at their new home—Cheerfulness in misfortune.

The summary is misleading because it inadvertently suggests that the father was (or that Parton thought he was) a drunk. He was not; he simply spent too much money on rum for his farmhands! Parton spoke ironically but not unkindly of his spending ways, not wishing to suggest that Horace had traumatic reasons to blame the father for the family's hard knocks: "The way to thrive in New Hampshire was to work very hard, keep the store-bill small, stick to the farm, and be no man's security. Of these four things, Horace's father did only one—he worked hard." And though the father, a good man, was a flawed man, the mother was a perfect woman. Parton reported of her that "her spirit never flagged. Her voice rose in song and laughter from the tangled brushwood in which she was often buried." So, with the help of both parents, Horace was able to grow up in the perfect milieu for greatness, the milieu of innocent, thoroughly moral financial trouble, together with a great plenty of physical and moral stamina to combat it.

As for Horace himself, Parton approached his character by referring to the fashionable phrenological judgments of the period. One phrenologist had described Horace's brain as "of the best form, long, narrow and high," indicating "small animality and selfishness, extreme benevolence, natural nobleness and loftiness of aim." Parton was not, however, wholly satisfied with phrenological assessments and may have been making fun of them (though he referred to them often). His own view of human character was an interesting amalgam of social and biological postulates about it, which he presented serially. "The character of man," he announced, "is derived, 1) from his breed; 2) from his breeding; 3) from his country; 4) from his time." He then reported on what Greeley had received from his mother, what he had received from his father, what he had received from a childhood "in republican, puritan New England, in a secluded rural region," and what he had received from his own maturing circumstances: "He escaped the schools, and so passed through childhood uncorrupt, 'his own man', not formed upon a pattern. He was not trained up—he grew up."

This last observation is a bit contradictory, since until Parton made it he had been promoting the benevolent influences upon Horace. But if one grants that one can have such influences and still be one's own man, then all is well, and the resultant Parton mixture of independence and social-cultural dependence emerges as much like Carlyle's. In effect, it was Carlyle's mixture, Americanized, and commercialized. Parton even ranked Greeley *with* Carlyle as a great dissenter from the surrounding political consensus, who was at the same time a representative of the age's underlying morality, a morality of simple, noble service to man and man's spirit, and of opposition to riches, fine clothes, the world's pomp. This high view was sufficiently like that to which both Carlyle and Goethe had paid homage that Parton could twice quote a line from Goethe about it, and end his volume with advice to the reader that included the quotation: "Reader, if you like Horace Greeley, do as well in your place, as he has in his. If you like him not, do better. And, to end with a good word, often repeated but not too often: 'The spirit in which we act is the highest matter.'"

But for Parton the "highest matter" kept turning up as something a little lower than matter in Carlyle and Goethe, kept turning unobtrusively into a consensus spirit paying homage to the dollar. Parton's real ideological hero was not Carlyle but Franklin, with whom he compared Greeley constantly. At one point he declared Greeley to be the "better man," but eight years later he wrote of Franklin for two big volumes—managing to squeeze in a complete history of the United States in Franklin's age—and in those volumes Franklin came out well indeed, one of the great success stories of all time.

Franklin's success was truly American. After a rocky start he left behind his "baser part," wrote Parton, and emerged into a "noble and intelligent manhood," a model of a public servant: "At the age of forty-two he was a free man; i.e., he had an estate of seven hundred pounds a year. He became, successively, the servant of Philadelphia, Pennsylvania, the Colonies, England, France, the United States, and mankind." Parton listed Franklin's services to society for four pages, from his being "the first effective preacher of the blessed gospel of ventilation" to his breaking "the spell of Quakerism" and waking Pennsylvania "from the dream of unarmed safety." And he made Franklin's services conclusively practical by quoting the man himself saying, "It is incredible the quantity of good that may be done in a country by a single man, who will *make a business* of it" (my italics).

While reading the Franklin biography I naturally kept looking forward to what was in store for me in Parton's biographies of the unheroic Aaron Burr and John Jacob Astor, though I thought I knew. When I came to them, I found I was only half right; Parton presented them *both* as bad models, whereas I had thought he would at least admire Astor's business sense. He was fascinated by the moral deficiencies of Burr, of whom a phrenologist had said that "his perceptive powers were prominent . . . his executive faculties were all strong . . . [but] his spirituality appears to have been weak . . . [and] his social brain unevenly developed." Parton supplemented the phrenologist's editorial by saying that Burr "had failed to achieve a character worthy of his powers," which "was a great pity. Think of the good he might have done his country." But then, with Astor, Parton became a thorough populist raging against greed. Writing right after Astor's death he took the man as a biographical opportunity, filled the account out to small-book size with twenty pages of Astor's last will and testament, and steadily affirmed that Astor was a skinflint who did no good for anybody except his close family. He had given no sums to charity; at age fifty he had "possessed his millions," but by sixty-five "his millions had possessed him." Parton concluded with the negative lessons to be learned from Astor's life and suggested looking forward to an America run by persons *un*like him. He recommended the building of "HOUSES FOR THE PEOPLE, which shall afford to an honest laborer rooms in a clean, orderly and commodious palace at the price he now pays for a corner of a dirty fever-breeding barrack."

All in all, Parton emerged for me as a likable professional moralist who mixed his high-mindedness with respect for the dollar, and just happened to be in biography. He was to be succeeded in the genre by a number of other prolific students of moral leadership, notably Elbert Hubbard, who may well have picked up his scheme for producing "little journeys" among the great from Parton. Parton's own little journeys included several collections of short biographies, of which his *Daughters of Genius* was representative. A very businesslike volume, it ranged through the whole Western world with its forty-three worthy biographees. (Here are eleven: Joan of Arc, Queen Victoria, Louisa May Alcott, the mother of Victor Hugo, Harriet Martineau, George Sand, Madame de Staël, the Brontë sisters, Fanny Mendelssohn, and the wife of Benedict Arnold.) Parton managed to package each one neatly in five to twenty-five pages, and if anyone should now complain that he turned each one into a simplified miniature of a woman the reply would have to be, yes, but other biographers have done this at much greater length, even Viennese psychobiographers. And Parton could do what he did extremely well. To give just one example, his account of Jane Welsh Carlyle's trials with her difficult husband summarized in twenty-five pages what Carlyle himself had provided in his long, long memoir of her, and Froude in his endless biography of Carlyle—nor did Parton misrepresent the bulky estimates of his predecessors. He had a talent for spaciousness in brief, and in his industrious career he covered a great deal of space. He was also, for his time, what we now uncertainly call a liberal—a very safe capitalist one. I mean that on the basic matters of human rights he seems to have been ahead of the population as a whole, but not worrisomely. He knew better than to be gloomy about the condition of man in America. He had faith in Progress. He respected the integrity of human motives. The same cannot be said of Henry Adams.

❖ ❖

I find that I own four copies of the *Education of Henry Adams*. I have lived with the book, argued about it, and written about it or near it, for most of my adult life. Yet I must work up to it here by way of an

Adams work thoroughly inferior to the *Education* that is nonetheless instructive in suggesting Adams's basic approach to biography. The work is his only full scale biography, his *Life of Albert Gallatin*. Together with three volumes that he edited of Gallatin's writings, the *Life* is essentially a part of his *History of the United States*, since it emerged as a by-product of that immensity. History, with Adams, always came first. He began with the forces of society, and he then turned to the people living with the forces.

This procedure is the reverse of Parton's in writing of Franklin, where history tagged along after Franklin. It is also opposed to Carlyle's thesis that "history is largely the story of the great men who have lived here." Adams was an admirer of Carlyle until the 1860s, when Carlyle's diatribes against America made it seem (Adams said in the *Education*) as if a "general darkness" had fallen on faith and the whole "habit of faith"; but it does not appear that Adams ever gave credence to the powers of individuals as Carlyle did. In the Adams view, great men, though important influences upon history, were great less because they influenced history than because they kept up with it. The difference here is relative, yet crucial to understanding Adams's approach to human character.

Gallatin was, for example, a hero for him, though no earth-mover, because he kept up. He performed as secretary of the treasury, and minister to France and then England. After government service of nearly forty years he retired, at age sixty-eight, to become president of the New York Historical Society, and at eighty-two became the founder of the American Ethnological Society. Thus, he was a statesman in the old Adams mode of statesmen. Like Franklin he served his country and humanity, but unlike Franklin—or Parton's version of Franklin—he was not a hero to Adams for his accomplishments so much as for his activities of mind. Right to the end of his life he was on top of the best thinking of his time. He was always ready to "grapple with the ideas and methods of the coming generation."

Adams himself was only in his forties when he wrote about Gallatin, and the obsessive "keeping up" theme of the *Education* had not yet taken over his dutiful historian's attention to the low daily business of bills, votes, speeches, and insider trading in Washington lobbies. Adams's own biographer in the *DAB*, Allen Johnson, said of the Gallatin life that it was weak on economics because its emphasis was "always on politics," but to me it does not seem short on economics but on vision, the kind of vision that Adams thought Gallatin had and that he would press for later among his fellow historians.* When he wrote of Gallatin, he was, as it were, only beginning his own education in vision. Not until he had finished the Gallatin life, and not until he had then suffered through the ineradicable private history of his wife's suicide in 1885, was he able to move seriously away from the fixed thoughts of a professional academic and make his contribution—definitely a major one—to biography, his own *Education*. Yet it seems to have been the character of Gallatin that began the stirring in him, Gallatin who had qualities that Adams found lacking in himself and lacking in his own famous forbears also, notably his grandfather John Quincy. The old president had had a wide-ranging mind, but when he suffered the political reverses accompanying the Jackson triumph in 1828, he became, though a sturdy combatant, a man with contempt for, and indignation at, the new ways of the world. As Henry Adams saw Gallatin, Gallatin had been able to avoid such a mind-set against the future.

And so he came to emulate Gallatin. He went off in many intellectual directions. He wanted to keep up with the sciences and lectured his fellow historians on their ignorance of science, much as C. P. Snow lectured literary folk in the 1950s. He wanted to know where the human mind as a collective evolutionary entity was going (Darwinism had hit him hard while he was serving his father in the London Embassy in the 1860s), and he kept being disappointed in his own mind, as it failed to help him to the degree that he thought it should. So in the *Education* and elsewhere, he convicted himself *and* his fellow scholars, in what are now mostly the humanities, of "mental indolence." In himself the indolence had been produced in part by his own physical and social milieu in the 1870s, when he was writing history (and biography) but looking at his subjects through a window on Lafayette Square, looking at them as a Washington insider. It had also been produced by the profession of history itself, which was his academic center and kept demanding intimate knowledge of all state crises, all public maneuvering in legislatures and governmental agencies, and leaving little scholarly energy for that which Adams did not call "real content" but had comparable phrases for, little energy for studies of character, of mind.

*Allen Johnson was general editor of the *DAB*. He took on Adams himself, just as Leslie Stephen of the *DNB* took on Carlyle. The parallel is striking; both Carlyle and Adams were attractively difficult biographer-models for biographers themselves.

On the south wall of the Hyattsville library the lack of such
energy—if "energy" is the word—is still evident in political biography
and national history. Aside from the inroads of the clinical, the south
wall remains largely populated by writers who assume of each of their
biographees, as Parton did, that their subject's principles were given
him by his breed and his breeding, and that he had the right bump
on his head. I mean that they think of character as a not-to-be-
worried-about quality. The subject did of course have to mature, but
he did not have to change his essentials. He did not have to change
because he was born with what he was and should be. Writing his
biography therefore properly consists largely of reporting on his tactics
of movement as he served his society. Such a biographical assumption
was the core of the Parton biographies, and it remains at the core of
the political biographies of our times (as well as the biographies of
generals, spies, and great entrepreneurs). It was also at the core of
Adams's *Life of Gallatin*, except that with Gallatin, Adams began to
see the possibilities of a different core, began to explore the mysteries
of "education" in the largest sense of that word.

His exploration never became an exploration of the unconscious or
subconscious—and it was definitely not an exploration of sex—but it
was indeed exploration of the human mind, of its assumptions and
fixities. The result was, eventually, his *Education*, which is as radical a
venture in the writing of a "life" as my book has to deal with.

But is the *Education* not autobiography rather than biography? In
an obvious sense, yes, since it is about the person who wrote it. Yet
Adams's *DAB* biographer, Johnson, points out that it was not even
labelled autobiography until after Adams's death, and Johnson does
not want to call it either biography *or* autobiography, but only what
Adams himself called it, "a study of twentieth-century multiplicity." Is
it so radical that that is the best we can do?

I don't like to disagree with either Johnson or Adams, but I find
the presence of "Henry Adams" in the title hard to ignore, and I note
that the book only *points* toward twentieth-century multiplicity, since
the writing of it began at just about 1900, when Adams was 62, and
since it was concerned for most of its five hundred pages with how the
nineteenth, eighteenth, and thirteenth centuries impinged upon the
life of this "Henry Adams." Would it not be better then to say that it
was a five-hundred page effort at making this "Henry Adams" a *classic*
(in the sense of representative rather than individual) American biographee? After all, it is in the third person.

Yes, I will be prescriptive and call it a biography, a novel experiment in describing the *real content* of an Adams life from 1838 to the twentieth century.

I use Freud's phrase not to assert Adams's nonexistent Freudianism but merely Adams's insistent questioning of a manifest content around him. Of course Freud would have found—perhaps did find—Adams's notions of real content laughably unreal, since Adams ostensibly limited himself throughout to a description of his Adamsian intellectual life, with the limitation entailing such omissions as thirteen years of marriage and the wife's suicide. Still, the inclusions are extraordinary and are what I am pointing to.

The book is too familiar to describe here in detail. It is indeed, as Johnson said, a study of cultural multiplicity growing out of earlier unities, from the unity of eighteenth-century thought out of which our Constitution and the Adams ideology grew, back to the very different unity of thirteenth-century faith, as described in Adams's companion volume, *Mont St. Michel and Chartres.* It is also a study of the effect of Darwinism upon the nineteenth century and beyond, as well as a speculative foray into the muddy new ages of thermodynamics and electricity. What is *not* commonly noticed about the book is that it is a major psychological study.

The book is so Adamsian, so seemingly remote, lofty and impersonal—and of course so cerebral—that to tie any meaning of the word *psychological* to it may seem ridiculous. The book seemed psychologically ridiculous to southern poet Allen Tate, for example, who took umbrage at Adams's account of a representative nineteenth-century Southern mind ("strictly," the Southerner, Ronnie Lee, "had no mind," Adams had said; "he had temperament"), and decided that Adams was too abstract to be quite human.* Yet the human predicament to which Adams introduces his reader on his very first page is hardly impersonal. He tells us that he—he is speaking of himself—"would scarcely have been more distinctly branded, and not much more heavily handicapped in the races of the coming century" if he had been "born in Jerusalem under the shadow of the Temple and circumcised in the Synagogue by his uncle the high priest, under the name of Israel Cohen." And later in the book he returns

---

*In conversation with the author. But see also Tate's remarks in the essay "Religion and the Old South," where he says, "There is the tragedy of *The Education of Henry Adams*, who never quite understood what he was looking for." (Tate, *On the Limits of Poetry*, 318.)

to the same backhandedly anti-Semitic comparison: "Not a Polish Jew from Warsaw or Cracow—not a furtive Yacoob or Ysaac still reeking of the ghetto, snarling a weird Yiddish to the officers of the customs—but had a keener instinct, an intenser energy, and a freer hand than he— American of Americans, with Heaven knew how many Puritans and Patriots behind him, and an education that had cost a civil war." Such remarks as these—and there are many equally self-interested ones scattered through the volume—belie his ironically announced purpose in his 1907 preface. There he borrows from Carlyle's *Sartor Resartus* and says that he is only trying to tailor his (mental) clothes for the manikin of a modern self, in order to help the manikin fit the modern world. The clothing analogy simply does not work. It is of the basic Henry Adams, not the manikin, that he speaks when finding himself unable to compete with Yacoob or Ysaac. His *Education* is first and foremost a study of his own educational failure, then of other Adams failures, and only then of any anonymous, representative, turn-of-the-century American self. Though full of Adamsian snobbery and annoyance at the new human energy around him, it is indeed a study, a probe of himself, and a profound one. If it were not deficient in the kind of analysis now taken as central to psychological study, it might even now be thought modern, since Adams was busy most of the time questioning his own assumptions with a fine fervor. This severity with himself is what interests me here. At his own hands he fared no better than the mindless Southerner. As a result, the *Education* displays a depth of probing for which neither biography nor autobiography was noted, up to its time.

Loosely, it can be said that Adams shifted the focus of these genres from attention to the subject's performances as a model in public life to the insuperable difficulties of being a model at all; and he labored so hard at those difficulties that he all but put himself in the clinic describing them. As he did so he sometimes came to sound a bit like Jean-Paul Sartre wrestling with his own contradictory, existential obligations to be what he had to be, while asserting himself and being what he willed to be.* The *Education* has no clean and safe character assessment on any page of it, not even of Ronnie Lee, who turned out

---

*Sartre made endless capital out of this philosophical-psychological crux in his biography of Jean Genet (*Saint Genet: Actor and Martyr* [Paris: George Braziller, 1963]), taking off from Genet's own remark, "I decided to be what crime made of me," and noting at very great length "the overlapping of the dialectic of doing and that of being." Adams would have been as surprised as Freud by Sartre's jargon, but it does point in the direction of the *Education*.

to be "simple beyond analysis; so simple that even the simple New England student could not realize him," as well as so ignorant that "no one knew enough to know how ignorant he was!" One of the book's most telling contradictions was aired early, where Adams announced that though he had had nothing at all to do with his coming into life, he had come into it as a "consenting, contracting partner." Further, he said he had no other plans for himself, even in old age, than to be a *useful* partner, that is, a social servant of the kind that Adamses had always been. At the time he was not being a useful partner at all. He was living all over the world in his own enforced isolation from service.

One way of looking at these congested proceedings of self-discovery is to put them in the context of Parton's four bases of biography: breed, breeding, country, and age. In relation to the first of these, Henry pointed monotonously to the Adams breed's waning leadership role over several generations, but managed to be snobbish about the decline even while damning it. (He had had, he reported, scarlet fever in childhood, and he described the sickness as having a permanent psychic effect, giving him "the habit of doubt.") Then in talking of breeding—which was for him interchangeable with education—he constantly complained of failure of vision while displaying a great deal of it. Then of his country he spoke as if it were an element in his life like an organ of his own body, while at the same time incomprehensible and running on its own steam. And finally, of his age—that is, of his times—he spoke like a man immersed in an alien medium who had nevertheless been swimming in it all his life. In sum he spoke as a singular, isolate being who was also a complex of beings, a complex that Sartre would have delighted in.

Most modern psychobiographers, including Sartre, would not, however, be happy with the limitations of that complex as Adams presented it. He omitted too much of what they think of as "real content" to be, for them, psychologically credible, omitted his extraordinary inhibitions and other aspects of his felt life in favor of exclusive attention to his ideological life. I can sympathize with their unhappiness and must point to an obviously vulnerable part of the *Education*, Adams's descriptions of his relationship with his father. Henry clearly understood that relationship in considerable depth, but he was hesitant to talk about it in depth. His focus was always on the father's influence upon him as educator in a quite formal sense, with the result that the father was frequently indistinguishable from other educators surrounding Henry, all ineffectual. Henry sometimes tried to spare the father the blame for the failed education, as he did not, for instance, spare Harvard,* but his sparing was perfunctory. Thus, he gave his father credit for being complicated, saying that the father's "mind and temper" were a constant subject of interest, and that the father "possessed the only perfectly balanced mind that ever existed in the name of Adams." But then he added: "His memory was hardly above the average; his mind was not bold like his grandfather's or restless like his father's, or imaginative and oratorical—still less mathematical; but it worked in singular perfection, admirable self-restraint, and instinctive mastery of form. Within its range it was a model."

Within its range it was a model! *There* was a real put-down, coming from someone always complaining about the absence of range among scholars.

Naturally Freud would have been pleased with the malice seemingly lurking in these remarks, and doubtless would have carried his pleasure into an account of father-son hostility. But while Freud might well have been right, the tension that does surface occasionally in the father-son relationship needs to be balanced against Henry's own complicated assessment of the relationship. Henry speaks warmly, for instance, of how the father took the son's Washington education in hand, at age twelve, by going along with him to Washington and showing him the insider sights of Congress, the White House, Mount Vernon, all the familiar haunts of Adamses, so that the boy could learn the attractions as well as the villainies of the slave South and on his own "deduce George Washington from the sum of all wickedness." He also praises the father's sensible influence on the son when the son took a postcollege hegira in Europe, spent too much money with too little result, and immersed himself in too many of Europe's deceptions of the period, such as the wonders of German transcendentalism. And Henry is as a whole exceedingly respectful of his father's handling of the embassy problems in London during the Civil War. The *absence* of friction between father and son, then, is notable, and while a Freudian reader may find the perhaps superficial harmony between them itself significant, a little research will show that Henry, always ready to qualify, found the harmony superficial too. Thus, he noted particularly his own lapses in sound skepticism about his father's capacities, saying that the difficult situation in London made it politically discreet for him to "imitate his father and hold his tongue," adding that he

*Nobody, he said, had ever received an education at Harvard.

carried his imitating to the point of believing in it, when he should have been able to imagine that the father "might make a mistake." These are not simple observations for a son to make, and though they do present the father as a sort of intellectual construct, it is clearly a construct to reckon with, not just a front, a facade for unrecognized hostility.

All in all, Adams seems to have been narrow in his understanding of self only because of his deliberate focus upon rational thought itself, a focus not respected in our current biographical climate except, as I have indicated, in the world of political and journalistic biography. Adams should, I think, be respected for knowing and specifying what his focus was, that is, knowing precisely the elements in himself that he *was* undertaking to measure. These elements are well summed up in a passage about himself at age sixteen:

> He finished school, not very brilliantly, but without finding fault with the *sum* of his *knowledge*. Probably he *knew* more than his father, or his grandfather, or his great grandfather had *known* at sixteen years old. Only on looking back, fifty years later, at his own figure in 1854, and *pondering* on the needs of the twentieth century, he wondered whether, on the whole, the boy stood nearer to the *thought* of 1904, or to that of the year 1. He found himself unable to give a *clear* answer. The *calculation* was clouded by the *undetermined* values of twentieth century *thought*, but the story [in the *Education* itself] will show his reasons for *thinking* that, in essentials like religion, ethics, philosophy; in history, literature, art; in the *concepts* of all science except perhaps mathematics, the American boy of 1854 stood nearer the year 1 than to the year 1900. (Italics mine)

For many psychobiographers all these italicized ratiocinative essentials are of course not essentials at all, and such writers feel they do not need to apologize for ignoring or demoting them.

◆ ◆

And now, with the psychoanalysts' attack on ratiocination and manifest content in mind, as well as Henry Adams's own quite different approach to essences, I find myself looking at the south wall again, scouring it for the last group on my American agenda: books by contemporary literary biographers. I see quickly that there are not as many such biographers on the wall as the country's literary biographers would like to see there. (More than any other group they like to think they have been "taking hold" of the genre in recent years, but the south wall, with its flavoring of the popular, does not confirm this opinion.) I can also see quickly—because I know this group; it is my own—that although they are not all Freudians, the grace of Freud is upon them and that their works are heavy with propositions about the real content beneath the skin. Yet they are mostly cautious biographers, and being themselves literary people, they do not flatly ignore or deny the *writing* skin. An author's work is their bread and butter.

But there are two problems here. One is that many literary people who might write biographies in good times are now looking for bread and butter elsewhere; bread and butter is scarce in such realms as poetry, for instance. And another is that a literary author's work is always in some measure autobiographical, hence not always readily separable from his life even by the sternest theorist of the autotelic in art, hence doubly demanding of the biographer: he must be literary critic as well as biographer. If the author's work happens to be all science fiction taking place on another planet, the earthly connections to the author's life in Ashtabula may well take some time to discover. But if the author's work is heavily naturalistic and takes place in an Ohio town with a name close to Ashtabula, then the work quickly invites probes, and the biographer may even soon discover, for instance, that the hero of one of the author's stories had the name of an actual person in the town, that that character ran a business exactly like the business run by that same person, and that that same person once sued the author for libel. (Therein lies a true tale from the life of William Carlos Williams in Rutherford, New Jersey.) Planetary or earthly, however, in our age a literary work's connection with its author's private life will soon absorb much of a biographer's attention.

In early literary biography the connecting of the two was usually perfunctory and mechanical, as when Samuel Johnson in his *Lives of the Poets* provided a Johnsonian vita at the beginning of each "life" (sometimes of only a paragraph, sometimes of several pages), and then turned to the serious business of assessing poems. A comparably formulaic approach can be seen in Giorgio Vasari's *Lives of the Artists* in the sixteenth century, where the lives were also taken care of abruptly, as mere preface to the business of locating and assessing paintings. Thus, Vasari conventionally described just two significant childhood moments in a "life." First he presented the artist-child as idly drawing something, perhaps on a rock, that was impressive to a parent or town elder; and second he arranged for an art patron—perhaps a cardinal—to pass through the town, see the child's work, and instantly carry the child off to fame and fortune. Such formulae could not persist in simplicity into modern times, but the arbitrary division between life and work hung on. It is still to be found in dictionaries of literary biography, in the English Men of Letters series (also, briefly, in its American equivalent), and in academic literary biographies with a publisher-prescribed format such as those published by Twayne.

The division persists because it is useful and practical. It is also, though, scholarly in a bad sense of that word, in that it is an obligatory feature of Ph.D. theses about individual writers, where examining committees *expect* the organization of a thesis to be mechanical. Worse, the division is deceptive, since the inevitable autobiographical element in a writer's work makes the work an organic part of the material *of* his life, not something separable.

Further, the autobiographical element makes the writer his own first biographer and, in turn, makes the biographer who follows him a sort of parasite. The relationship between a literary figure and his biographer is simply different from that between, say, Roger Tory Peterson and his biographers. Literary persons may or may not be better *auto*biographers, but they do leave more in print about themselves than other persons, with the result that the biographer following after is simply not in a position to move into his subject's inner life on his own hook. At least he has first to reckon with his subject's having already publicly, in writing, been there.

And if the biographer is himself a literary man, he is usually beholden to his subject; he is more than apt to like and be respectful of his subject's writings, unlike Freud and Bullitt with Wilson's writings. He will therefore usually think of himself as a mediator between the writings and the life, rather than a penetrator of a facade.

A good summary of the modern complications of such doubleness appeared in Arthur Mizener's biography of F. Scott Fitzgerald, *The Far Side of Paradise*, nearly forty years ago. Mizener did provisionally separate, at the outset, Fitzgerald's life from his work, and he also added, as a third "area of interest," the "time and place in which [Fitzgerald] lived"; but having noted these divisions, he then proceeded to ignore them, and sometimes also to fight off critics who insisted on them. Fitzgerald's work, he argued, was always central and crucial for Fitzgerald and so "inextricably bound" to the life that "nothing was quite real to him until he had written about it."

Yet Mizener was also at pains to assess the work as work, and as he went on he regularly complained about literary journalists and social scientists who wanted to concentrate on Fitzgerald's high living at places like the Plaza and reduce him to the status of a jazz-age symbol, neglecting him as an artist. Mizener was trying to be a combination of New Critic and biographer, with the result that he was sometimes fighting what he was wedded to. But since biography *is* lives, and since Fitzgerald's exotic life made such good copy that it was an obvious candidate for the south wall, Mizener's life of him became a bestseller for the usual nonliterary reasons,* and was followed by other biographies of Fitzgerald (and of Zelda) that paid almost no attention to literary assessment of his novels and stories.

The issue of whether a literary biographer can or should play literary critic does not go away. Whenever a writer becomes a celebrity for reasons other than his writing, biographers who are looking for a slot on the south wall take note of the fact and become aware of the dubious merits of mere literary talk. Irving Stone, for instance, must have taken note of the fact when he chose to write *Sailor on Horseback*, a best-selling biography of Jack London. Stone liked London's writing and said so, but he was a popular biographer—a good one—and was not neglectful of what good nonliterary copy London was—as a maverick, a patriot, a socialist, an adventurer, a noisy orator, and a drunk. Similarly, from the times of Shelley, Shaw, and Wilde to the time of Kerouac, Plath, and Robert Lowell, popular literary biographers have been thoroughly aware of their subjects as *news*. They have sometimes even neglected the subject's writings entirely.

And aside from the diversions of good newscopy, there are always the biographer's own interests and ego to distract him from his announced hero. Sartre is probably the most celebrated literary biographer of modern times, yet he spent almost no time at all *being* a biographer. For most of his pages he avoided either the biographic or the literary, except referentially, in favor of being an independently philosophical, psychoanalytical, socio-anarchical (i.e., existential) exhibitionist, writing, as if incidentally, of writers who fitted his own

---

*When Mizener later took on a biography of Ford Madox Ford in the same balanced manner, the result was a publishing failure.

plans, chiefly Baudelaire and Genet. Perhaps luckily, no American biographers have achieved Sartre's lustre, for though we love authoritative authors dearly, we have not—or so it seems—wanted their biographers to "take hold" of the genre as conspicuously as Sartre was impelled to do. In general we have expected them to assume a role of reportorial modesty.

But the genre's chief characteristics in our culture are nowhere more perplexing than in English department lounges, where the double obligation to text and to life is always an issue, and where also the usual obligations of dryasdust scholarship keep butting up against obligations to be readable, to take positions, to make plain unacademic sense. How, after all, can one be modest and scholarly as a biographer while at the same time passing out Johnsonian literary judgments? And how can one be anything but arrogant while passing out such judgments and being a Freudian prober too? Two of our most eminent practitioners, Richard Ellmann and Leon Edel, have confronted these problems quite differently.

◆ ◆

Ellmann—who died in 1987—was a student of Mizener's, but in choosing Yeats, Joyce, and Oscar Wilde as his chief targets he had writers more clearly in need of textual explication than Fitzgerald. He must have wanted to be critically on top of their work—he was good at explicating—but he was also full of Freudian impulses to go beyond explication, and he was, as it turned out, an excellent historical prober too, ready to wander all over Ireland for anecdotal data. He was in fact so good at the latter that Edel has described Ellmann's Joyce opus—wrongly, I think—as having been written in "the old-fashioned Victorian chronological manner." The chronology is there all right, and in great plenty, but so is all the rest. In all his works Ellmann steadily observed his double obligation, as in this usefully illustrative passage from an essay by him on Oscar Wilde's *Salome*:

> The general problem that I want to inquire into is what the play probably meant to Wilde and how he came to write it. Villainous women were not his usual subject, and . . . the choice of Salome would seem to inhere in her special relationship to John the Baptist and Herod. Sources offer little help in understanding this, and we have to turn to what might be called praeter-sources, elements which so pervaded Wilde's imagination as to become presences. Such a presence

Amadis was for Don Quixote, or Virgil for Dante. In pursuing these I will offer no *explication de texte* but what may well appear a divagation, though I hope to define a clandestine relevance. It includes at any rate those furtive associations, often subliminal, which swarm beneath the fixed surface of the work, and which are as pertinent as is that surface to any study of the author's mind.

One simply should not believe Ellmann when he says there is to be no explication. What he means is that he assumes the reader is familiar with the play—admittedly an esoteric assumption—and does not need to be introduced to basics such as its plot, or how Wilde deviates from the Bible story in it. Granted, Ellmann does then move quickly away from the text to considerations of the author's view of women before undertaking the play at all, but at the end of the essay he comes back forcefully from his "divagation" *to* the text, and the divagation is then employed to explicate. In other words the divagation is not a random diversion; it is aimed at *both* Wilde's text and Wilde.

Ellmann introduces it as a divagation because it is not directly about Wilde himself or *Salome*, but about the attitudes toward women of two of Wilde's celebrated mentors, Ruskin and Pater. Ruskin had a perverse opinion of womanhood that enabled him to imagine that the infidelity he attributed to his own wife (with whom he may never have had sexual relations) was the norm in all women, as well as the cause of the moral and physical decline of great cultures. Walter Pater, on the other hand, found beauty and humanity in women, and busily espoused high passions and "great experiences." Two-thirds of the Ellmann essay is devoted to this opposition, but then Ellmann moves to its "clandestine relevance." He proposes that the crazy figure of John the Baptist in the Wilde play is Ruskinism, while the "perverse sensuality [of *Salome*] is related to" Paterism. He even goes so far as to call the play a psychodrama—that is, a drama within the mind—and to find Wilde portraying his own mind there, especially in the character of the play's indeterminate Herod (Herod is attracted to both Salome and John the Baptist). He points out that Aubrey Beardsley, in providing illustrations for the printed play, gave Herod the author's own face, and he concludes, "In Herod Wilde was suggesting the *tertium quid* which he felt to be his own nature, susceptible to contrary impulses but not abandoned for long either."*

*Dictionary definition of *tertium quid*: Literally, third something, something related to but distinct from two other things; intermediate person or thing.

No Wilde authority, I was impressed with these remarks, partly because they are indeed explication of a truly tricky text, and partly because they suggest at the same time Ellmann's notion of the literary biographer's proper modern role, which is hardly that of Victorian chronologist. Ellmann sees the biographer as the *tertium quid* existing between text and life, like Wilde between Pater and Ruskin, partaking of both but identifying with neither. His essay on *Salome* is a critical-biographical fragment only, but the postulates behind it are not fragmentary. They affirm the double role of which I have been speaking, and which Ellmann elsewhere actively describes as mediational. Thus, in his Joyce biography he says that the biographer's duty is to "reflect [the] complex, incessant joining of event and composition" in his artist's life and work.

This joining process is immensely demanding, and if the biographer is as scrupulous about detail as was Ellmann, and if the details are, as in the case of Joyce's life and work, copiously available, it can also be nearly endless. Joyce said of himself that he had a "grocer's assistant's mind" about detail; and Ellmann had such a mind too. Though capable of generalizations like those in the *Salome* essay, he became dutiful in the extreme as he approached full-scale biography, and duty for him meant, aside from textual explication, infinite care for trivia such as the names and numbers of streets, precise familial relationships, who said what to whom in what bar, and so on. Here is a typical passage out of the Joyce biography's early pages:

> But Joyce was very much a part of things. He was in a play at Eastertime, 1891, as an 'imp,' he sang at a Third Line concert about 1890, and took piano lessons beginning before February 1891. About this time, too, he and Thomas Furlong, the second-smallest boy in the school, were caught out of bounds raiding the school orchard, and the word went round that 'Furlong and Joyce will not for long rejoice,' a pun that he became fond of in later life.

Joyce, of course, became more than "fond of" puns "in later life"— he became obsessed by them—and Ellmann was onto a big early influence upon *Finnegans Wake* (comparable to Leonardo's vulture?) in the above episode. And with his grocer-assistant's memory he had an immense amount of verbal "trivia" from the life to line up with the writings. Almost any passage finds him mixing "event and composition," with the mixtures ranging from such trivia as the source of Leopold Bloom's name in (*a*) a friendly signorina's father in Trieste and (b) a Catholic Jewish dentist in Dublin, to major connections like those between Joyce's own character and his created characters.* Thus, though the historical detail in the biography is usually interesting in itself, as Irish anecdotalism tends to be, in Ellmann's hands it usually has a mission. I know no better place for a sophisticated reader of *Ulysses* and *Finnegans Wake* to go for illuminations of life *and* text than Ellmann's effort. It is a continuous demonstration of what can be done with the mixture.

But it is also a demonstration of how professionally esoteric the literary game can now be. Reading around in it recently, with Freud's sallies into art and literature in mind, I decided that Freud himself would have been driven away from it by some of its detailed interplay between "event and composition," which requires the reader to perform like a conscientious graduate student and keep the "composition" constantly at his elbow. The fault, if it is that, may be more Joyce's than Ellmann's, but here it is, something the non–graduate-student reader is not apt to expect as he picks a biography off the south wall. Freud would probably have preferred the fragmentary Ellmann of the essay on *Salome*. After all, though Freud spent much time with Leonardo's vulture, he did not undertake to supply an orderly discussion of the undercurrents in the whole of Leonardo's *Notebooks*. He had a clear sense of limits and wanted merely to spotcheck Leonardo's art so that he might study Leonardo's uncertainties about it. Ellmann, working on Joyce, had a modern literary scholar's obligations to completeness in his head. Completeness does not jibe with Freud's clarity and essential simplicity of intent.†

Nor does it jibe with Leon Edel's plans and claims for the biography. Edel has said a good deal *about* the genre while also producing

---

*Ellmann saw Joyce himself as a kind of merger of Bloom and Stephen Dedalus, much as he found Wilde a mixture of Ruskin and Pater. In the large, Ellmann's thematic mission is that of tying the amalgam of Bloom and Dedalus to the whole scheme of values in *Ulysses*, with both characters serving as the base for the novel's mighty "yes."

†A recent anthology of essays on biography edited by Jeffrey Meyers is a fine source of plaintive comment on the biographer's scholarly trails. Some of the contributors—and notably William Murphy, who took thirteen years to produce a fine biography of Yeats's father—can be amusing about their labors, but most have become so committed to scholarly thoroughness that they do indeed think of their labors as like those of Hercules.

one of the most massive biographies of modern times, his five-volume opus on Henry James. Most of what he has said about the genre has been summed up in his late volume, *Writing Lives*, where he speaks optimistically of the "new biography." I confess that I cannot see the newness in his own James, though there are interesting departures in it, but I can see the novelty of his theories. When he achieved them, he was not, I think, sitting in an English department lounge and hearing the confusions there, for he refers to the lounge's confusions as if they were something in the primitive past when biography "suffered . . . from a lack of definition, a laxity of method." He must instead have been sitting where Sartre, Mailer, and Freud have sat, amid those who have felt it the biographer's job to take hold of biography, rather than muddle, chronologically, through. In his *Writing Lives* he enunciated four principles for biography, and it is to be noticed of them that they are all in some measure aimed at establishing and asserting the literary biographer's role beyond that of literary historian and critic.

First, he said, the biographer "must learn to understand man's ways of dreaming, thinking and using his fancy." Second, he "must struggle constantly not to be taken over by his subjects, or to fall in love with them . . . [but must] learn to be a participant-observer." Third, he "must analyze his material to discover certain keys to the deeper truths of his subject—keys . . . to the private mythology of the individual." And fourth, he must, since "every life takes its own form, . . . find the ideal and unique form that will express it." The focus here is unlike Ellmann's, even though both Ellmann and Edel are always to be found ferreting out "deeper truths" in the Freudian mode. Ellmann's focus upon mediation made him always ready, like Mizener before him, to find that his author had *himself* uncovered the deeper truths. In contrast, Edel assumes—at least in his theory—that it is the biographer who is the truth-finder. He constantly echoes an odd remark by James himself, who said, "Men of genius never can explain their genius."

The remark is odd because James, something of a genius surely, was not the narrow, intense kind who becomes a chess champion, but a genius of broad view who was immensely occupied, as Edel is at pains to point out, with self-understanding. In other words, he was an analyst after Edel's own heart, was in fact the partial source of Edel's control principles—though James's theories were directed at fiction (and drama), not biography. In any event, the Edel principles provide steps by which the biographer may and should go beyond the biographee's own perceptions.

Like a good psychoanalyst? In commenting on his first principle Edel issues a strong disclaimer, saying, "This does not mean that a biographical subject can be psychoanalyzed; a biographical subject is not a patient and not in need of therapy." He then destroys the disclaimer by talking of the biographer in scientific terms as an analyst and saying that the dreams, thoughts, and fancies of the biographee are useful to him just as they would be if the analyst had the biographee on the couch. They are, that is, useful to him "for the revelations they contain" (so long as the analyst is properly equipped "to see through the rationalizations, the postures, the self-delusions and the self-deceptions" to "the manifestations of the unconscious"). And where does a literary analyst chiefly go for his biographee's delusory dreams, thoughts, and fancies? To the biographee's writings. So it is with those writings that biographical analysis must concern itself, not, however, because of the perception they openly display, but because of what Edel calls the biographee's "private mythology" that they contain, that is, the public facade by which the writer hides himself from the world *and also himself*. The "deeper truths" of Edel's third proposition lie behind the facade.

Later in *Writing Lives* Edel provides two perfunctory but startling illustrations of what he means by a private mythology. Choosing Hemingway and Thoreau as his targets, he predictably first finds Hemingway to have been, behind his hair-on-chest mythology, "a troubled, uncertain, insecure figure, who works terribly hard to give himself eternal assurance," and Edel curiously then adds, "The biography of Hemingway that captures the real portrait, the portrait within, still needs to be written"—curious because Edel's confident tone proclaims that he has just done the writing himself. (See below for comments on Kenneth Lynn's Hemingway biography.) Perhaps a little less predictably, Edel discovers of Thoreau that behind "the solitude-loving, nature-loving, eternally questing self-satisfied isolate" who was the *mythical* Thoreau, there was "a lost little boy of Concord, a loner, a New England narcissus." And with Thoreau, Edel also professes that the biography catching the real Thoreau still needs to be written.

What strikes me most about his observations is that in both cases the writings of these men are flatly described as facades that conceal their opposites, the "figure *under* the carpet."* All of Hemingway's writings simply present us, he tells us, with the "manifest myth" of masculinity, which includes "courage, resignation, heroism and perseverance" plus avoidance of "too much feeling," the myth being the false Hemingway, the Hemingway that Hemingway wanted to be but was not. As for Thoreau, his *Walden* consists merely of "beautiful rationalization," and Edel asks us to ask ourselves, "Why did he *really* go to Walden Pond?" Whatever one may think of these pronouncements, one cannot escape their denial of the authors' own understanding of their inner selves.

With the remark about Thoreau's beautiful rationalizations I am reminded of the way in which Freud and Bullitt dismissed Woodrow Wilson's writings as ideological nonsense; yet in defense of Edel, I must say that his descriptions of the "real" Hemingway and Thoreau are intended, in context, as illustrations only, illustrations of a prime aim of analysis, to *find* that "real." And though the illustrations are more than that (I have to assume that Edel does not like the writings of Thoreau and Hemingway much!), I also have to acknowledge that Edel does not treat James as equally imperceptive. Obviously he would not have chosen to study and write about James for several decades if he had thought him so.

If I may now psychoanalyze Edel's relationship with James, let me say (and then abandon the role) that he seemed to develop admiration for "the master" as he went along. In the first volumes, when he is discussing James's early works, he does not give James much credit for character analysis or worry about the meaning of the psychological thinness of these fictions. It is when James himself begins to move inward that Edel does too; and it is then that Edel blossoms with admiration, but also violates his own principles.

Edel's handling of *Daisy Miller* is a simple instance of his early approach. With it he gravitates quickly to the heroine as a quintessentially open American girl, and he conventionally goes about describing her thematic relationship, in James's symmetrical character-scheme, to the opposing, closed Europeans. I have no quarrel with his remarks so far as they go, but note that they do not extend far into the "felt life" of Daisy, that quality of which both James and Edel talk much. For example the remarks do not probe the possibility of Daisy's deviation from the typical in her conversation with others. Would her

*Edel's phrase, converted from James's story "The Figure in the Carpet."

remarks ever have been made by a "real" Daisy? Are they anything *other* than thematically typical? Edel does not bring such matters up, does not move beyond Daisy's representativeness.

In discussing *The Princess Casamassima* he is equally inattentive to the felt lives. He insists that James had done his homework before he wrote the book, that he had prowled the slums of London and had also studied the ideological radicalism of the period, but he does not look seriously at how James's characters in that world live, or fail to live, on the page. Particularly, he fails to note the woodenness of the dialogue in the novel and only includes a few instances of James's clumsy attempts, in a revision, to toughen the talk by having someone say, for instance, "What the hell am I to do with seventeen shillings?" rather than "What the plague am I to do with seventeen shillings?"

Later, Edel is equally inattentive to the dialogue in James's several dreadful plays before the really disastrous *Guy Domville.* Always the Edel analysis of a play moves out and away from the nuances of speech into submerged essences in the characters speaking, and in their creator. Thus, at the end of Edel's third volume, *The Middle Years,* he moves away from the plays, and particularly *Guy Domville,* to tell us that James's failure in the theater was not that he couldn't write dialogue, or couldn't in other ways master the medium, but that he "despised the theater too much to give it of that best of which he was capable."

Yet in the fourth volume, *The Treacherous Years,* Edel appears to have had a new insight upon James's own insights. The volume has a "moody, misanthropic, melancholy, morbid, morose" James at its center,* a writer whose efforts in the theater have failed and whose subsequent suffering eventually emerges as the triumph that is *The Turn of the Screw. The Treacherous Years* is probably the high point of Edel's opus, a most readable account that introduces James's melancholy with a well-staged description of the *Guy Domville* first-night failure,† followed by brief accounts of a series of short James fictions with recurrent character types (types remain Edel's interest), all leading to the characters in *The Turn of the Screw*—especially the two

*The words were James's own, in a letter to Edmund Gosse.

†In brief, there were malcontents, apparently drunk, in the gallery, and distinguished reviewers (Shaw, Wells, and Arnold Bennett) below. There was a good deal of first-night confusion on stage, and pretty soon the gallery reacted. To one of the key lines in the play, Guy Domville saying solemnly, "I am the last of the Domvilles," a "strident voice somewhere in the gallery" responded, "It's a bloody good thing y'are."

children and the governess. Then Edel explicates that work more clearly and simply than anyone else I have read, being in his element—as was James himself—with the complications of a story told from the point of view of an unreliable, mythologizing observer, the governess. And, having described the results of her psychic impositions upon the children, he inevitably moves to the psychological connection with James's own troubles at the time and (of course) in childhood. One does not have to go along with all the connections that Edel makes with James's way of coping with the theatrical disaster (and with his having been treated in childhood as a girl) to be impressed by the energy and fullness of Edel's account. He is fully committed here to the sort of mediation between event and composition that I described in Ellmann's work, and he is a less recondite explicator than Ellmann in that he is not referential; the materials of the James texts are well summarized.

I assume that Edel's energy with the late works derives from his enthusiasm for his biographee's own probings of human character. In his introduction to *The Treacherous Years*, and then again later on in the volume, he even compares James's explorations of human character to those of Freud at about the same time—and throws in Proust's simultaneous efforts for good measure:

> . . . On the level of art James was probing the same human experi-
> ence—and in an analogously systematic if unconscious way—as Sig-
> mund Freud, who was making his discoveries at this very moment in
> Vienna. And also at this same moment, in Paris, James's fellow-artist,
> Marcel Proust, was engaged in examining that part of reflective expe-
> rience which relates to association and memory. Proust in the footsteps
> of Bergson, discovered for himself and demonstrated how a calling up
> of the past (which Freud was asking of his patients) establishes man in
> his time, can give him an identity and reveal to him the realities of his
> being. Thus in three different cities of the Old World three different
> men were embarked at this singular moment of the history of the
> mind and psyche on journeys into a personal "dark backward and
> abysm."

The connection between the three men is striking, and Edel's enthusiasm about making the connection is evident. He feels he has located a crucial moment in human history (rather like Yeats's "Great Year" of "terrible beauty"). In *Writing Lives* he is still enthused and, in effect, moves the crucial moment over into the history of biography, it being *after* this moment, in his opinion, that the muddled genre picked up order and direction. Yet to me the odd feature of his handling of the crucial moment is that he keeps insisting that James himself was somehow unconscious of what was going on. Shades of Iran-Contra know-nothingism! The evidence that James *was* aware of the dimensions of *The Turn of the Screw*, for instance, is in the text itself.

◆   ◆

Probably the first rule of biography, ancient and modern, has been that the genre must adapt itself somehow to the visible, publicly known and celebrated character of a life. If the character is that of an Attila, so be it. If that of a saint, so be it. The biographer takes what there is. The probings of psychobiography have now seriously undermined that rule—or perhaps, some would say, liberated it—but even the most earnest modern prober is still encouraged by the forces of biographical tradition to reconcile his version of a life's "real content" with the public version. He is encouraged, that is, to take on the life sympathetically and not allow what Edel calls the "life myth" to be destroyed by his probing. Even Professor Edel acknowledges the importance of such sympathy and says, after he has battered Thoreau's myth, that a "new" biography "would have to be written, not in debunking spirit but in compassion," by someone who can see how Thoreau "was able to transcend his losses and create an American myth and the work of art known as *Walden*."

I agree about the need for compassion, and I see the current rise in numbers of simple muckraking biographies as a symptom of general journalistic greed—anything for a story—but the Thoreau instance provided by Edel troubles me. Is not the "transcendence" of which he speaks itself tarnished, whether compassionately or not, by a lack of "real content," if in fact there is a lack? How can a biographer truly respect a biographee's writings if he finds the poor chap's understanding deficient? (The problem of an Attila does not enter here. His public image was not tied to understanding.)

On the whole, literary biographers do respect the understanding of their subjects, and they do so by showing a respect for their writers' works—by reviewing, commenting on, explicating them seriously. The result is that while biographical approaches to literary figures are as various as our literature, most of them are quite naturally spawned by more than compassion, since compassion can be sympathy without admiration. Let me insert a few instances here intended to represent, though skimpily, a spectrum of literary biographers' admiring stances.

First, a recent biography of E. B. White, by Scott Elledge(1986). The book participates warmly but hard-headedly in White's affirmations, which are an American mix of material and spiritual values that a dedicated psychoanalyst might demolish in one session. It participates because Elledge's own psyche participates. Elledge takes the real content of the fable *Charlotte's Web* to be what he believes White thought it to be; he thinks his biographical duty is primarily that of reporting on the resilience of that content. And White's tricky ironic mode also delights him, becoming something to emulate.

Similarly, Townsend Luddington's biography of John Dos Passos (1980) is conditioned by Luddington's general acceptance of the Dos Passos approach to character, which he compares to Thackeray's: "[Thackeray's] intention was to define by actions and surfaces, not to present psychological studies." While Luddington duly reports what the severe critics of Dos Passos said of his satiric, "outside" novels ("If Dos Passos is a *novelist*," said Louis Bogan, "I'm a gazelle!"), he does defend the novels and tries to demonstrate that the characters in them have, beyond representativeness, "roundedness and complexity—in a word, lifelikeness."

And an extremely detailed biography of Edith Wharton by R.W.B. Lewis (1976) is similarly participatory. Lewis probes the nuances of Wharton's relations with the social figures of New York, Newport, Bar Harbor, Lenox, Paris, and other high places with energy, skill, and above all persistence, estimating each character's character at length as well as Wharton's response to the character. For a hundred pages or so he is in control, managing to move Wharton's literary development forward in conjunction with all her comings and goings, attachments and detachments. Obviously Lewis was attracted to Wharton's complicated relationship to all the glitter, but after a hundred pages, somewhere in midstream, he seems to me to have lost control. He might well have chopped out a few years and books to get it back: scholarship's loss perhaps, but not Wharton's.

Much less academically, Ann Charters' biography of Jack Kerouac (1973) reports on Kerouac from the point of view of a young admirer. She tells us that she did not like his work at first, became interested in him slowly, then began to have dreams about him, and finally became a sort of disciple, even dreaming that a Parisian bookseller told her, "That man Kerouac is a model for the young." Literarily he became such a model for her that when she describes his books, she describes them in *his* ebullient, unanalytical manner. In characterizing his style she merely reports that he tried imitations of detective story writers, then of William Burroughs, and then of Thomas Wolfe, and that he told her of a "huge novel" that he was writing "explaining everything to everybody." Otherwise, she lets it be understood that the art of writing is indeed mainly spontaneous overflow, because her model so understood it.

Nor does she complain of Kerouac's immense fantasy life, or of his failure—which she acknowledges—to comprehend it. He was "directed by what he felt under his skin," she says admiringly. An unsympathetic critic of Charters' stance obviously has a good deal to complain about here. If he is a moralist, he can be indignant at her setting up Kerouac as a model. If he is a political scientist, he can ridicule the effectiveness of countercultural protest when practiced by drunks, druggies, and floaters. If he is a New Critic, he can complain of the thinness of Kerouac's prose, its lack of resonance, its persistent anecdotal drift. And if he is a psychoanalyst, he can take the Edel position strenuously and show how deficient was Kerouac's understanding of the real content of his rebellion. The Charters biography is unusually vulnerable critically because of its strong emotional allegiance to the biographee, and yet a participatory biographer like Charters is a familiar, thoroughly defensible toiler in the "life" field. She is as much a phenomenon of the genre in our time as the severe probers certainly, and closer to the main tradition of the genre than they. After all, the main literary tradition has assumed a biographer's essential willingness to ride along with the biographee emotionally, intellectually, morally.

Sometimes, though, it is useful for a biographer to be presented with impediments to riding along. An excellent 1960s biography of Dylan Thomas was undertaken by a non-Welshman, Constantine Fitzgibbon, who begins by telling us that he does not know Welsh, though it is extremely important for an understanding of Thomas to do so. He adds, "Language not only expresses thought, but also affects it," and says, to the detriment of his own case, "The Welsh did not, and still do not, think exactly like the English." From there on he has the obligation of asserting the peculiar Welshness of Thomas's poetry and thought (even though Thomas himself never wrote in Welsh), and he faces up to it strongly because he is a strong believer in the participatory nature of his job.

I can speak personally of the importance of coping with such obligations, from my experience in writing a biography of William Carlos Williams. From the beginning I had a minor psychic impediment to riding along, since I had not on my own decided to "do" Williams, but had been asked to do so by a publisher. Luckily, I liked Williams' work, had met him, and had been able to publish a number of his poems in a magazine I had edited. I had no trouble with early Williams poetry and no trouble with the confused political Williams of the 1930s, since I was old enough to have been politically at sea in the 1930s too. I was not, though, a disciple, and of the postwar Williams of the long poem *Paterson* I was no fan at all. The deeper I dug into my hero's late life the more I felt that I was losing touch with him, and with my book. I wished—as I think most biographers wish toward the end, if only because of fatigue—that I was in a position to write a biography of the early Williams only, for I could sense the shape and drive of *that* book. It was not that I had come to dislike my hero—for there were poignant moments in his late life that made me feel thoroughly at one with his troubled psyche. It was that I was a poet writing of another poet and finding that our poetic ways, at a certain point, significantly parted. What to do? I did my best, and muddled through. To this day I respect my judgment about *Paterson*— and regret that the Williams industry that has grown up around his works persists in making so much of that poem—but I also know how important it is for the biographer to find a deep well of communion with his subject from which he can dependably draw.

And now the question arises, can a dedicated psychobiographer find such a well? Or rather, *how* can he? How can he participate, if his own professional ideology prescribes that he "take hold" of the biographee rather than ride along? Kenneth Lynn's biography of Hemingway presents a reader with all the tensions that such a dilemma creates.

Fortunately, Hemingway is an excellently battered subject, and fair game. The Hemingway industry is like Marilyn Monroe's in having much of the sensational in it, including suicide, so that the problems having to do with Hemingway as a writer, good or bad, can always be put on the back burner for a few chapters while Hemingway the braggart and liar performs. Lynn is a knowledgeable money writer and capitalizes on these features, bringing forth a major Freudian item from Hemingway's infancy. Yet he happens also to be a literary biographer interested in literary matters. He therefore attends to the

Hemingway texts too. He even says something new (it is new to this Hemingway amateur) about Hemingway's style.

Several generations have now grown up with Hemingway's mode of understatement and have taken it to be his most distinguishing mark (unless they have only seen the movies). Happily Lynn does not, I believe, ever even characterize this oversold device *as* understatement, or as a device, but he does talk about it frequently in more precise ways, describing Hemingway's "hostility to bombast," his revisionary impulse to delete "words that display emotion" in a text, and, most importantly, his capacity for establishing, in deadpan fashion, "an inner drama of terrific intensity." Lynn then proceeds to chase after that inner drama as a Freudian, searching for its real content. Pretty soon, sure enough, he has the reader back with Ernest's mother as she clothes the infant Ernest in dresses (right up to the age of kindergarten), and as she makes a game of pretending that little Ernest is his big sister's twin sister. Androgynous feelings subsequently swamp Hemingway for the rest of his life and become, in Lynn's estimation, perhaps the greatest source of the inner drama Hemingway became so good at "understating" in his fictions. Pages of illustrations.

Here then is Freudian explication by an analyst who respects texts, knows Hemingway's texts intimately, and admires them. Furthermore he admires them because he thinks they demonstrate, if erratically, Hemingway's own *awareness* of what he was doing to achieve inner drama and of where the personal sources of his fictions were. Repeatedly Lynn points to clear connections between Hemingway family life and Hemingway texts, in the process demolishing the early theory of such critics as Cowley and Schorer about sex in Hemingway—the theory that Jake Barnes's sexual incapacity, for instance, in *The Sun Also Rises*, stemmed from a trauma suffered by Hemingway when he was himself wounded in the war. No, says Lynn, it was mother who did this for him, and he pushes the point relentlessly for 600 pages.

He even pushes it in his incredibly detailed index, where he has more than two hundred topical references under Hemingway's name, starting with "as accident prone" and moving through such references as "mother figures in the relationship of" to "twinhood as obsession of." Lynn is an extremely thorough scholar, and his volume might well be held up as a graduate-school model in firm academic procedure, yet he tries, while being thorough, not to be a prosecuting attorney. He expresses genuine admiration for Hemingway's work at its best, a feeling that cannot be shown convincingly for long by any critic who thinks himself superior in understanding to the author he explicates.

Even so, Lynn's insistent causative thrust keeps bringing to the fore the question of how far one can carry Freudian rules—or any other strenuous rules for "taking hold" of biography—and remain a participator in a biographee's life rather than a judge on high.*

◆ ◆

I began my now two-volume exploration of biography because I had been tantalized, while writing about Williams, by the endless problems connected with trying to be both thorough and readable. (Did one start at the beginning, and plod to the end, without looking to right or left?) As I plodded deeper, I became learnedly of the opinion that the trouble with most modern literary biographies was that they were shapeless, that they had *not* been taken hold of by their authors, that they were books to be referred to, not read. In other words, I came to share the Edel sense of the need for order in the genre, except that I did not do so as a Freudian but as a poet of sorts, an aesthetic orderer looking for authorial control because I had come into biography in the first place from literary forms where control was—or so I believed—crucial. In my book *Pure Lives* I therefore duly looked at the ancient forms of control in the form, and I particularly noted the limiting effect of moral control. But I also looked, as I progressed from Plutarch to Boswell and Sterne, at the anticontrol forces at work. I came to the end of the project wondering which was worse as a model, a Boswell or an Aelfric.

And here I am at the end of this second volume, still on the fence. The formlessness of much honest biographical scholarship is most disconcerting. It is Carlyle's dryasdustness brought up to date; it is intellectual absenteeism. Yet the ordering forces, especially of psychobiography, are disconcerting too, sometimes being as limiting and prescriptive in their way as the old moral forces.

Furthermore, the new ordering forces have a way of undercutting biography's greatest resources, none other than the philosophers,

---

*In an essay in *Daedalus* in 1971, "Adulthood in Amerian Literature" (reprinted in the same journal in the summer of 1988), Lynn did play judge, describing both Fitzgerald and Hemingway as adolescents. Interestingly, he also disposed of Thoreau, finding him guilty of "incorrigible puerility."

churchmen, scientists, artists, writers, scholars, and so on who came to be on the south wall simply because they were understanding, were wise. Out of this titanic group, my own interest has of course focused on the writers, and when I consider the great ones, I am instantly aware that every one of them has come down to me for *being* wise, not for being a great craftsman or purveyor of great beauties or clever tactician (though certainly those virtues can be thought to be part of wisdom.) I am familiar with Plato's complaints about poets, as well as with my own college philosophy teacher's complaints about poets,* but I am talking here only about the few great literary persons upon whom literature as a whole rests, and I am saying of them that they have been seen to be great by many generations because of their conscious, manifest, expressed understanding of people and the world. So I ask myself, has all that now been declared factitious? Does "real content" replace it?

Or, more relevantly, does the psychoanalytical mechanism for understanding take away the understanding of the great biographees themselves and give it over to the psychoanalysts?

I can hardly deny the basic psychic forces from childhood that model character, or the subversive ways in which they work on us all, and I assume that a biographer who ignores such material is not doing his job. But I am now convinced that the biographer who allows his probings to eliminate the biographee's final, controlling role threatens the poor mixed-up genre itself. The literary biographer as a prober is particularly fearsome here. If he cannot accept from the start that the venture is just not wholly his—or, rather, that the whole he is struggling to create is not his—he is a threat to his particular subject and to the model principle with which biography began and upon which it still, though restlessly, rests. For though he can and should assert a measure of control over detail and chronological plod (throwing out a few years and books perhaps), he also has, I think, a duty to abandon control at the heart of the material he has chosen. In other words, he has to learn where *not* to take hold.

*In his mind poets were mostly useful for imitating the sound of a babbling brook.

Notes

Full publication information for the sources cited in the notes is given in the Readings. Notes have not been supplied when sources are clearly indicated in the text, nor when succeeding quotations in a given text paragraph derive from the same source as the first quotation.

Introduction

4   "The writer is entertained": Edith Hamilton, *Mythology*, 92.

4   "the soul's progress": Apuleius, *The Golden Ass*, 22.

7   "You, a mere boy": ibid., 126.

I: Carlyle and His Great Men

11   "The river Annan": James A. Froude, *Thomas Carlyle*, 1:1.

12   "the manners of": Froude, *My Relations with Carlyle*, 16.

12   "public principle is gone": Carlyle, *Selected Works*, 21.

12   "natural man": ibid., 518.

12   "more than three minutes": ibid., 524.

13   "When I declined": ibid., 548.

14   "one of those persons": Froude, *My Relations*, 18.

14   Goethe as substitute father: Fred Kaplan, *Thomas Carlyle*, 168.

14   "that select number": Caryle, *Life of Schiller*, 3.

15   "Hitherto Schiller": ibid., 42.

15   "hovering between the Empyrean": ibid., 43.

15   "distinguished alike": ibid., 34.

15   "frightful" . . . gifted: Kaplan, *Carlyle*, 50.

16   "advanced state of culture": Carlyle, *Sartor Resartus*, 3.

16   "indeed an illimitable one": Carlyle, *On Heroes*, 1.

16   "God-given mandate": *Sartor Resartus*, 184.

16   "zeal": Kaplan, *Carlyle*, 136.

16   "net result": *Sartor Resartus*, 163.

16   "eternal maxim": Carlyle, *Selected Works*, 558.

16   "sheep nibbling": ibid., 559.

17   "close-muffled": *Sartor Resartus*, 72.

18   "lit up a blazing": Carlyle, *Selected Works*, 699.

18   Freud's approval of *Sartor Resartus*: Ronald Clark, *Freud*, 35.

19   "steam engine": *Sartor Resartus*, 164.

19   "Den of Lies": ibid., 156.

19   "Quackery, Puffery": ibid., 110.

21   "another and more advanced": J. S. Mill, *Autobiography and Literary Essays*, 21.

21   "this is the divider": Carlyle, *Selected Works*, 540.

22   sit with him in class: ibid.

22   "Alas! such": ibid., 548.

22   "I have thought": Mill, *Autobiography*, 5.

22   "not only the ordinary": ibid., 39.

22   "bookish turn": ibid.

22   "severity sooner or later": ibid., 313.

23   "one of the very few examples": ibid., 49.

23   "regard for the public good": ibid., 43.

23   "I felt that he was a poet": ibid., 183.

25   "fairest unhappy Queen": Carlyle, *The French Revolution*, 132.

25   "insurrection of Women": ibid., 162.

25   "Universal history": Carlyle, *On Heroes*, 3.

26   "read the world": ibid., 80.

26   "messengers sent from": ibid., 45.

26   "at the bottom": ibid., 156.

26   "mass of men": ibid.

26   "entirely unexceptionable": ibid., 55.

27   "entirely obscure": ibid., 147.

27   "ruin and death": ibid., 190.

27   "books, like himself": ibid., 186.

27   "fatal charlatan": ibid., 241.

27   "a poor barren country": ibid., 145.

28   "vital relations": ibid., 2.

28   "practically the summary": ibid., 196.

29   "written at height of Carlylism": Mill, *Autobiography*, xxxii.

29   "to play bo-peep": Emerson, *English Traits*, 524.

30   "poor Irish folk": ibid., 531.

30   "manifold, inextricably complex": Carlye, *On Heroes*, 167.

30   "would have to be possible": ibid., 168.

31   "Thirty to Fifty Thousand": Carlyle, *Oliver Cromwell's Letters and Speeches*, 1:2.

31   "the most impossible": ibid., xx.

31   "O Dryasdust": ibid., 10.

31   "a man of extreme imbecility": ibid., 15.

32   "soul of the Puritan": ibid., 13.

32   "Histories are as perfect": ibid., 7.

32   "was taken with Sir Marmaduke . . . Antichristian Interest": ibid., 1:396, 247, 249, 305; 4:71.

33   "Oliver is gone": ibid., 4:207.

35   "J. Sterling": Carlyle, *The Life of John Sterling*, 29.

35   "without in the least": ibid., 30.

35   "his outlooks": ibid., 123.

36   "superior excellence": ibid., 195.

36   "intrinsically no depth": ibid.

36   "Artist not Saint": ibid., 124.

37   "Rhapsodio-Reflective": ibid., 109.

37   "like older and younger": Kaplan, *Carlyle*, 300.

40   "fait accompli": ibid., 412.

40   "the last of the Kings": Carlyle, *History of Frederick the Great*, 1:1.

40   "exploded past": ibid., 17.

41   "grim hirsute": ibid., 323

41   "economy to the very bottom": ibid., 377.

41   "miniature image": ibid., 411.

41   "verses, stories": ibid.

42   "Course of Education": ibid., 422.

42   "All-Serenest": ibid., 2:349.

42   "among his fellow creatures": ibid., 331.

42   "blockhead": ibid., 380.

43   "very few women": Carlyle, *Selected Works*, 562.

44   Frank Harris caricature: Harris, *Contemporary Portraits*, 28.

II: Leslie Stephen's *DNB* and the Woolf Rejoinders

48   "our most important modern person": Carlyle, *On Heroes*, 165.

48   "the Reality which lies at the bottom": ibid., 165.

49   "for a few plain words": James Stephen, *Essays in Ecclesiastical Biography*, 2:448.

50   "My mental and moral development": Leslie Stephen, *The Mausoleum Book*, 6.

51   "did not belong to either": Noel Annan, *Leslie Stephen*, 6.

51   "grinding economy": ibid., 185.

51   "muscular Christian": ibid., 185.

52   "a family magazine": ibid., 68.

52   "fine generous fellow": Stephen, *Mausoleum Book*, 109.

53   "direct and immediate": Annan, *Stephen*, 40.

53   "confined him to": ibid., 60.

54   "gyrated in orbits": ibid., 61.

54   "Suppose I": ibid., 133 (quoting a British Museum MS of Virginia Woolf's).

55   "had received a terrible shock": Leslie Stephen, *Studies of a Biographer*, 3.

55   "small type": Stephen, *Mausoleum Book*, 93.

55   "second-rate people": Stephen, *Studies of a Biographer*, 22.

56   "When I am by myself": Annan, *Stephen*,, 111.

56   "causeway": Stephen, *Studies of a Biographer*, 7.

56   "unmixed benefit": ibid., 11, 17, 22.

56   "I used rigidly": ibid., 22.

57   "The difference may be": ibid., 24.

57   "a most detestable fellow": ibid., 114.

58   "laying bricks": ibid., 7.

61   "It would be altogether unjust": Stephen, *Thomas Hobbes*, 23.

61   "A man who is above all": ibid., 24.

62   "I fancied": Stephen, *Mausoleum Book*, 87.

62   "If I felt": ibid., 89.

63   "hideous fancies": ibid., 57, 23.

64   "face was always ill-drawn": ibid., 16–17.

64   "her purest happiness": ibid., 36.

65   "best of nurses": ibid., 37.

65   "loathed the Dictionary": Annan, *Stephen*, 41.

65   "his life would have entirely ended": ibid., 135.

66   "had been noble": Virginia Woolf, *Orlando*, 3.

66   "Happy the mother": ibid., 14.

66   "confusion of passions": ibid., 16.

66   "sights disturbed him": ibid., 15.

66   "fulfill the first duty": ibid., 61.

67   "The image of writer-father": Annan, *Stephen*, 131.

67   "There are no crannies": ibid., 132–33.

67   "flopped, foully": Woolf, *Orlando*, 117.

68   "Often the paper": ibid., 113.
68   "one was as well favored": ibid., 170.
68   "women are but": ibid., 213.
68   "negresses are seductive": ibid., 258.
69   "This method of writing": ibid., 266.
69   "The true length": ibid., 305.
70   "a special bond": Quentin Bell, *Virginia Woolf* 1:89.
70   "from two angles": Lyndall Gordon, *Virginia Woolf*, 17.
70   "so crude, so elementary": Woolf, *Moments of Being*, 126.
70   "panoply of life": ibid., 83.
70   "I was looking at": ibid., 71.
71   "no idea of what": ibid., 126.
71   "when the Carthaginians": Woolf, *Flush*, 12
72   "His head must be": ibid., 72.
72   "Before he was well out": ibid., 16.
72   "the most formidable": ibid., 51.
73   "No human figure": ibid., 66.
74   "Mr. Carlyle!": ibid., 151.
74   "took credit for the result": Bell, *Virginia Woolf*, 2:182.
75   "The drudgery of making": Woolf, *Moments of Being*, 85.
76   "But though the scientific": Woolf, *Roger Fry*, 220.
77   "Biography has been the wayward": Leon Edel, *Writing Lives*, 24.

Chapter III: Sigmund Freud and His Disciples

79   "We must also": Ronald Clark, *Freud*, 314.
80   "an inclination to concentrate": Freud, *An Autobiographical Study*, 17.
80   "with the fate of being": ibid., 14.
81   "expected to feel inferior": ibid., 82.
81   "secessionists . . . repellent findings": ibid., 50.
81   "laid stress upon the significance": ibid., 37.
82   "with a cold, strange, ideal": Freud, *Leonardo da Vinci*, 80.
82   "specially gifted as a translator": Ernest Jones, *Freud*, 1:55.
83   "not inhibited": Richard Ellmann, "Freud as Biographer."
83   "only truly beautiful thing": *Freud and Andreas-Salome Letters*, 90.
83   "highest realization": Freud, *Leonardo*, 84.
84   "under the limitations": Freud, "A Disturbance of Memory," 319.
84   "as an addition": ibid., 320.
85   "ideals . . . transcended": Jones, *Freud*, 377.
85   "fix [his] gaze": *Freud and Andreas-Salome Letters*, 11.
85   psychoanalysis as pornography: Clark, *Freud*, 51.

85   "It contains": Freud, Foreword to *Interpretation of Dreams*.

86   "already been more open": Freud, *Autobiographical Study*, (later postscript), 125.

87   "application of methods": Alan Tyson, Introduction to Freud's *Leonardo*, 8.

87   "It seems that": Freud, *Leonardo*, 32.

88   "among the people of antiquity": ibid., 33.

88   "substitutive expression": ibid., 35.

89   "learned editor and commentator": ibid., 39.

89   "if vultures were described": ibid., 40.

89   "decisive time": ibid., 42.

91   "into the general urge": ibid., 82.

91   "kissed into precocious sexual": ibid., 81.

91   "acknowledged that the comprehension": Ellmann, "Freud as Biographer."

92   "as a neurotic": Freud, *Leonardo*, 81.

93   "rash, poorly prepared campaign": Clark, *Freud*, 475.

95   "still freshly under": Freud. *The Wolf Man*, 153.

95   "an uneducated old woman . . . normal life": ibid., 154 ff.

96   "one of the richest landowners": ibid., 4.

97   "originated in what might be called": Ellmann, "Freud as Biographer."

97   "The Freudian method can do much": quoted in Clark, *Freud*, 477.

98   "the result of much combat": ibid., 476.

99   "agreed to eliminate": Freud and Bullitt, *Thomas Woodrow Wilson*, viii.

100   "was everything that the son": ibid., 6.

100   "sickly, spectacled, shy": ibid., 11.

100   "left scars": ibid., 12.

100   "badly prepared": ibid., 17

101   "He could rest": ibid., 25.

101   "In this psychological study": ibid., 106.

104   "The voice of the intellect": Auden, *The English Auden*, 342.

105   "with its slipshod writing": Strachey, *Biographical Essays*, 35.

106   "accurate" and "interesting": ibid., 16.

106   "natural gift of style": ibid., 16.

106   "pomp and flourish": Lyndall Gordon, *Virginia Woolf*, 94.

106   "the visit of Voltaire": Strachey, *Biographical Essays*, 56.

109   "we . . . have learned": Erikson, *Young Man Luther*, 18.

110   "were hard, thrifty": ibid., 50.

110   "most decisive contribution": ibid., 45.

110   "A creative man": ibid., 46.

112   "A clinician can and should": ibid., 55.

112   "fair to assume": ibid., 56.

114   "to his father's secular": ibid., 102.

115   "the metabolism of generations": ibid., 253.

115   "grow into the social process": ibid., 253.

115   "We say the tradition": ibid., 254.

Chapter IV: American Biography

118   "half way between": John C. Devlin and Grace Naismith, *The World of Roger Tory Peterson*, xvii.

118   "It is possible": ibid., 9.

120   "I go back": Iacocca, *Autobiography*, 340.

122   "of every phase of childhood": Anne Edwards, *Judy Garland*, 18.

123   "was in the modern sense": Albert Britt, *The Great Biographers*, 134.

123   "How delicate, how decent": Paul Murray Kendall, *Encyclopaedia Britannica*, 15th ed., Macropaedia, s.v. "Art of Literature."

125   "a species of novel": Mailer, *Marilyn*, 20.

125   "A biography is considered complete": ibid., 18.

126   "We are all steeped": ibid., 37.

127   "If the law of passion": ibid., 256.

127   "for he, like many another": ibid., 248.

128   "generous in a spontaneous": Steinem, *Marilyn*, 58.

128   "If I am a star": ibid., 70.

129   "a queen of a castrator": Mailer, *Marilyn*, 97.

129   "without the artificial language": Steinem, *Marilyn*, 135.

129   "If you have difficulty": ibid., 137.

130   "Children who are not the focus": ibid.

131   "refusal to marry for money": ibid., 140.

134   "The way to thrive": James Parton, *The Life of Horace Greeley*, 20.

135   "of the best form": ibid., 15.

135   "The character of man": ibid., 30.

135   "He escaped the schools": ibid., 40.

136   "better man": ibid., 440.

136   "At the age of forty-two": Parton, *The Life and Times of Benjamin Franklin*, 20.

136   "It is incredible": ibid., 648.

136   "his perceptive powers": Parton, *The Life and Times of Aaron Burr*, 688.

136   "possessed his millions": Parton, *The Life of John Jacob Astor*, 464.

137   "Houses for the People": ibid., 473.

138   "general darkness": Adams, *Education of Henry Adams*, 131.

141   "had no mind": Adams, *Education*, 55.

142   "Not a Polish Jew": ibid., 238.

143   "consenting, contracting partner": ibid., 4.

143   "the habit of doubt": ibid., 6.
144   "His memory was hardly": ibid., 27.
144   "imitate his father": ibid., 115.
145   "He finished school": ibid., 53.
147   "time and place": Arthur Mizener, *The Far Side of Paradise*, xii.
148   "inextricably bound": ibid., xi.
149   "the old-fashioned Victorian": Leon Edel, *Writing Lives*, 185.
149   "The general problem": Ellmann. *Golden Codgers*, 41.
150   "great experiences": Pater quoted by Ellmann, ibid., 53.
150   "perverse sensuality": ibid., 56.
150   "In Herod Wilde": ibid., 58.
151   "reflect complex, incessant": Ellmann, *James Joyce*, 1.
151   "grocer's assistant's mind": quoted by Ellmann, ibid., 28.
151   "But Joyce was very much": ibid., 30.
153   biography "suffered": Edel, *Writing Lives*, 24.
153   the biographer "must learn": ibid., 28.
153   "Men of genius": ibid., 167.
154   "troubled, uncertain, insecure": ibid., 166.
154   "the solitude-loving": ibid., 165.
157   "On the level of art": Edel, *Henry James: The Treacherous Years*, 15.
159   Thackeray's "intention": Townsend Luddington, *John Dos Passos*, 64.
159   "If Dos Passos is a novelist": ibid., 35.
160   "That man Kerouac": Ann Charters, *Kerouac*, 15.
160   "huge novel . . . explaining everything": ibid., 65.
160   "directed by what he felt": ibid., 22.
160   "Language not only expresses": Constantine Fitzgibbon, *The Life of Dylan Thomas*, 4.
162   "hostility to bombast": Kenneth Lynn, *Hemingway*, 168.

Readings

General

Altick, Richard. *Lives and Letters: A History of Literary Biography in England and America*. New York: Knopf, 1966.

Apuleius. *The Golden Ass*. Translated by Jack Lindsay. Bloomington: Indiana University Press, 1932; Midland Edition, 1962.

Bettelheim, Bruno. *Freud and Man's Soul*. New York: Knopf, 1982.

Bridges, Robert. *Eros and Psyche*. London: George Bell & Sons, 1885.

Britt, Albert. *The Great Biographers*. New York: Whittlesey House, 1934.

Edel, Leon. *Writing Lives: Principia Biographia*. New York: W. W. Norton, 1984.

Ellmann, Richard. *Golden Codgers: Biographical Speculations*. New York: Oxford University Press, 1973.

Hamilton, Edith. *Mythology*. New York: New American Library, 1969.

Kendall, Paul Murray. "The Art of Literature," in Macropaedia section, *Encyclopedia Britannica*, 15th ed.

Carlyle

Campbell, Ian. *Thomas Carlyle*. London: Hamish Hamilton, 1974.

Carlyle, Thomas. *The Life of Friedrich Schiller* (1825). Vol. 25 of the Edinburgh Edition. New York: Scribners, 1903.

———. *Sartor Resartus: The Life and Opinions of Herr Teufelsdröckh* (1831). Edited by Charles Frederick Harrold. New York: Odyssey Press, 1937.

———. *The French Revolution* (1837). New York: Modern Library, 1934.

————. *On Heroes, Hero Worship, and the Heroic in History* (1841). Edited by Carl Niemeyer. Lincoln: University of Nebraska Press, 1966.

————. *Oliver Cromwell's Letters and Speeches, with Emendations* (1841). 4 vols. (Vols. 6–9 of the Edinburgh Edition). New York: Scribners, 1903.

————. *The Life of John Sterling* (1851). Vol. 11 of the Edinburgh Edition. New York: Scribners, 1903.

————. *History of Frederick the Great* (1858–65). 8 vols. (Vols. 12–19 of the Edinburgh Edition). New York: Scribners, 1903.

————. *Selected Works, Reminiscences, and Letters*. Edited by Julian Symons. London: Rupert Harte-Davis, 1955.

Emerson, Ralph Waldo. *English Traits*. In *Complete Essays*. New York: Modern Library, 1934.

Froude, James Anthony. *Thomas Carlyle: A History of the First Forty Years of His Life*. 2 vols. New York: Scribners, 1882.

————. *My Relations with Carlyle* (1903). Reprint. Freeport, N.Y.: Books for Libraries Press, 1971.

Harris, Frank. *Contemporary Portraits*. New York: Mitchell Kennerly, 1915.

Kaplan, Fred. *Thomas Carlyle: A Biography*. Ithaca: Cornell University Press, 1983.

Mill, John Stuart. *Autobiography and Literary Essays*. Parallel Reading Text, edited by John Robson and Jack Stillinger. Toronto: University of Toronto Press, 1981.

Neff, Emory. *Carlyle and Mill*. New York: Octagon Books, 1964.

Stephen and Woolf

Annan, Noel. *Leslie Stephen: The Godless Victorian*. London: Weidenfeld & Nicolson, 1984.

Bell, Quentin. *Virginia Woolf: A Biography*. 2 vols. New York: Harcourt Brace & Jovanovich, 1976.

Gordon, Lyndall. *Virginia Woolf: A Writer's Life*. New York: W. W. Norton, 1984.

Stephen, James. *Essays in Ecclesiastical Biography* (1849). 2 vols. Reprint. Hank, England: Gregg International, 1972.

Stephen, Leslie. *The History of English Thought in the Eighteenth Century*. London, 1881.

————. *Studies of a Biographer*. London: Duckworth, 1898.

————. *Thomas Hobbes*. English Men of Letters. London: Macmillan, 1904.

————. *John Locke*. English Men of Letters. London: Macmillan, 1904.

————. *Men, Books, and Mountains: Essays*. Collected and with an introduction by S.O.S. Ullman. Minneapolis: University of Minnesota Press, 1956.

———. *The Mausoleum Book*. Oxford: Clarendon Press, 1977.

Woolf, Virginia. *To the Lighthouse*. New York: Harcourt, Brace, 1927.

———. *Orlando: A Biography*. New York: Harcourt, Brace, 1928.

———. *Flush: A Biography*. New York: Harcourt, Brace, 1933.

———. *Roger Fry: A Biography* (1940). New York: Harcourt, Brace & Jovanovich, 1976.

———. *Moments of Being: Unpublished Autobiographical Writings*. Edited by Jeanne Schulkind. New York: Harcourt Brace & Jovanovich, 1976.

Freud and His Disciples

Auden, W. H. *The English Auden: Poems, Essays, and Dramatic Writings, 1927–1939*. Edited by Edward Mendelson. New York: Random House, 1977.

Clark, Ronald. *Freud: The Man and the Cause*. New York: Random House, 1980.

Ellmann, Richard. "Freud as Biographer." *The American Scholar*, 53, no. 4 (1984):465–78.

Erikson, Erik. *Young Man Luther*. New York: W. W. Norton, 1957.

Freud, Sigmund. *Interpretation of Dreams* (1900). Translated by A. A. Brill. New York: Modern Library, 1950.

———. *Delusions and Dreams in Jensen's "Gradiva"* (1907). Vol. 9 of the Standard Edition of *The Collected Works of Sigmund Freud*. New York: W. W. Norton, 1964.

———. *Leonardo da Vinci and a Memory of Childhood* (1910). Translation by Alan Tyson. Vol. II of the Standard Edition. New York: W. W. Norton, 1964.

———. *Totem and Taboo* (1913). Vol. 3 of the Standard Edition. New York: W. W. Norton, 1964.

———. *An Autobiographical Study* (1925). Translated by James Strachey, 1935. Vol. 20 of the Standard Edition. New York: W. W. Norton, 1963.

———. "A Disturbance of Memory" (1937). In *Character and Culture: Selections from Freud*. Edited by Philip Rieff. New York: Basic Books, 1963.

———. *Civilization, War, and Death*. Edited by John Rickman. Hogarth Press, 1939. (Selections from five works by Freud.)

———. *The Letters of Sigmund Freud*. Selected and edited by Ernest L. Freud. New York: Basic Books, 1960.

——. *The Wolf Man.* Edited by Muriel Gardiner. New York: Basic Books, 1971.

——. *Sigmund Freud and Lou Andreas-Salome Letters.* Edited by Ernst Pfeiff. New York: Harcourt, Brace, 1972.

Freud, Sigmund, and Bullitt, William C. *Thomas Woodrow Wilson: A Psychological Study.* Boston: Houghton Mifflin, 1967.

Johnson, Roger A., ed. *Psychohistory and Religion: The Case of "Young Man Luther."* Philadelphia: Fortress Press, 1977.

Jones, Ernest. *Freud: The Life and Work of Sigmund Freud.* 3 vols. New York: Basic Books, 1953–57.

Strachey, Lytton. *Eminent Victorians.* New York: Harcourt, Brace, 1918.

——. *Queen Victoria.* New York: Harcourt, Brace, 1921.

——. *Biographical Essays.* Edited by James Strachey. New York: Harcourt, Brace, 1949.

——. *The Really Interesting Question, and Other Papers.* Edited by Paul Levy. New York: Coward, McCann, 1973.

American Biography

Adams, Henry. *The Life of Albert Gallatin.* (1879). Reprint. New York: Pepter Smith, 1943.

——. *The Education of Henry Adams* (1918). New York: Modern Library, 1931.

Britt, Albert. *The Great Biographers.* New York: Whittlesey Books, 1936.

Charters, Ann. *Kerouac: A Biography.* San Francisco: Straight Arrow Books, 1973.

Devlin, John C., and Naismith, Grace. *The World of Roger Tory Peterson.* New York: New York Times Books, 1977.

Edel, Leon. *Henry James: The Treacherous Years (1895–1901).* Philadelphia: Lippincott, 1969.

——. *Henry James: A Life.* New York: Harpers, 1985. (A condensed version of separate earlier volumes that included *The Treacherous Years.*)

Edwards, Anne. *Judy Garland: A Biography.* New York: Simon & Schuster, 1975.

Elledge, Scott. *E. B. White: A Biography.* New York: W. W. Norton, 1984.

Ellmann, Richard. *James Joyce.* New York: Oxford University Press, 1959.

——. *Golden Codgers: Biographical Speculations.* New York: Oxford University Press, 1973.

Fitzgibbon, Constantine. *The Life of Dylan Thomas.* Boston: Little, Brown, 1965.

Iacocca, Lee, with William Novak. *Iacocca: An Autobiography.* New York: Bantam, 1984.

Lewis, R.W.B. *Edith Wharton: A Biography.* New York: Harper & Row, 1975.

Luddington, Townsend. *John Dos Passos: A Twentieth-Century Odyssey.* New York: E. P. Dutton, 1980.

Lynn, Kenneth. *Hemingway.* New York: Simon & Schuster, 1987.

Mailer, Norman. *Marilyn: A Biography.* (With "Pictures by the World's Foremost Photographers.") New York: Grosset & Dunlap, 1973.

Mizener, Arthur. *The Far Side of Paradise.* Boston: Houghton Mifflin, 1951.

Parton, James. *The Life of Horace Greeley* (1855). New York: Arno Reprint, 1971.

———. *The Life and Times of Aaron Burr.* Philadelphia: Mason Brothers, 1858.

———. *The Life and Times of Benjamin Franklin* (1860). Boston: Houghton Mifflin, 1892.

———. *The Life of John Jacob Astor* (1857). Reprinted in James Parton, *Famous Americans of Recent Times.* Boston: Houghton Mifflin, 1883.

———. *Daughters of Genius.* Philadelphia: Hubbard Brothers, 1886.

Steinem, Gloria. *Marilyn.* Photography by George Barres. New York: Henry Holt, 1986.

Stone, Irving. *Sailor on Horseback: The Biography of Jack London.* Boston: Houghton Mifflin, 1938.

Tate, Allen. *On The Limits of Poetry.* New York: Swallow Press, 1948.

Whittemore, Reed. *William Carlos Williams: Poet from Jersey.* Boston: Houghton Mifflin, 1975.

Index

Fielding, Henry: Stephen writes *DNB* biography of, 55

Finnegans Wake (Joyce), 151–52

Fitzgerald, F. Scott, 147–48

Fitzgerald, Zelda, 148

Fitzgibbon, Constantine, 160

Fliess, Wilhelm, 79, 81

Flush: A Biography (Woolf), 71–74

Franklin, Benjamin, 136, 138; Parton on, 136

Frederick the Great, 13, 24, 35, 39; Carlyle on, 39–43

Frederick the Great (Carlyle), 39–40

French Revolution, The (Carlyle), 20, 24–25, 45

Freud, Martha Bernays (Mrs. Sigmund), 85, 99

Freud, Sigmund, 2, 8, 19, 20, 65, 77, 79–102, 109, 130, 141, 144, 146, 147, 152, 153, 155, 157; and collaboration with Bullitt on Wilson biography, 98–102; and development of new biographical style, 79–82, 94, 104–5; Erikson on, 110; influence on Mailer, 126–27; and the Parthenon, 82–84; on *Sartor Resartus*, 18; and translation, 82–83; and the "wolf man," 95–97

Froude, James Anthony, 12, 13, 14, 47, 123, 137

Fry, Roger, 74–76

Gallatin, Albert, 138–39

Garland, Judy, 121–23

Genet, Jean: Sartre on, 149

Goethe, Johann, 39, 41, 47, 48, 135–36: influence on Carlyle, 14, 16, 39; death of, 16

Golden Ass, The (Apuleius): J. Lindsay translation of, 4

Gordon, Charles George ("Chinese"), 107

Gordon, Lyndall, 70; on Strachey, 106

Gosse, Edmund, 105

Gradiva (Jensen): Freud on, 94–95

"Great Year" (Yeats), 157

Greeley, Horace, 133–36

Guy Domville (James), 156

Hamilton, Edith: on Apuleius 4–5

Hardy, Thomas, 52

Hare, Archdeacon, 36–37

Hawkins, Sir John, 57

Hemingway (Lynn), 154, 161–62

Hemingway, Ernest, 154, 155, 161–63

Henry James: The Middle Years (Edel), 156

Henry James: The Treacherous Years (Edel), 156, 157

History of English Thought in the Eighteenth Century (Stephen), 52

History of the United States (Adams), 138

Hobbes, Thomas, 60: Stephen biography of, 59

Homer, 3, 21

Horace, 21

Hubbard, Elbert, 137

Hume, David, 27; Stephen's treatment of, 53

Iacocca (Iacocca and Novak), 120–21

"In Memory of Sigmund Freud" (Auden), 104

Interpretation of Dreams (Freud), 81, 85–86: and Oedipus complex, 93

Intimate Papers of Colonel House (Seymour), 100

James, Henry, 153–54

Jeffrey, Francis, 16

Jensen, William, 94

Jewsbury, Geraldine: on Jane Carlyle, 14, 16, 43–44

John Dos Passos: A Twentieth-Century Odyssey (Luddington): compares Dos Passos to Thackery, 159

Johnson, Allen: and *DAB* biography of Henry Adams, 138, 139, 140, 141

Johnson, Samuel, 1, 2, 12, 16, 25, 30, 48, 57, 105, 146; Stephen writes *DNB* entry on, 55

Jones, Ernest, 82, 84–85; on *Thomas Woodrow Wilson: A Psychological Study*, 98

Jowett, Benjamin: relationship with Stephen, 51–52

REED WHITTEMORE is author of the biography *William Carlos Williams: Poet from Jersey* and twelve books of poems, short stories, and essays. Former literary editor of the *New Republic* and twice the poetry consultant to the Library of Congress, he is also Poet Laureate of the State of Maryland and professor emeritus of English at the University of Maryland, College Park. His *Pure Lives: The Early Biographers* is also available from Johns Hopkins.

Designed by Martha Farlow
Composed by BG Composition, Inc., in Goudy Old Style, with
display lines in Goudy Handtooled
Printed by R. R. Donnelley & Sons Company on S. D. Warren's 50-lb. Cream White
Sebago and bound in Joanna Kennett with Multicolor Antique endsheets